Chin-Lushai Land. With maps and illustrations.

Adam Scott Reid

Chin-Lushai Land ... With maps and illustrations.
Reid, Adam Scott
British Library, Historical Print Editions
British Library
1893
x. 235 p. ; 8°.
010057.h.10.

The BiblioLife Network

This project was made possible in part by the BiblioLife Network (BLN), a project aimed at addressing some of the huge challenges facing book preservationists around the world. The BLN includes libraries, library networks, archives, subject matter experts, online communities and library service providers. We believe every book ever published should be available as a high-quality print reproduction; printed on- demand anywhere in the world. This insures the ongoing accessibility of the content and helps generate sustainable revenue for the libraries and organizations that work to preserve these important materials.

The following book is in the "public domain" and represents an authentic reproduction of the text as printed by the original publisher. While we have attempted to accurately maintain the integrity of the original work, there are sometimes problems with the original book or micro-film from which the books were digitized. This can result in minor errors in reproduction. Possible imperfections include missing and blurred pages, poor pictures, markings and other reproduction issues beyond our control. Because this work is culturally important, we have made it available as part of our commitment to protecting, preserving, and promoting the world's literature.

GUIDE TO FOLD-OUTS, MAPS and OVERSIZED IMAGES

In an online database, page images do not need to conform to the size restrictions found in a printed book. When converting these images back into a printed bound book, the page sizes are standardized in ways that maintain the detail of the original. For large images, such as fold-out maps, the original page image is split into two or more pages.

Guidelines used to determine the split of oversize pages:

- Some images are split vertically; large images require vertical and horizontal splits.
- For horizontal splits, the content is split left to right.
- For vertical splits, the content is split from top to bottom.
- For both vertical and horizontal splits, the image is processed from top left to bottom right.

1

CHIN LUSHAI LAND

A. SCOTT REID.

CHIN-LUSHAI LAND

CHIN-LUSHAI LAND

INCLUDING

A DESCRIPTION OF THE VARIOUS EXPEDITIONS INTO THE
CHIN-LUSHAI HILLS AND THE FINAL ANNEXATION
OF THE COUNTRY

BY

SURG.-LIEUT.-COL. A. S. REID, M.B.

*Indian Medical Service: Medical Officer in charge 2nd Battalion
4th Gurkha Rifles.*

WITH MAPS AND ILLUSTRATIONS

Calcutta
THACKER, SPINK AND CO.
1893

CALCUTTA:

PRINTED BY THACKER, SPINK AND CO.

DEDICATED
TO
S. V. R.

PREFACE.

IN a campaign or expedition into a new country, it can easily be understood that the matters regarding military operations, political negotiations, or characteristics of the people concerned, which come within the personal observation of a medical officer, must, from the nature of his duties, be of very limited extent, and that he is usually debarred, by his position, from acquiring an accurate knowledge of the undertaking as a whole.

It is therefore almost entirely owing to the kindness of Colonel W. P. Symons, C.B., of the South Wales Borderers, Colonel V. W. Tregear, C.B., of the 9th Bengal Infantry, and Colonel G. J. Skinner, D.S.O., of the 3rd Bengal Infantry, who commanded the Chin Force, Lushai Force, and Northern Column of the latter respectively in the expedition of 1889-90, and who placed the information in their possession at my disposal, as well as to that of Mr. G. M. Chesney, Editor of the Allahabad *Pioneer*, who allowed me to search the files of his paper for former records of the Chin-Lushai Country, that I am enabled to place the following volume before the public.

I have also to thank Colonel R. M. Clifford, I.S.C., Lieutenant E. W. M. Norie, Intelligence Officer, Lieutenant M. E. Willoughby, 2nd Bengal Lancers, and Surgeon-Captain A. G. E. Newland, of the Indian Medical Service, for generously furnishing me with information, etchings and photographs.

A. SCOTT REID.

CALCUTTA,
   October 1893.

CONTENTS.

CHAPTER I.
Geographical and Ethnological 1

CHAPTER II.
The Lushai Expedition of 1871-72—Operations of the Cachar Column 13

CHAPTER III.
The Lushai Expedition of 1871-72 continued—Operations of the Chittagong Column 29

CHAPTER IV.
The Lushai Expedition of 1889—Attack on Lieut. Stewart's Party and other Lushai Raids 38

CHAPTER V.
The Lushai Expedition of 1889 continued—Advance on Howsata's Village 48

CHAPTER VI.
Military Operations in the Northern Chin Hills, 1888-89 ... 60

CHAPTER VII.
The Chin-Lushai Expedition of 1889-90—On the March with the 2nd Battalion, 4th Gurkha Rifles 71

CHAPTER VIII.
The Chin-Lushai Expedition of 1889-90 continued—Concentration of the Southern Chin Column at Pakokku and Advance to Kan 84

CONTENTS.

CHAPTER IX.
The Chin-Lushai Expedition of 1889-90 continued—Advance of the Southern Chin Column to Haka—Rawvan ... 95

CHAPTER X.
The Chin-Lushai Expedition of 1889-90 continued—Advance of the Southern Chin Column to Haka—Yokwa ... 122

CHAPTER XI.
The Chin-Lushai Expedition of 1889-90 continued—Advance of the Southern Chin Column to Haka—Haka ... 140

CHAPTER XII.
The Chin-Lushai Expedition of 1889-90 continued—Advance of the Southern Chin Column to the Tashon Capital and Close of the Operations ... 161

CHAPTER XIII.
The Chin-Lushai Expedition of 1889-90 continued—Operations of the Southern Lushai Column ... 184

CHAPTER XIV.
The Chin-Lushai Expedition of 1889-90 continued—Operations of the Northern Lushai Column ... 209

CHAPTER XV.
General Information regarding the Chins ... 225

LIST OF ILLUSTRATIONS.

	PAGE.
BRIDGE ON THE BARAK RIVER	16
GURKHAS BUILDING A "BASHA" OR REST HOUSE	50
HAKA WOMEN	93
BARGAINING WITH CHINS	128
THE POST AT HAKA	144
RAFTING ON THE KLANG DONG OR DHALESWARI RIVER	210
SYLU MEN AT LIENPUNGA	216
A TASHON CHIEF'S HOUSE AT FALAM	230
MAP OF THE CHIN-LUSHAI COUNTRY.	
MAP ILLUSTRATING COUNTRY TRAVERSED BY CHIN FIELD FORCE	71
MAP ILLUSTRATING COUNTRY TRAVERSED BY LUSHAI FIELD FORCE	184

CHIN-LUSHAI LAND.

CHAPTER I.

Geographical and Ethnological.

Prior to 1889, the interior of the tract of country known as the Chin-Lushai Hills, was a *terra incognita*, and, even now, there are probably many members of the general public included in the class of well-educated to whom the title conveys but little meaning, and in whom it arouses still less interest.

Consisting of parallel mountain ranges rising to heights of over 9,000 feet, this, the most recent acquisition to Her Majesty's dominions, embraces every variety of physical feature and climate, from the dense and deadly jungles below, through the tangled mazes of which the ponderous elephant and rhinoceros push their way, to the invigorating summits, crowned with pines, where the sheen of the pheasant's wing catches the eye, as, with lightning speed, he skims down the mountain side.

People this region with dusky tribes, almost as numerous in dialect and designation as the villages in which they live, owning no central authority, possessing no written language, obeying but the verbal mandates of their chiefs, hospitable and affectionate in their homes, unsparing of age and sex while on the warpath, untutored as the remotest races in Central Africa, and yet endowed with an intelligence which has enabled them to discover for themselves the manufacture of gun-powder.

Such in general outline is the Chin-Lushai country, and such were its inhabitants until some three years ago they were touched by the transforming wand of civilization. The world moves rapidly in these times, and, before many decades shall have passed, the descendants of Lienpunga and Jahuta may perhaps be seen peacefully wending their way along roads, formerly the lines of "Kuki" paths, and used principally for murderous raids, but now leading to trim railway stations, whence the powerful engine and pioneer of progress conveys them to Rangoon or Calcutta as candidates for University degrees and Government appointments.

No less strange things have happened within comparatively recent years In the words of a writer in the *Englishman* : " The future of Lushai-land may be foreseen from what we know of the Khasia Hills that lie to the north of it. Sixty years ago the Khasias, who are the bravest and most warkike of all the wild tribes of India, were more bloodthirsty than the Lushais. On the 4th of April 1829, they rose in arms, and murdered Lieutenants Bedingfield and Burlton and some sepoys. That led to the inevitable military expedition which was protracted through several cold seasons, and the accounts of which differ from the accounts of the present Lushai Expedition chiefly in the determined resistance offered by the brave hill-men armed only with bows and arrows and *dhas*. The last of the Khasia chiefs did not tender his submission till 1833, and for the next twenty years Colonel Lister was Political Agent with the tribes. In his time Welsh missionaries entered the hills, learned the strange language, and reduced it to writing, prepared a grammar and vocabulary, introduced a printing press and opened schools.

"Now the Khasias are running the Bengalis a close race as clerks and accountants in the *cutcherries* (Government offices) at Shillong; they have beaten them in both the high schools there; their foremost youths are aspiring to University degrees; and in female education they are officially stated to take the lead of all the Indian races. There can be no doubt that the future of the Lushais will be similar, whichever missionary denomination enters the field. A few years will see the hill-sides dotted with schools, while the garrisons at Haka,

Sangal Klang and Fort Tregear will be asked for subscriptions to build churches."

The above reads like a page from Mark Twain's "A Yankee at the Court of King Arthur," but is none the less true as to facts and probable as to speculation.

The Chin-Lushai country is said to extend generally between latitudes 21° and 24° north, and longitudes 92° and 94° east; to be bounded on the north by Manipur and Cachar, on the east and south by Burma, and on the west by Arakan and the Chittagong Hill Tracts, being some two hundred and sixty miles in length, with a maximum breadth of about one hundred and twenty.

Since beginning this work, however, I have received a note from Lieutenant E. W. M. Norie, of the Middlesex Regiment, late Intelligence Officer with the Southern Chin Column, in which he says, referring to the Chins: "They extend very far to the north—to parallels 28° or 29°, or further. Since I saw you, I made a trip up the Chindwin, about 150 miles beyond where any white man had been before, and they were there and to the north, living quite distinct from the Kachins and entirely in the hills. The Kachins called them by the Burmese name of 'Chins,' and say they extend north as far as they know anything of the country. Of course they are distinct tribes, but of the same stock, I fancy.

"The women wear a different style of dress from the Baungshès, and very little of it. In many parts men and women tattoo their faces."

Considerable confusion arises from the various names under which the inhabitants of the Chin-Lushai Hills have been described.

Previous to the Expedition of 1871-72, the wild tribes which had been in the habit of raiding our North-Eastern Frontier, were generally spoken of as "Kukis"—a Bengali word meaning hill-men or highlanders. Since that event, however, the term "Lushai" has come into more common use; and although originally applied to the tribe or tribes occupying the tract immediately to the south of Cachar, is now employed, in a comprehensive sense, to indicate all those living to the west of the Koladyne river, while those to the east are designated Shendús. On the other hand, to any one approaching them from the Burma side, the Shendús would be known as Chins, and I think it would therefore be better to drop the term Shendú, and divide the people with whom I am going to deal in the following pages into the two broad classes of Lushais and Chins, the course of the Koladyne river forming the line of demarcation. Various derivations have been suggested for the word "Lushai," among which are "Lu" meaning head, and "Shai," to cut, or "Shai," long-haired, and I leave it to philologists to decide the question. I believe the Lushais call themselves "Zao." "Chin" is a Burmese term, and, on the authority of Colonel Woodthorpe, synonymous with Khyen (pronounced "Chin.")

That officer states that when surveying the Chindwin

river, he was informed that it was so called from the fact of its forming the eastern limit of Chin raids in Burmese territory. The Chins call themselves "Lai." While exhibiting distinctive characteristics in dress and dialect, there can be little doubt that the Chins and Lushais are practically one race; although it is true that the language of the latter is not understood by the people living east of the Koladyne. On the other hand, tribes are found among the Chins themselves, separated by only a few miles, whose dialects are so dissimilar as to be mutually unintelligible. As regards dress, one of the most conspicuous distinctions exists in the manner of arranging the hair. The Lushais and Northern Chins gather it in a knot on the nape of the neck, and the Baungshès on to the forehead. This remark applies only to the males. The Paitès or Soktès wear their hair short and standing out like the tresses of Medusa.

It is only since the annexation of Upper Burma in 1885 that we have come into practical contact with the Chins, and been forced, much against our inclinations, to cultivate their acquaintance. Until the extension of the British rule to the banks of the Maw and Myittha, their name, if it even penetrated to English territory, excited little interest.

Not so with the Lushais. Since the days of Warren Hastings the various tribes whom we now include under this term have, at long and uncertain intervals, reminded us of their presence in a manner not calculated to

GEOGRAPHICAL AND ETHNOLOGICAL. 7

inspire mutual regard or confidence. The first record of the raids of these savages dates from 1777, when the chief of Chittagong, a district which had been ceded to the British under Clive by Mir Kasim in 1760, applied for a detachment of sepoys to protect the inhabitants against the incursions of the Kukis as they were then called.

In December 1844, a party of the Sylhet Light Infantry under Captain Blackwood, and assisted by a Kuki chief Lalmi Sing, attacked Lalchokla, another chief and cousin of the latter, in reprisal for a raid committed during the preceding April on a Manipur colony settled in Pertabghar in British territory. The motive of the outrage committed by Lalchokla was, as we shall also see in some succeeding instances, to obtain heads to place on the tomb of his father Lassu, who had died a short time before.

Lalchokla on this occasion took twenty heads and six captives, but paid dearly for his temporary triumph, as his village was surrounded, and he himself transported under circumstances, which, in the minds of the Lushais, appear to have implied a breach of faith, a promise of life having been interpreted by them to mean free pardon.

Cachar had been taken possession of by the British in 1830, the pretext being the death by assassination of the last of the native rulers without heir, and, twenty years after, a second expedition was rendered necessary on account of a raid which had been committed by the Lushais, the victims in this instance being a tribe of their own kinsmen, who had settled within our territory.

Colonel Lister, Political Agent in the Khasia Hills, assisted by one subaltern, led the force of six native officers and two hundred and twenty-nine rank and file which, in the month of January 1850, was sent out to exact retribution. He destroyed the village of a chief named Mullah, about eighty miles south from Cachar. Following this military operation a powerful chief Sukpilal, whose name will become more familiar as we proceed, paid a friendly visit to the Deputy Commissioner of Cachar, and more amicable relations than had formerly existed were established between our people and the Lushais.

Peace reigned until 1862 when Sylhet was disturbed, three villages being attacked and burned, and their inhabitants as usual either killed or carried into captivity. On this occasion Sukpilal was appealed to, and his friendship strengthened by a small annual subsidy.

Meanwhile it had been discovered in 1855 that the tea plant was indigenous to Cachar, and soon after gardens, for the cultivation and production of this important article of commerce, began to be opened out in the southern part of the district, with rather a disquieting effect upon the neighbouring tribes, who fancied they saw possible encroachments upon their hereditary hunting grounds. The suspicion found expression in a raid upon the tea gardens of Loharband and Monierkhal in the beginning of 1869. The usual military demonstration followed, but on this occasion, owing to delay in the despatch of the force, lateness of the season and other causes, the troops employed were obliged to retire with the object in view unattained, and, as a result, our prestige with the wild tribes on our frontier considerably diminished.

A weak policy of concession and conciliation was then tried, and between December 1869 and March 1870, Mr. Edgar, then Deputy Commissioner of Cachar, and Major MacDonald visited Sukpilal at his home, and between them fixed a new boundary, which, as after events will show, was not recognised by the tribes whom the chief represented.

The outrages which soon followed exceeded in magnitude and ferocity all that had gone before. Raids, almost simultaneous in date but emanating from different tribes, were made on the Chittagong Hill Tracts, the semi-independent state of Hill Tipperah, Sylhet, Cachar and Manipur.

The first raid occurred in the Chittagong Hill Tracts near the Chima outpost, and was supposed by Captain Lewin, Political Officer of that district, to have been effected by a party of Shendús or Eastern Lushais two hundred strong.

Poyakookie in Hill Tipperah was burnt on the 21st January 1871.

Alexandrapore, a tea garden in Cachar, shared the same fate on the 23rd January, when Mr. Winchester, a planter on a visit from a neighbouring estate, was killed, and his daughter Mary, a little girl of six, carried off by the Howlongs. On the same day the adjoining garden of Katli Chura was attacked, but the assailants were driven off.

The village of Ainakhal, in Western Cachar, fared worse, twenty-five persons being killed, thirty-seven taken captive, and the houses burned.

The Lushais attacked the garden of Monierkhal on the 26th January, and afterwards the stockade and coolie lines at the same place, the loss on our side being seven killed and about as many wounded. The fight lasted for seventeen hours, and from the vigorous and sustained nature of the attack, it was supposed that the raiders had old mutineers among them. They were finally driven off with a loss of fifty-seven killed and wounded.

On the following day Nugdigram was raided, eleven persons killed and three carried off.

On the 28th a party of eight sepoys were attacked, and all but one killed; not, however, before they had accounted for twenty-five Lushais.

The last place attacked in Cachar was the Jalnacherra tea estate, where, on the 23rd February, seven coolies were killed and wounded.

Outrages continued to occur in Sylhet, Tipperah and Manipur until well on in March.

At the beginning of the incidents which I have related, Mr. Edgar was paying Sukpilal a second visit, but apparently neither his presence in the country nor the efforts of the friendly chief had any effect in checking the intended raids, and for a time considerable anxiety was felt regarding the safety of the representative of the British Government. As I have already said, the theoretical frontier laid down by Mr. Edgar a few months before and acquiesced in by Sukpilal, was not recognised even by the subjects of that chief, and, on the present occasion, the alleged grievance of the Lushais was that the tea planters cleared forests on the Cachar frontier, under the promised protection of the civil authorities, in tracts which were claimed by the former as their rightful hunting grounds, although regarded by us as well within the newly defined line.

Whatever the justice or otherwise of the original *casus belli* from the Lushai point of view, such deeds as I have described, could not be passed over without further and more effectual steps being taken to punish the offenders and put a stop to future possible raids. The season was, however, now too far advanced for extensive military operations, and all that could be done in the meantime was to summon troops from the garrisons of Shillong and Dacca for the protection of the frontier, and to make preparations on a larger scale than had even hitherto been done for the despatch of a force into the enemy's country, when, with the return of the cold weather, the climate should again become safe for our troops, and the paths practicable.

The plan formed was that two columns should start as early as possible in November 1871—one from Cachar, and the other from Chittagong.

Brigadier-General G. Bourchier, C.B., was selected for the command of the former force, and Brigadier-General C. Brownlow for that of the latter.

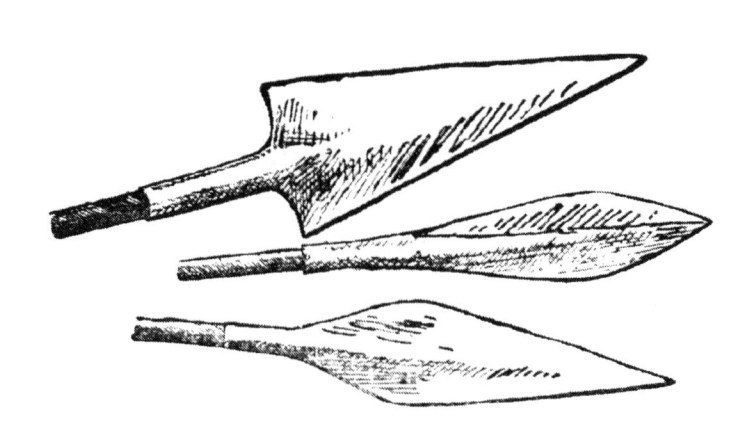

LUSHAI SPEAR HEADS.

CHAPTER II.

THE LUSHAI EXPEDITION OF 1871-72.

Operations of the Cachar Column.

A REVIEW of the work done by each column appeared in the *Pioneer* at the close of the Expedition, and as the article will serve my purpose better than any narrative I can construct from the information scattered through the letters of special correspondents and the meagre paragraphs of communicated telegrams, I take the liberty of quoting it here.

"The strength of each column of the Expedition was fixed by the Commander-in-Chief at half a battery of Mountain Artillery (with rockets), one company of Sappers and Miners and three regiments of Native Infantry.

"The regiments selected for the Cachar side were the 22nd, 42nd and 44th, consisting mainly of Punjabis, Sikhs and Gurkhas—races especially adapted for the work before them, and equally expert with the mattock and the bayonet. Carriage was reduced to a minimum, for the way was long and rough, and the routes uncertain. Tents were dispensed with, each man being furnished with a waterproof sheet for his bedding and left to cut branches and bamboos to keep the dews from his pillow. One maund (80lbs.) of personal baggage sufficed for the General; 6srs. (12lbs.) were allowed to the soldier.

"We need not tarry to explain how elephants and coolies were got together and sent up, how boats were seized and boatmen impressed, how the commissariat toiled and district officers went almost wild, and how the fell scourge of cholera threatened at one time to mar the whole.

"By the end of November the column had fairly started into the hills, and on the 6th of December the civil officer, Mr. Edgar, had left Silchar to join the troops.

"Before accompanying them on their weary progress, it will be well to understand the dispositions made in support of their advance, and the instructions which we gather were given them for their guidance. The goal which the left (Cachar) column had (if possible) to reach was the village of Lalburah, son of Vonolel, who had been mainly concerned in the raids of Monierkhal. It was known that this chief dwelt far within the hills to the south-east of Tipai Mukh, the trijunction point where Cachar, Manipur and Lushai-land join their boundaries. The line by which he had to be reached lay therefore to the extreme east of the district of Cachar and up the course of the Barak river, which there runs northwards from the hills.

"The whole southern frontier of Cachar stretched westwards from the column's right flank and had of course to be properly protected. This was done by stationing strong guards at the points where the ordinary Lushai routes debouched on the district.

"Beyond the hills again to the east of the line of march lay the territory of Manipur, the confines of which towards the south-west pointed towards Lalburah and the other Lushai clans of that neighbourhood, the only intervening tribes being those of the Soktè Kukis, a race hostile to the Lushais and friendly to Manipur. Advantage was taken of this to move a strong Manipur force down towards the south, with orders not to invade or attack the Lushais, but merely to serve as a threatening demonstration against them and as a support to the Soktès.

"This Manipur contingent was the net into which subsequent events drove all the captives held by Lalburah and many other chiefs.

"Having thus stationed permanent supports, as it were, on both flanks, General Bourchier prepared to carry out the plan of the Expedition entrusted to his conduct. It was a task requiring much political discrimination as well as military skill. The information which Government had as to the perpetrators of the raids was at the best incomplete.

"The names of the leaders were, it is true, pretty well ascertained; but our knowledge of their tribal relations was admittedly imperfect, and it was impossible to say with certainty that *this* village shared the guilt while *that* was undoubtedly altogether innocent. Hence it was evident that the Expedition could not merely march into Lushai-land to plunder and to ravish, careless of where its blows might fall, and eager only to burn and slay. If during its progress guilt were with certainty brought home to any particular villages, the General's orders were to punish without scruple.

"The surrender of chiefs known to hold British subjects in captivity was to be demanded rigorously, and in the event of non-compliance, their houses and property were to be unhesitatingly destroyed. Restoration of captives was also to be insisted on.

"Should it appear that some only of the inhabitants of a village had joined in the raids without complicity on the part of the village as a whole, the payment of a fine and the surrender of the guilty were the punishment to be inflicted. Hostages were to be demanded did this appear necessary. If hostility was met with, resisting villages were to be attacked and burnt, and the surrounding crops laid waste.

"It was, however, strongly impressed on all that retaliation was not the main object of the Expedition.

"It was the desire of the Supreme Government to show the Lushais that they are completely in our power, to establish permanent friendly relations with them, to induce them to promise to receive our native agents, to

BRIDGE ON THE BARAK RIVER.

make travelling in their country safe to all, to demonstrate the advantages of trade and commerce, and to prove to them in short, that they had nothing to gain but everything to lose by acting against the British Government. This was the general programme on which both columns had to work; and with this before us we may at last venture to set out from the sudder station of Cachar.

"For all that portion of their journey which lay between Silchar and the first Lushai villages it may be roughly said that the force had to follow the course of the Barak.

"For fourteen miles or so from the station they had a fair track due east to Luckeepore, where the river takes its great southern bend; but here the difficulties of the road commenced, and the troops had actually to begin their pioneering labours one day's march from their head-quarters. At the frontier post of Mynadhar the force was fairly on the verge of the wild country, and from the depôt here established the stores required in front were regularly despatched thereafter.

"The second grand depôt was at Tipai Mukh, on the junction of the Barak and the Tipai, between which and Mynadhar were four distinct stations or camps.

"Up to this point water carriage was to some extent available, though the river was rapidly falling and not to be depended upon. On the 21st November the 44th had marched to Luckeepore. By the 9th December it had cut its way to Tipai Mukh.

"There was much to do here in the way of building hospitals, store-houses and stockades. But they were now close upon the Lushai fastnesses, and it was deemed expedient to show the enemy without delay what the force was capable of effecting.

"Accordingly, on the 13th December, the General pushed on the Sappers and a wing of the 44th to a camp five miles out, and commenced therefrom the ascent of the Senvong range through fine timber forests, encamping ultimately at an elevation of 4,000 feet.

"From this point looking southward, the Tuibhoom river was seen flowing from the east into the Tipai.

"Across the latter stream to the west stretched the 'jooms' and cottages of Kholel, while far away on the south-eastern hills perched the more advanced villages of Poiboi.

"From its lofty camp on the Senvong the little party descended by a long day's march towards the confluence of the Tipai and Tuibhoom, crossing the former stream by a weir, in spite of the yells and threatening demonstrations of a crowd of armed Lushais. It was in vain the General assured them that his intentions were not necessarily hostile; that if they did not molest his men he would do them and theirs no injury. Nothing succeeded in producing confidence, and with a final yell of defiance they at last disappeared to take counsel for the work of the morrow.

"Next day (the 23rd December) the troops commenced

the ascent of the hill on which the Kholel villages lay, and were received at the first clearing by a volley from a Lushai ambuscade. This, of course, prevented all hope of peaceful negotiation. Had they remained quiet, we should merely have marched into their villages, interviewed their chiefs, and settled our relations for the future. As it was, the village was taken with a rush, fired, and its granaries destroyed.

"Another village, a mile further along the ridge, was occupied as a camp, and a third village at the summit of the mountain was captured and burnt before evening closed.

"Next day and the next the troops were occupied with raids on the surrounding villages and granaries, and a lesson was read to the unbelieving men of Kholel which they are not likely soon to forget.

"It was disappointing to be met with hostility at the outset, especially from villages with the chief men of which Mr. Edgar had had some apparently friendly palavers before the Expedition started.

"Mora, the 'muntri' (envoy) of Impanu, the old lady who at present rules these villages, had indeed met the General at the crossing of the Tipai, but had disappeared with the rest when the troops crossed over.

"On the 26th December the force evacuated Kholel and returned to the camp in the valley below near the stream; but being still constantly harrassed by firing from the surrounding jungles, a second foray was made on the 29th; the mountain was again scaled more to the west by a party of the 42nd which had now come up, and the blaze of fresh villages and granaries would soon have followed had not the enemy suddenly, unexpectedly and very dramatically made complete submission.

"As the troops advanced they were met by Dharpong, a muntri of the still distant Poiboi, who had been with them at an early part of the Expedition. This gentleman clad in orange-coloured garments, and decked with a lofty plume, now came and interceded for Kholel, and by anticipation for Poiboi. Assured that it was not the wish to continue hostilities which we had not begun, he climbed up a tree, and from its summit emitted an unearthly yell that echoed from the surrounding peaks, put a sudden stop to the dropping fire in the jungles, and brought in the Lushais in crowds to fraternize with their late opponents.

"The muntris declared that the elders of the tribe had never wished for war, that the young braves had rashly commenced hostilities and brought all this sorrow on their homesteads. On the 30th and 31st Mora and other muntris came in, peace offerings were offered and accepted, and the year closed in comparative quiet.

"The camp was soon thronged with Lushais, young and old, bringing pumpkins, fowls, and ginger, for barter, and curious to examine the appurtenances of civilization in the shape of watches and burning glasses. Every effort was made to gain their confidence, and messengers were sent to the tribes ahead to explain more fully to them the objects of the Expedition.

"On the 6th of January the force advanced from the Tuibhoom east by south towards the Tuitoo, another affluent of the Tipai, crossing the intervening ridge at a height of 3,400 feet. Thence almost due south over a difficult road they marched to the village of Pachnee, the ninth station out from Mynadhar, overhanging a sudden bend of the Tipai. Here they could see to the eastward the precipitous cliffs on which stood the principal northern villages of Poiboi, while, as far as the eye could reach, to the west lay villages and 'jooms.'

"Waiting here for reinforcements and stores the General took the opportunity of making an excursion to the old site of Kholel, where was the village of Vonpilal, the former Chief of that clan. The village had been burnt six days before our arrival, but the tomb was intact, and consisted of a stone platform twenty feet square and four feet high, surrounded by poles on which hung skulls of wild oxen, deer and goats, enigmatical representations, drinking vessels, and the skull of a pony slaughtered at the funeral.

"On the 13th the force made preparations for its onward march. It was but 2½ miles from Pachnee down to Tipai, but it gave two wings of the 42nd and 44th hard work to clear a road. So steep was it naturally in places that the Lushais had been wont to let themselves down by ropes of cane, which primitive aids to locomotion were hanging down the fall of the rock when our men arrived. The force was now coming close upon Poiboi, already referred to as one of the most powerful Chiefs of this quarter, whose attitude, notwithstanding the presence in camp of his muntri Dharpong, was still uncertain.

"Two wings had been left to overawe Kholel in the rear. There was a wing at Tipai Mukh and a wing in the two stations immediately in rear of the advance, which itself consisted, as we have seen, of two wings with the General and head-quarters. Small detachments held intermediate posts, and the artillery had got as far as the camp at the confluence of the Tuibhoom and Tipai, but was fast pushing on to the front, and had, indeed, joined the General before he crossed the bend of the Tipai below Pachnee. It was well, as it turned out, that he was in a position to make a good display of force at this point.

"The Lushais were evidently very unhappy at his determination to proceed. The village of Chipooee and Tingridong, which lay on the mountain across the river, were nominally subject to Poiboi, but were situated so far from his chief village as to be, to some extent independent.

"We were anxious therefore to secure their neutrality, but, at the same time, they were half afraid to treat us well lest Poiboi should resent it hereafter.

"As the force scaled the hill to Chipooee they were

met by Dharpong and a crowd of Lushais, who pretended that Poiboi himself had come to meet the General. The man put forward as the chief turned out, however, to be an impostor, and, as a punishment for the deception, the General warned them that he would now listen to none but Poiboi himself in his principal residence. Leaving a strong party to watch these doubtful villages, and taking the headmen on as hostages, the force again set out south-eastward.

"The road as usual led over a lofty ridge down to another affluent of the Tipai, and then up a mountain chain on the other side. The reconnoitring party in advance came here upon two paths—one running along the ridge, the other turning down to the east. Across the latter was suspended a rude imitation with figures *sus. per coll.*, and a block roughly cut into the representation of a body with the scalp off.

"These were intended as warnings not to take the path so guarded—warnings, however, which were afterwards known to be treacherous and deceitful. Fortunately the leaders of the advance were not easily frightened, and they forthwith selected the tabooed road, which they explored without accident. On the road left open the Lushais were lying in wait and ready for an attack!

"Next day (the 25th January) Dharpong who had been sent on to summon out Poiboi, appeared in camp and warned the General that he would be attacked if he went on. This, of course, had no effect; but attacked he was on all sides, in the midst of one of the worst bits of ground yet traversed by the troops. The men, however, behaved splendidly, and although the General himself was wounded, the enemy was driven off and severely punished, and the road in advance secured.

"This attack proved that Poiboi and Lalburah had actually coalesced, and had determined to oppose the further march of the column. Accordingly, as a foretaste of what they might expect, parties were sent out to burn Poiboi's villages on the neighbouring heights, and here, for the first time, the artillery made play, and struck terror and wonder into the minds of the Lushais, who fled from their stockades in panic, and left their homesteads eventually undefended.

"It is worth mentioning here that on the bodies of some of the Lushais slain in this skirmish was found ammunition taken from the Sepoys killed at Nugdigram in the Cachar raids—proof positive that the Expedition was on the right track, and that the tribes who now opposed us were actuated rather by despair of pardon than hope of success. The lessons thus taught him seem, however, to have convinced Poiboi that he had better separate himself from his ally Lalburah.

"He was warned that a heavy fine of hill oxen and other things, with complete submission, could alone condone his rash resistance, and that his villages would all be burnt unless he came in.

"He began sending in presents forthwith, but the General replied that he would only treat in Sellam the chief village of the tribe; and for Sellam, on the 1st February, the column marched, crossing three ridges— one 5,850 feet high—to the top of the Lengting range, where they came in sight of Sellam and its dependencies, crowning the hill over against them, and stretching with 'joom' and clearing for some three or four miles. Here again Dharpong, the muntri, appeared bearing offerings, but nothing served to stay the advance, and Sellam deserted by Poiboi and his followers was entered in peace.

"The very furniture from the chief's house—a great hall 100 feet long—had been removed. Skulls and antlers alone hung on the deserted walls.

"Next day, however, the Lushais came fearlessly to the camp, and were given to understand that only Poiboi's submission could eventually save their villages. Poiboi with his guilty fears had, it now appeared, sent embassies to General Nuthall and the Manipuris; but his submission to General Bourchier in Sellam was what was uniformly insisted on, and to Sellam he seemed determined not to come.

"Here the preparations were made for the final dash upon Lalburah. Two guns and four hundred men were the force detailed for this service; baggage was almost entirely got rid of. Time was pressing, and the work required to be speedily done with. On the 12th February the troops started upon the last stage of the Expedition. Five days marching almost due south, through an elevated mountain region over ridges in some places 6,600 feet high, brought them at length in full view of the valley of Champai, the head-quarters of Lalburah, son of Vonolel, leader of the raids on Monierkhal. On the 17th February they reached the village. But other invaders had been before them; and signs of war and slaughter greeted them on every side.

"The withdrawal of the Manipur contingent from the front owing to sickness, had set free the Soktè Kukis, old enemies of the Lushais, who seizing the opportunity and knowing the panic caused by the advance of the British column, made fierce onslaught on Lalburah under the guidance of Kamhow their chief. Lalburah had, it is true, beaten them off with loss; but their attack had probably prevented his occupying a strong position which he had stockaded and prepared, across the route by which the column came, and frustrated the hopes he entertained of entangling them in the mountains. His village was now found deserted, and was forthwith burnt to the ground, only the tomb of his father Vonolel escaping the flames.

"On the neighbouring height dwelt the widow of Vonolel, herself a powerful and wise old woman, who had in vain urged her sons to submission. From her a fine was levied of war-gongs, oxen, goats and such like, which she did not refuse to pay. Besides this, it was stipulated that three headmen should return as hostages to Tipai Mukh ; that they should receive Government agents in their villages when required ; that either the twelve muskets taken at Monierkhal and Nugdigran should be given up, or a similar number of their own fire-arms be surrendered.

"On the 20th February the conditions were complied with, and next day the force, its task accomplished, set out on its return. Poiboi, in nervous dread of punishment, had, we may notice, been hovering round the camp all the way from Sellam, and had even met the native assistants of the civil officer, but nothing had induced him to come in and sue for peace. This is the one failure in the operations of this column.

"It was ninety-two days since the head-quarters of the Expedition had left Cachar. During that time they had been almost constantly on foot, cutting the roads by which they advanced over lofty mountains, ridge after ridge, crossing and recrossing numberless streams, scaling fastnesses of hostile tribes, burning their villages and destroying their crops when punishment was demanded, proving at the same time to the peaceably-disposed that conciliation was more agreeable to us than scourge.

"The return march was rather a festal than an armed progress. Molested by no enemies, the column retraced its steps, attended by crowds of admiring Lushais, who thronged its camps and bartered their country produce for articles valuable to them and costing little to us.

Headmen and muntris from all the tribes attended the General to Tipai Mukh.

"By noon on the 10th of March the last man had left that station, and the column withdrew to Cachar, leaving behind it some hundred miles of mountain road to testify to the perseverance and pluck of the gallant corps who had cut and blasted a path from Mynadhar to Champai and avenged the outrage of Monierkhal at the tomb of Vonolel."

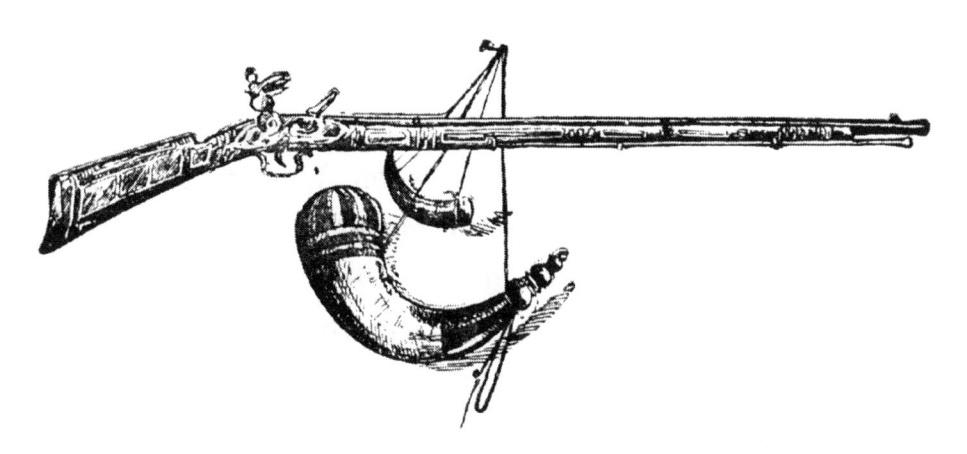

GUN AND POWDER HORNS USED BY CHINS AND LUSHAIS.

CHAPTER III.

THE LUSHAI EXPEDITION OF 1871-72—(*continued*).

Operations of the Chittagong Column.

"In treating of the doings of the left column, we set forth the general principles by which the Expedition as a whole was to be guided. We may now note that while the main object of the left column was to get at and punish the tribes who had raided on Monierkhal and East Cachar, it was the aim of the Chittagong force to reach the Sylu chief Savunga, who was known to have been concerned in the raids on West Cachar, the sack of Alexandrapore and the murder of Mr. Winchester. With the Howlongs too we had a score to settle, but it was not at the outset certain which column could most effectually deal with them.

"Mr. Edgar had hoped that the Cachar troops would have penetrated by tolerably easy roads to Lalburah's village, and remaining there, would at leisure have subdued the neighbouring tribes, including the Howlongs, who were supposed to be near.

"But the difficulties of the way made it late in the season when Lalburah was reached, and the site of the village was found to be so far to the east that General Bourchier at Champai had over thirty miles of mountain ridges between himself and General Brownlow at the most easterly point to which the latter attained.

"To the Chittagong column, therefore, fell the task of dealing both with Sylus and Howlongs, and although the two branches of the Expedition never met among the hills, we shall see that each did its work thoroughly and well, and we shall find that, in the end, their failing to unite was a matter of very secondary importance.

"The great advantage possessed by the right column as compared with the left was, that it had the sea or rather Calcutta as a tolerably convenient base, and that it had water carriage up to a point in the almost immediate vicinity of its active operations. The Kurnafulee, which cleaves the north of the Chittagong Hill Tracts, is navigable by river steamers up to Rangamatti, a distance of seventy-one miles; thence to Kasalong, seventeen miles further up, light country-boats of 18 inches draught could go; and beyond that twelve miles further on to Lower Burkal, small boats and canoes, carrying about five maunds each, could very well be used. The troops selected for this column were the 2nd and 4th Gurkhas and the 27th Punjab Infantry with half a mountain battery and a company of Sappers and Miners—a force precisely the same in composition and character as that with General Bourchier.

"On the 28th October General Brownlow landed in

Chittagong, and no time was lost in completing the commissariat arrangements already well advanced, and in pushing on provisions as far as Kasalong. The course of the Kurnafulee above this place is broken at intervals by dangerous rapids, the first of which is situated between upper and lower Burkal. From Kasalong to Burkal the river runs due east. At Burkal it takes a sudden northward turn, and above the rapids is found a clear, deep, sluggish stream navigable by boats for nineteen miles to the rapids of Ootan Chutra.

"By dint of great labour boats were dragged up the Burkal falls, and a river service established on the reach above. Beyond Ootan Chutra to Demagiri the course of the stream as we ascend turns again to the east, till we reach Demagiri, a point where the great Ohephum range abuts on the Kurnafulee from the south, and the Sirtay Klang meets it from the north. Canoes it was found could be got up the Ootan Chutra rapids as far as Demagiri. It was well indeed that this boat service between Burkal and Demagiri was possible, for the land route between those places was all but impracticable. Only sixteen miles apart as the crow flies, it was a five days' march of forty-one and a half miles to traverse by the ordinary Kuki path, two-thirds of which lay along the beds of torrents, the rest being through all but impervious jungle. By dint of great labour a road was cut passable for unladen elephants and coolies, but laden elephants were to the last unable to traverse it. From the ranges on either side of Demagiri a fine view was obtained of the Sylu and Howlong country. Five ranges lay before them to be crossed rising to 4,000 and 5,000 feet covered with forest to the very top. In every intervening valley was a stream now rushing fiercely shallow amid its boulders, and now flowing deep and unfordable between large silent woods.

"At Burkal the General was joined by Rutton Puya, the Kuki chief of whom we have heard so much, and who since 1860 has been our more or less faithful ally.

"His present villages lie on the Ohephum range south of Demagiri, and he offered to lead the force by land as far as that place. What the road he led them was like we have seen above.

"At Demagiri there was much to do; a standing camp had to be cleared, and provisions for the whole force got up in anticipation of an advance. Demagiri was to the Chittagong column what Tipai Mukh was to that from Cachar. It was the 1st of December before there was food enough in store to warrant a forward movement.

"For four miles above Demagiri the river was impracticable, but canoes were placed on the reach above, as they had been above Burkal, and ten miles more of water carriage was thus secured.

"Some little way above this point the force left the valley of the Kurnafulee and turned northward along the Sahjuck. From the furthest point on this stream to which canoes could go, the troops commenced their regular hill work, marching north by east to attack Vanunah, the first great Sylu chief on the Belkai range, and to commence that severe course of discipline which in time taught the Sylu that the way of transgressors is hard.

"On the 14th December Vanunah was captured by surprise—surprise common both to the Lushais and to our reconnoitring party, which came suddenly on the village from above after losing its way in the woods.

"The Sylus had, in reply to our overtures, already intimated their full intention of fighting, and had made no signs of submission. On the contrary, a few days later they vindicated their reputation as warriors and braves by attacking in force three little Gurkhas carrying the post-bag, and were very much astonished to find that, after shooting one of them from behind a tree, the other two did not run away, but showed effective fight until a rescue came. From Vanunah's village Colonel Macpherson with three companies was sent on a five days' raid to the east. Down into the valley below and up the range beyond, his men toiled scrambling, and on the third day they made Lal Heera, only eight miles from Vanunah as the crow flies. This they burnt with two other villages beyond, and destroyed vast quantities of grain, getting back to Vanunah on Christmas Day.

"Another raiding party had been out during their absence to the north-east, and done equally good service of a similar kind, and returned home "driving off ta' cattle" to assist the stores of a much-tried commissariat.

"On the 27th the head-quarters moved northward along the range from Vanunah for thirteen miles, and thence a few days later turned eastward on its way to Savunga (the head village of the Sylu tribe) and the Howlong fastnesses beyond. From Upper Hoolien a captured village *en route*, a full view was obtained of the country they had to traverse, and it was seen that there were still three ranges to cross with the intervening valleys.

"While the force rested at Hoolien a party raided north, and took villages and stockades defended with some energy although without persistence.

"On the 13th of January Sylu Savunga was occupied and found deserted, and the conquest of the Sylus was then complete. The position of this village was singularly fine. Lying on a hill 3,200 feet high with the Klang Dong or Dhaleswari flowing under it on its way to Cachar, a tributary of the Gootai rising at its western base, and a branch of the Kurnafulee taking its course southward close by.

"The Sylu chief dwells, as it were, at the very omphalos of the hills, and sends out his war parties north and south to plunder in Cachar or slay in Chittagong.

"We have spoken of the troops raiding and burning in the course of our narrative as things of course, but in fact no effort was spared to induce the Sylus to come in and make terms. By messengers and notices, by shouting parleys across rivers and amid the woods, they were warned and encouraged and invited to come in ; but their hearts were guilty, and their hands not clean, so savage-like they doubted of that which should happen unto them. Their doubts were their destruction, and in truth, politically speaking, it was better for the future peace of the hills that things were as they were. Punishment has more effect when felt than when fancied, and if we have one regret in connection with the whole Expedition it is this, that the more easterly villages of the Southern Howlongs (the most formidable of the tribes) were wise enough to submit at the first summons, as we shall see below, and that the residence of their principal chief Vandula was never occupied even for an hour. Bloodshed and burning we do not affect; but peaceful occupation to vindicate our power and policy was much to be desired. We are, however, anticipating. The rest of our narrative we must condense. From Savunga the destruction of other Sylu villages to the north was effected, and Rutton Puya was despatched as a messenger to the Northern Howlongs dwelling across the Dhaleswari.

"Rutton Puya travelled by a more southern and roundabout road to avoid the refugee Sylus, and was met by messengers from the Howlongs bringing in Mary Winchester as an earnest of peace. General Brownlow waited patiently at Savunga from the 12th January to the 11th February to give his emissary time to work upon the Howlong mind. Then finding that no reply had come from the northern section of the tribe, though the southern chiefs said they would come in at Demagiri, the force at last crossed the Dhaleswari.

"No resistance was offered, though the villages were fired by the inhabitants as they advanced. On the 16th, however, Sungbhunga and Benkoea, the great chiefs of the clan, came into camp and submitted, agreeing to give up their captives and to admit our troops to their villages. Two days later Lalburah (not he of Champai) Jatoma and Lienrikum, other leading chiefs, came in, and the same day the first instalment of the returned captives rewarded the exertions of the force, and testified to the sincerity of the Lushais.

"A detachment of Gurkhas attended the survey officers through the villages, and on the 23rd the troops set out on their homeward march accompanied for a time by crowds of Howlongs, male and female, clad many of them in dark cotton tartans, and wearing as ornament the true Highland sporran.

"With curious inconsistency, the Sylus having been utterly harried and ruined, came in as the force retired, and made full submission.

"On arrival at Demagiri General Brownlow started with four companies eastwards to quicken the movements of the Southern Howlongs who had not yet appeared. Forty miles march over a peaceful country and a final climb of 4,000 feet brought them to the village of Sypora, an inferior chief, who at once submitted.

"At the Dhaleswari beyond, the General was met by Vantonga, one of the leading chiefs, and by the sons of the great Vandula who brought in captives and did homage on their father's behalf.

"The season was now late, and General Brownlow accepted this and returned, to save the force the three days' eastward march which lay between the river and Vandula.

"We cannot blame him for this, but of all the chiefs in that quarter Vandula is the one we should have most wished to see humbled.

"There are, however, good grounds for hoping that the permanent establishment of a strong post at Demagiri will secure his good behaviour for the future.

"The right column had now done its work. Its four months' campaign had reduced two powerful tribes and brought in fifteen chiefs, rescued many captives and added to our maps in detail three thousand square miles of hill country."

CHAPTER IV.

The Lushai Expedition of 1889.

Attack on Lieutenant Stewart's Party and other Lushai Raids.

The lessons taught by the Expedition of 1871-72 appeared to have made a considerable impression upon the Lushais, for although, in pursuance of hereditary feuds, or in retaliation for recent insults and injuries, they still continued to raid upon each other, such disturbances were, for a long time, confined to their own territory.

In January 1882 a body of two or three hundred men described as Shendús and Malliam Puis, headed by a chief named Howsata, attacked and took a village belonging to a Lushai chief Lalseva, situated about four miles beyond our border. Twenty-nine Lushais were killed, seven wounded and ninety-nine persons carried off as prisoners. Lalseva applied to us for help, but this was refused on the ground that the village did not lie within British territory.

On the 18th November of the following year a party of police travelling from Burkal to Demagiri were set upon by Kukis, who were afterwards ascertained to be

Malliam Puis acting as scouts for a large body of eastern Lushais. A follower was shot, and two of the police drowned from the capsizing of a boat, while the enemy got off with only one casualty.

After this the country remained quiet until the early part of 1888 when a head hunting party from the tribes beyond the Koladyne ventured once more to cross the frontier and to commit, in this instance, a most unprovoked outrage upon a small survey party commanded by Lieutenant J. F. Stewart, of the 1st Battalion, Leinster Regiment, who, in conjunction with Lieutenant J. Mc.D. Baird, of the 2nd Battalion, Derbyshire Regiment, was making a reconnaisance to the south-east of Rangamatti, with a view to a new road being opened up, and this part of the frontier, admittedly the weakest, strengthened by the establishment of additional posts.

Lieutentant Stewart was to use Rangamatti as his base, and from there work southwards along the Belaisuri Tong range as far as the Rang Kyong river, where Lieutenant Baird starting from Demagiri was expectedto meet him.

Lieutenant Stewart was accompanied by two men of his own regiment.—Lance-Corporal McCormik and Private Owens—to assist in the survey operations, and he had as an escort one naick (corporal) and ten sepoys (Gurkhas) of the border police.

He left Rangamatti on the 16th January, and two days after, information was received at Demagiri, from a friendly chief Saipuya, that a large body of men, from

Malliam Pui, Tlan Tlang and Lungten, were on the warpath and proceeding in a westerly direction.

Although such alarms had come to be regarded somewhat in the light of the traditional cry of "wolf," parties of police were sent to the north and south of Demagiri, and a warning of the rumour conveyed to Lieutenant Stewart.

On the 2rd February he had worked along the Belaisuri Tong and was then encamped on a flat piece of ground, about eighteen miles in a direct line from Rangamatti, on a spur which connected it with the Saichal range.

By this time he had received information of a second impending raid, but with such contempt did he regard either the probability of an attack or the valour of his enemies, that when pressed by the naick of the escort to be on his guard and to take additional precautions he replied: "Kuki log ane se hamara salaam do" (give my compliments to the hill men and let them come on), and persistently declined even to post a sentry. He had left five sepoys of his small guard behind him, one to return with his elephants, another to take back his letters, and three to look after part of the provisions and form a depôt a few miles to the rear.

The hour of dawn, when the vital tide appears to be at the ebb and the senses are still under the drowsy influences of the night, is the one almost invariably chosen by the Chins and Lushais to attack their unsuspecting victims.

The camp was so arranged that the sepoys slept in advance, then came the stores, next the huts occupied by Stewart and the two European soldiers, and in the rear the coolies.

In the early morning Lieutenant Stewart awoke, dressed, and gave the usual orders for the move, but had not left his hut or put on his boots. The two soldiers were still asleep in their own quarters, and the sepoys of the escort were beginning to move about, one lighting a fire, and the others engaged in the various preparations which precede the striking of a camp in the east.

Suddenly a shot was fired which hit one of the sepoys in the thigh, breaking the bone; then two more followed, one of which wounded another of the escort in the arm. Taken thus by surprise some confusion ensued, and a few seconds passed before the fire of the enemy was returned. Mr. Stewart's servant with the guide and coolies ran away, and I regret to have to record that one of the sepoys followed their example. Two, as I have stated, had already been wounded, one had gone into the jungle before the attack commenced, and there were thus left only Mr. Stewart, the two European soldiers, Naick Kali Sing, and Sepoy Gaja Ram.

The European soldiers took no part in the defence from beginning to end, and the explanation of their inaction afterwards given by Sepoy Gaja Ram, was that their ammunition was with the coolies—surely a strange arrangement when raiders were reported to be about!

Lieutenant Stewart began firing as soon as he emerged from his hut—first with a revolver, and afterwards with his breech-loading gun. He was immmediatly joined by the two remaining men of the guard, and the three kept up a brisk return to the shots of the Lushais, until poor Stewart received a bullet in the chest and fell back dead, not, however, before he and the two men had accounted for several of the enemy. Such was the story told by the survivors, but, as Stewart's body was afterwards found at the foot of a precipice twenty or thirty yards from the huts, some of the particulars are probably inaccurate.

The two Gurkhas had now nearly come to the end of their ammunition, and, as their commander was beyond the reach of human aid, they considered that they were justified in looking after their own safety, and, accordingly, retired through the jungle towards the depôt where the provisions had been left. As they retreated, they heard the exultant yell which probably marked the discovery of Stewart's body.

Throughout the attack that officer preserved the intrepid coolness and disregard for personal safety which had marked his previous conduct.

Although the naick and sepoy tried to induce him to take cover under a clump of bamboos near the pathway, he refused to do so, either because he did not wish to leave his cartridges, which were in the hut, or because he thought he could do more execution where he was.

The naick and sepoy met the three men who had been left at the depôt, and who had been informed of the attack by the fugitive coolies. With them they returned to the scene of the late conflict, which they reached shortly after noon.

All was then quiet, and they found the bodies of the two European soldiers stripped and decapitated. A further search by Mr. Murray, District Superintendent of Police, who visited the spot shortly afterwards, revealed the headless trunk of the sepoy who had been shot in the thigh, and who had dragged himself to a stream close by.

No trace of Mr. Stewart could be obtained, although the body of one of the European soldiers was at first mistaken for his. The camp had been thoroughly looted, and among the spoil were included three Snider rifles belonging to the sepoy (Theka Ram) who had been killed, the man (Jangbir Thapa) who had been absent when the fight began, and Narbir Thapa who had run away; also the two Martini-Henry rifles of the British soldiers, Lieutenant Stewart's double-barrelled gun, his pistol, and some other personal effects. The bodies found were buried on the morning of the 7th February, wooden crosses being put up to mark the spot.

On the 25th, a party of hill men instigated by a promised reward of Rs. 200 offered by Mr. Lyall, Commissioner of Chittagong, discovered the body of Lieutenant Stewart lying at the foot of a precipice down which it had apparently fallen. It was headless but not stripped, and was identified by the clothes, decomposition being advanced.

The motive of the above murders arose, not from any alleged grievance against the British Government, but to fulfil an obligation under which Howsata, one of the chiefs of the Malliam Puis had placed himself to his father-in-law Jahuta, of the Tlan Tlang or Tantin Clan.

The story goes that Howsata had quarrelled with his wife who then took refuge with her father Jahuta, and that the latter, with some hesitation, only agreed to restore the lady to her legal owner on condition that he presented him with the heads of two foreigners, the idea, I believe, in the minds of these simple savages, being that the original owners of the ghastly trophies become the slaves of their final possessors in a future state of existence.

It was therefore by accident that the raiding party came across Stewart's camp, and, finding it unguarded, considered the opportunity of attaining their object too good to lose. Had ordinary precautions been taken for the safety of the party, there is little doubt that the attempt would not have been made, for neither Chin nor Lushai cares much for fighting unless the chances are all in his favour.

As in the case of the raids of 1871, the season was too far advanced for immediate retributive measures, and the despatch of a punitive expedition had to be postponed untill the following cold weather.

During the summer of 1888 a scheme of operations on the Chittagong frontier was framed by a committee under the orders of His Excellency the Commander-in-Chief, which embraced the despatch of a small force to Demagiri, from which a flying column was to be sent to meet another from the Burma side at Haka, with smaller expeditions in different directions from the base.

On the 22nd September, however, the Government finally decided that, owing to the unsettled state of the Chindwin district, it would be inexpedient to take any further action against the Shendús or Eastern Lushais for the present, but, at Mr. Lyall's suggestion, sanctioned the despatch of a small military force to act as a reserve to the police.

With this object in view, during the following November 250 men of the 9th Bengal Infantry were sent up to strengthen the police outposts. Such half measures in dealing with uncivilised races are almost invariably unsatisfactory, and generally have to be followed up by operations more elaborate and expensive than would have been required had the original offence been promptly and effectually punished. It was very soon found that the presence of 250 additional sepoys was not sufficient to put a stop to further raids.

On the 13th December, an attack, characterised by unusual ferocity, was made on a village, only four miles from our outpost of Demagiri and within British territory, belonging to a chieftainess called the Pakuma Rani.

Here indiscriminate and purposeless slaughter seems to have been indulged in, simply from the savage love of bloodshed. Neither age nor sex was spared, and, to complete their work of destruction, the raiders set fire to the village comtaining the headless corpses of their unfortunate victims. The Rani and twenty-one of her subjects were slain, while fifteen were carried off captive. It was subsequenty ascertained that the three Sylu chiefs, Nikama, Lungliena, and Kairuma, were responsible for the deed. The event was speedily followed by a series of raids, on a larger scale and marked by similar acts of cruelty, which took place in the Upper Chengri valley, about forty-three miles north-west of Rangamatti, between the 8th and 10th of January 1889. Twenty-four villages were raided, 101 persons killed, and 91 carried into captivity, the number of assailants, who belonged to the Sylu tribe, being estimated at 600.

The story told by two women who were taken prisoners, but afterwards escaped, well illustrates the ferocity of the savages. In describing her experiences in the retreat of her captors one of them said : " In the morning as we were starting, finding that I was unable to carry the brass plates and other things they had taken from my house, a Kuki came up and seized my elder boy who clung to my clothes. The man grasped him by the hair, forcibly dragged him away a few yards, and killed him with his *dha*. Then he returned and seized the infant at my breast, and killed him in the same manner before my eyes." The other woman had also her child snatched from her arms and killed, ten children being thus massacred.

At this time our old friend, the Sylu chief Sukpilal, had gone over to the majority, and his sons, eight in number, reigned in his stead. Either he had failed to impress them with a just appreciation of the majesty of the British power, or time had dimmed the memory of the parental precepts, for it was ascertained that the unfortunate captives had been carried off to the village of Lienpunga, one of the sons of Sukpilal, and that therefore he, aided probably by one or more of his brothers, must have been implicated in the raid on the Chengri valley. Forbearance was no longer possible, and it was determined to employ what remained of the cold weather in the organisation and despatch of a punitive force. Time, however, permitted of only the village of Howsata, one of the chiefs implicated in the raid on Lieutenant Stewart's party being visited, and most of the other objects which it was desirable to attain had to be left to a more convenient season.

CHAPTER V.

The Lushai Expedition of 1889 (*continued*).

Advance on Howsata's Village.

The column which was ordered to concentrate at Demagiri, and which was to be styled the "Lushai Expeditionary Force," comprised the following troops:—

2nd Bengal Infantry	250 men.
9th Bengal Infantry	250 "
2nd Battalion 2nd Gurkha Regiment	400 "
4th Madras Infantry (Pioneers)	200 "
Two guns of No. 2 Bombay Mountain Battery	

The whole under the command of Colonel V. W. Tregear, General List, Infantry.

Ammunition.—Seventy rounds in pouch, thirty on coolies and one hundred in reserve. Total, 200 rounds in regimental charge.

Transport.—A corps of 1,000 coolies to be raised in the Punjab and North-Western Provinces, with such additional coolies as it might be found possible to engage locally. Thirty-eight elephants were also to be sent.

To the frontier post of Demagiri the route to be followed was almost identical with that taken by the right or Chittagong column of 1871-72, *viz.*, from Chittagong to Rangamatti, up the picturesque course of the Kurnafulee river by steamer, and thence, for the troops, by land in four marches, *viâ* Burkal to Demagiri, while stores were transhipped to smaller boats at Rangamatti and conveyed to their destination by water, dug-outs being used for the latter part of the journey. A break in the continuity of the river carriage, to the extent of nearly two miles, occurred at the Burkal falls.

The boats had to be unloaded at the lower end known as Peshgiserra, and the goods carried by coolies to the Burkal stockade where they were re-embarked. Above this point there are some further obstructions in the shape of strong rapids, especially at Ootan Chutra and the Bara Harina Khal, but through all these the dug-outs could be dragged, although with considerable difficulty when the water was low.

With the exception of the detachment of the 9th Bengal Infantry, which, as we have seen, had been sent up early in November to strengthen the Frontier Police, the components of the force arrived at Demagiri, the base of operations, on the following dates :—Detachment 2nd Bengal Infantry on 11th and 12th January 1889; two guns, Bombay Mountain Battery, on 22nd and 28th January; Detachment 4th Madras Pioneers on the latter dates; and the 2nd Battalion, 2nd Gurkha Regiment, on the 4th and 15th February.

The three objects of the Expedition were defined in

Government letter No. 65L, dated 6th February 1889, as under :—

(1.) To construct a road in the direction of the Shendú country.

(2.) To punish Howsata and Jahuta for the murder of the late Lieutenant Stewart.

(3.) To establish an advanced post to be garrisoned during the season.

The second of the above orders was subsequently modified by a telegram received on the 3rd March, which directed that no punitive expedition was to be undertaken unless further circumstances rendered it absolutely necessary; but ultimately, much to the delight of the officers and men engaged, a final message which arrived on the 12th March permitted them to make Howsata's village the objective of the column.

Meanwhile the troops, assisted by upwards of 2,500 Chakma (a dark-skinned race in the Chittagong Hill Tracts) and Bengali coolies, who had been engaged by the civil authorities, were employed in the construction of a road from Demagiri to Lungleh, a distance of forty-one miles; the latter place, due east from the former, having been selected as the site for an advanced post.

The task of driving a road through such a country was no light one, large cuttings having to be made on the hill side, and temporary bridges to be erected over the numerous streams and nullahs which intersected the path. In addition to the above work the Chakma coolies

GURKHAS BUILDING A BASHA OR REST-HOUSE.

were at first employed in building temporary huts for the accommodation of the troops at the different halting places, but soon the sepoys learnt to do this for themselves, the Gurkhas especially possessing a natural aptitude for this sort of work and being able to turn their "kookeries" to any kind of cutting operation from the sharpening of a lead pencil to the felling of a tree.

The formation of the road was begun on the 16th January and completed to Fort Lungleh on the 11th March 1889, the result being a solid pathway from four to six feet wide over easy gradients and practicable for laden elephants.

While the above undertaking was in progress, several reconnaisances into the surrounding country were carried out by members of the force.

Captain Shakespear, Field Intelligence Officer, with Mr. Murray, twelve men of the Frontier Police and a few signallers, visited the village of the Howlong chief Saipuya on the 28th January returning to the headquarters on the 8th February. The chief renewed offers of friendship which he had formerly made and sent men to explore the route taken by the Expedition of 1871-72.

It will be remembered that this chief had already given proof of his friendly feelings towards us by sending intimation of the impending raids prior to the attack on Lieutenant Stewart's party.

Mr. Murray accompanied by fifty police, under the command of Mr. Walker, again left Demagiri for Saipuya's village on the 17th February, and afterwards extended his visit to the chief's eldest brother Vandula. As on the former occasion, the party were received with every outward mark of friendship, Saipuya supplying them with guides to show the way to his brother's village.

On arriving at Vandula's village the party were met by two men who forbade them to enter, to which prohibition a message was returned to the effect that enter they would, and that it remained with the chief to decide whether it was to be as friends or foes. The position was soon relieved by the appearance of the old gentleman himself with profuse apologies for the stupidity of his servants in offering such an inhospitable reception. Under the influence of Lushai spirit and rice-beer, the friendship so happily begun rapidly matured, and, among other interesting items, Mr. Murray was informed that the Shendús were making vast preparations for our attack, and that the Koladyne had been fortified with three tiers of stockades behind which three hundred warriors were waiting to conquer or to die. It was not, however, a case of *in vino veritas*, for the fortifications and their brave defenders were afterwards found to have existed only in the old man's imagination.

Vandula had at one time been one of the most powerful of the Howlong chiefs, but lately old age had overtaken him, and he had split up his villages among his sons. Still there is no doubt that his name carried weight among the tribe, and that his submission influenced others in following his example.

On leaving Vandula's village Mr. Murray and his party went on over Teriat, Moisum, and Bol Pui, across the Mat river, a tributary of the Koladyne, and over another range some 1,500 feet in height to the Koladyne itself.

A chieftainess name Darbilli, a near relative of Howsata, had sent two guides to point out the way to her kinsman's village, probably with an eye to future favours for herself. From one of these men Mr. Murray heard the rumour confirmed that Howsata had been dead for some time, and that Lieutenant Stewart's gun had been buried by his side. The same man also said that he had seen Stewart's revolver, but did not know where it then was.

The heads of the men killed had been sent for safety to another chief called Paona who lived further east, and who was one of the five implicated in the raid, the others being Howsata, his two sons, and Jahuta.

During this reconnaisance Mr. Murray was met by delegates from Dahuta and Jacopa, two chiefs of the Malliam Puis—a large tribe lying in the loop of the Koladyne river—with offers of submission. They were told that the chiefs should visit Colonel Tregear and make their terms with him as officer in supreme command.

The Howlongs had heard about Sir George White's fighting among the Chins, and described him as a

"Great White Raja," who had come from Burma and was destroying all he came across.

Perhaps the report may have reached the neighbouring tribe of Malliam Puis and stimulated their submission.

Before returning to Demagiri Mr. Murray got so near to the enemy that he could hear them peacefully clearing their "jooms" in the jungle.

The force selected for the advance on Howsata's village consisted of one gun and three hundred men, and at starting, was divided into two parties. The first of these, under the command of Lieutenant-Colonel Nicolay, was composed of 150 men of the 2nd Battalion, 2nd Gurkha Regiment, 40 Frontier Police, 20 Madras Pioneers and a few Sappers and Miners; the second comprised 50 men of the 2nd Bengal Infantry and one gun, under Major Channer, D.S.O., and was accompanied by Colonel Tregear, Mr. Lyall, Political Officer, and Staff.

Both parties left Lungleh on the 15th March within a few hours of each other and marched, the former to a camp below Bol Pui, and the latter to a camp near Moisum.

Next day Colonel Nicolay's party moved on to the Mat river, and Major Channer's to the camp below Bol Pui.

The two bodies of troops were united at the former halting place on the 17th, and on the 18th the advance was continued to the Koladyne, the mules being left behind, and the gun having to be carried by coolies on account of the bad condition of the road.

The original plan was that Howsata's village should now be surprised by a night march, but this idea had to be abandoned on account of the difficulties of the road and the professed inability of the guides, who had been supplied by Darbilli, to find the way in the dark.

The advance was accordingly postponed till daybreak of the 19th. On descending to the Koladyne, which was not reached until after dark, a flanking party of Gurkhas, under Major Begbie, came in sight of the fires of a picquet of the enemy, which bolted on our approach, leaving behind them a gun, knife, and powder flask, the gun being an old match-lock stamped with a crown, "G. R.," and tower on the lock.

After crossing the Koladyne two miles of easy going brought the force to the Darjow stream, the course of which they followed for three-quarters of a mile, when the foot of a spur which ran straight up to Howsata's village was reached. From this point the ascent was very steep, and the column, but especially the coolies, suffered much from want of water.

Three miles from Howsata's village the force arrived at a small one belonging to Jahuta, and it was decided to halt there for the night and go on to Howsata's early next morning. The houses were clean and afforded fair accommodation for the men.

The march was resumed at 5-30 on the morning of the 20th, and passing through the sites of Howsata's and Jahuta's old villages, a knoll, about a thousand yards from the modern residence of the former chief, was arrived at. The village was found to be divided into two parts, an upper and lower, the former being about 400 yards further off.

A couple of shots from the enemy apparently were intended as a signal for firing the village, for a number of the houses were soon seen to be in flames, and it required a few shells from the gun and a number of volleys from the Martinis to put a stop to further acts of incendiarism.

On entering the village it was found deserted, and two stockades which commanded the approach undefended, except in so far as the presence of a dog, which had been cut in half, while his blood was smeared on the posts of the first, might be supposed to deter our advance.

The guides pointed out a house of superior size and construction as the residence of the late chief, and on digging into a flat space in front of it, the body of Howsata was found dressed in robes and turban. In the grave had been placed his weapons, powder flask, and some food to provide for the wants of the departed warrior in a future world, while underneath the corpse was found Lieutenant Stewart's double-barrelled gun.

The principal objects of the Expedition had now been attained, and the column retraced its steps to Lungleh burning Jahuta's village as it passed.

A spot had been selected for the advanced post on the ridge which connects Lungleh with the site of Saipuva's old village, at 3,500 feet above sea-level, and on it was erected a stockade 167 yards by 40 to be called Fort Lungleh.

Within the stockade barrack accommodation was constructed for 200 men, with quarters for four officers, hospital, godowns for stores, magazine, and telegraph office.

There was an abundant supply of good water, and, after rationing it for eight months, the post was handed over, on the 15th April, to the Frontier Police who were to form the garrison.

Before leaving the country a durbar was held at Fort Lungleh on the 3rd April which the following Howlong chiefs attended :—

(1) Saipuya
(2) Lal Thuabunga. } *Brothers.*
(3) Lal Lunga.
(4) Sangliena—Son of Vandula, eldest brother of Saipuya.
(5) Lal Ruma.

In an address, which was translated to the chiefs in their own language by Mr. Murray, Mr. Lyall dwelt upon the events of the Expedition, and the causes which had led to it, pointing out the punishment which had been inflicted on the village of Howsata for the complicity of the late chief in the raid upon Lieutenant Stewart's party.

The meeting ended with the bestowal of rewards on those who had helped us, not forgetting a liberal distribution of rum without which no Lushai or Chin considers any ceremony complete.

The Malliam Pui chiefs had not yet come in, giving as their reason the unfriendly terms they were on with the Howlongs, but it was hoped that they would afterwards tender their submission to Mr. Murray who was to remain at Fort Lungleh.

In his despatch Colonel Tregear says: "The health of the troops during the four months the Expedition lasted was, I consider, marvellously good. There is no doubt, however, that the climate was beginning to tell on both officers and men towards the close of the operations, and that the health of the transport coolies who were very hard-worked, being incessantly employed in bringing up provisions, was seriously deteriorating, and that a very large number of them were what might be termed "played out."

The following table will help to show pretty accurately the amount of sickness in the force for the four months the operations lasted.

Details.	Number serving with the force.	Daily average number of sick.	Number sent on sick leave or invalided.	Number of deaths.
British Officers	45	0·16	1	2
British Warrant and Non-commissioned Officers	12	...	...	1
Native Troops	1,225	35·26	6	4
Transport Coolies	2,300	76·22	167	21
Public Followers	386	3 00	1	1

The two officers whose deaths are recorded were Lieutenant Pollen, R.E., belonging to the Government Survey of India, and Lieutenant A. T. Ward, Royal Irish Regiment, doing duty with the Transport Coolie Corps.

Both died of the remittent form of malarial fever, the former at Chittagong on the 26th March while proceeding to Darjeeling on sick leave, and the latter at Demagiri on the 2nd April after only ten days' illness.

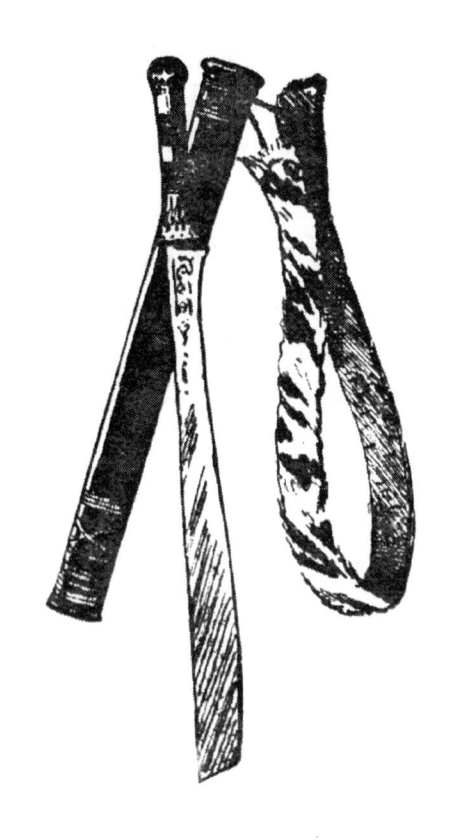

CHIN-LUSHAI DHA, SCABBARD AND BELT.

CHAPTER VI.

MILITARY OPERATIONS IN THE NORTHERN CHIN HILLS, 1888-89.

As has been seen the annexation of Upper Burma at the close of 1885 had brought us into contact with the Chins along the course of the Myittha and Chindwin rivers. It had also saddled the Government of India with the responsibility of protecting Her Majesty's new subjects from the inroads of the savages who had been in the habit of raiding the Burmese villages on the frontier, and carrying the inhabitants into captivity and slavery.

Hitherto the villagers had offered but a feeble resistance to these outrages, and it had not yet been brought home to the minds of the wild hill men, that the reins had dropped from the nerveless grasp of Theebaw, and that they were now held by a stronger hand.

During the month of October 1888, twelve of our subjects were said to have been killed, several wounded, and over a hundred and twenty carried off into slavery.

The Government of India had, however, strong objections to the undertaking of an extensive Chin Expedition this year, their hands being already full with two large expeditions in India. The Chief Commissioner of Burma, with Sir George White, therefore decided instead, to immediately occupy all the frontier stations with troops, while a small force was to be sent into the Northern Chin Hills, where dwelt the most ferocious and aggressive of all the tribes.

At the same time the Government of India had sanctioned the raising of an additional Military Police Battalion to be called the "Chin Levy" for the purpose of protecting the frontier.

This corps was to be about 600 strong, and to consist chiefly of Gurkhas and Punjabis, Lieutenant Rainey, Commandant of the Pakôkku Police Battalion, being selected to proceed to India to enlist the requisite number of recruits. It was not expected that the new corps could be got ready to take charge of the posts for which they were intended, earlier than February or March of the following year, and meanwhile the garrisons at the different positions had to be formed from the already existing body of police, supplemented by detachments of regular troops.

The chain of military posts to be occupied extended from Tammu and other stations in the Kubo Valley to Gangaw, Minywa, and Tilin on the Yaw border.

The force to operate in the Chin Hills was placed under the command of Brigadier-General Faunce who was accompanied by Major Raikes as Political Officer, the latter a gentleman who had had considerable experience on the frontier, and to whom was now entrusted full discretion in dealing with the tribes.

The General with 232 rank and file of the 10th Madras Infantry left Myingyan on the 9th November, and proceeded by steamer to Pakôkku near the junction of the Chindwin with the Irrawaddy, where he was joined by Major Leader with 100 more men of the same regiment. This column was further augmented by the addition of 50 Madras Lancers, who had been detailed as a personal escort to the General, while the right wing and head-quarters of the 42nd Gurkha Light Infantry under Colonel Skene, which was on its way to Assam, were ordered to stand fast in the Myittha Valley.

The force left Pakôkku on the 14th November, and reached Kambale on the 3rd December, the latter post, on the left bank of the Myittha river, having been selected as the immediate base of operations into the hills. The infantry were dropped to garrison the intermediate stations on the way.

At Kambale, in addition to the 50 Lancers who had accompanied him, General Faunce found 159 rifles of the 42nd Gurkha Light Infantry, 2 guns with 70 rank and file, No. 1, Bengal Mountain Battery, and 48, No. 2 Company, Queen's Own Madras Sappers and Miners.

One hundred and fifty-eight rifles more of the 42nd Gurkhas were at Sihaung, two marches south of Kambale, and he only awaited the arrival of Colonel MacGregor, who was marching *viâ* Manipur with 500 men of the 44th Gurkhas and expected on the 15th December, to commence the march into the hills.

The telegraph wire was being rapidly pushed on to Kambale, and on the 5th December the formation of a road into the Chin Hills, which was to lead the force to the head village of the Siyins, the first objective, was begun.

While engaged in this work Lieutenant Palmer, R.E., was mortally wounded on the 7th December, and died the following evening.

The Chins poured a volley into the road-making party guarded by 40 men of the 42nd Gurkhas, which was then establishing the first stockade about six miles from Kambale.

This event was followed by a number of almost simultaneous attacks along the Chin border.

On the 10th December a large party of Tashôn Chins attempted to surprise the camp of the 42nd Gurkhas at Sihaung at daybreak, but only succeeded in mortally wounding two followers.

Captain Westmoreland, Commanding, then sent out two parties of Gurkhas. His own, in which he was accompanied by Mr. Hall, Extra Assistant Commissioner, consisted of 25 Gurkhas. They found a body of 500 Chins or more surrounding the village of Kyawzwa one mile from camp. The Gurkhas got to within forty yards unseen, when they poured in a volley, and charged the enemy pursuing them for a mile. The Chin loss was twenty to thirty killed and many wounded. Three Burmese women, who were being taken away captive, were recovered, as also several guns. On the return of the Gurkhas the Sihaung villagers turned out *en masse*, and cheered the gallant little party.

On the same day the camp at Indin was fired into from the opposite bank of the Myittha but without result.

On the 11th December Kangyi, near Yazagyo, further to the north, was attacked by some sixty Chins, one sepoy of the military police being slightly wounded.

Colonel MacGregor, with the head-quarters of the 44th Gurkhas, arrived at Kambale on the 15th December, having done the distance from Manipur in twelve marches. They were sent to relieve the 42nd Gurkhas at Sihaung, who were ordered in.

The road had now been completed for a distance of twelve miles, and was being steadily pushed on, although under considerable difficulties, for the Chins took every opportunity of harassing the working parties and occasionally inflicted slight losses. No. 2 stockade had been completed at the 12th mile on the 10th December, and on the 22nd a position for No. 3 was selected at a place called Thyetbin Sakān six miles further on, and at an elevation of 3,700 feet. Two days later a sepoy of the 42nd Gurkhas belonging to the escort of a party working beyond this point was killed.

On the 25th December an unusually determined attack was made on a working party with an escort of the same regiment under Lieutenant G. H. Butcher. The Chins were estimated to number nearly a thousand. After two hours of fighting the enemy were repulsed with about forty killed and wounded.

On the 30th December the working part of the force was augmented by the arrival of 43 more Madras and fourteen Burma Sappers, an assistance much required.

Fifty men of the Norfolk Regiment, who had joined the column with 190 rifles of the 42nd Gurkhas, reconnoitred towards Siyin on the 22nd January. After passing Ehsin Sakān, the future site of No. 4 stockade and five miles from No. 3, their progress was obstructed by a stockade placed across the path, while another had been constructed on the *khud* and a third concealed in the jungle.

Here some firing took place, one sepoy being killed, and five wounded.

On the same day a convoy coming up from No. 2 to No. 3 stockade was attacked with the loss of one private Norfolk Regiment killed and one slightly wounded.

The village of Mawklin was attacked on the 24th January, and taken almost without opposition, 50 men of the Norfolk Regiment and 125 rifles of the 42nd Gurkhas being engaged.

On the 27th a working party with a guard of 40 rifles of the Norfolk Regiment, and 100 of the 42nd Gurkhas, were attacked by a large body of Chins. The working party was sent back to No. 3 stockade. The enemy were driven to the stockades formerly mentioned, which had been rebuilt, and where they made a stand.

Major-General Sir George White, v.c., Commanding in Upper Burma, who had come up to personally superintend the operations, joined the party with 30 men of the 42nd Gurkhas, and, in a charge brilliantly led by Colonel Skene, the Chins were driven from the stockades, the casualties on our side being only one lance-corporal of the Norfolk Regiment severely wounded.

On the 31st January No. 1 Mountain Battery, 162 rifles, Norfolk Regiment, 252 men of the 42nd Gurkhas, with 98 Sappers, proceeded to establish the post called No. 4 stockade at Ehsin Sakān. No. 5 stockade was erected on a knoll overlooking the water supply of No. 4.

All the preliminary measures had now been prepared for the final advance on the head village of the Siyins, the tribe which had been the most aggressive and persistent in their encroachments on our frontier.

The force detailed for the undertaking was composed as follows :—

	Officers.	Men.
Norfolk Regiment	5	176
42nd Gurkha Light Infantry	6	250
No. 2 Company Sappers and Miners	2	91
No. 1 Bengal Mountain Battery	1	2 guns.

The column moved forward on the 4th February, meeting with no opposition beyond a few shots fired from "Sangas"—loosely built shelter walls.

On arriving at Siyin it was found that the Chins had

themselves fired their village, only about twenty-six out of two hundred houses escaping the conflagration.

The troops were now working at a considerable elevation, and the cold had become proportionately severe, the water in the men's bottles freezing at night, while the thermometer stood at 38° at seven in the morning.

The villages of Tokhlaing and Bweman were occupied on the 6th February almost without resistance, the whole force moving to the former on the 13th. Some 400 feet above and a little to the south-west of Tokhlaing, a site was selected for the position of the permanent post which was christened Fort White in honour of the Commander of Upper Burma. The choice of locality turned out to be more unfortunate than that of name, for the place was afterwards found to be a hot-bed of sickness, and the quarters had to be ultimately shifted to a more favourable spot.

To describe in full the successive captures of the various Siyin, Sagyilain, and Kanhow villages would involve a somewhat wearisome repetition of detail, and I shall therefore merely run over briefly the principal events and movements of the troops, which brought the operations to a close.

On the 17th February Colonel Skene attacked the two villages of the Sagyilains, a small tribe which lived contiguous with, and to the south of, the Siyins.

The larger and more powerful tribe of the Kanhows who dwelt to the north, was next dealt with.

The village of Waukālè was occupied by the force, which had been reinforced by the arrival of 150 men of the 44th Gurkhas, on the 8th March, with but three non-fatal casualties on our side.

On the 10th Tsayan (300 houses) was captured, the enemy losing fifteen killed, with thirty to forty wounded. On the 12th Tigyin (250 houses) was attacked and occupied. The village had been fired by the Chins, but its destruction was arrested after about one-third of the houses had been burnt.

On the 16th the force marched for Tanka, which was found deserted but not fired.

Walawun opposite to Tigyin was visited on the 18th and on the 19th the force bivouacked on the Letha range.

On the 20th March the force divided into two columns and again turned southwards, one proceeding to Tokhlaing and the other visiting the villages of Yon, Phonon, and Taungwè.

The attack and capture of the Siyin village of New Tātan followed on the 4th May, and is of more interest than the preceding occurrences from the comparatively stubborn resistance offered by the Chins on the occasion.

The force selected for the purpose was composed of 65 men of the Norfolk Regiment and 60 rifles of the 42nd Gurkhas, and was placed under the command of Captain O. Mayne of the former corps.

This small column left Fort White at 4-40 A.M., and by nine had occupied, without opposition, the heights above the village, a covering party of 15 Norfolks and 10 Gurkhas having been left at the end of the Siyin spur.

Leaving a further party of the Norfolk Regiment to hold the heights, the rest of the column then advanced on the village, which was three or four hundred feet below and appeared to have been deserted.

Captain Westmoreland led with a few of his men followed by Captains Mayne and Donne, 2nd Lieutenant Michel being in rear with the main body. While descending a Chin was heard shouting. The main body was then ordered to advance and the troops in front began to double with the intention of rushing the village. On reaching it, fire was opened by the Chins, who were posted in two stockades at the bottom.

Michel who, with a few men, had descended by the spur to the east of the ravine, came suddenly on the lower of the stockades, and was mortally wounded by a shot from it. His party halted near where he fell, and began firing on the stockade. The rest of the men advanced right up to the upper stockade firing.

The upper of the two stockades consisted of a log hut the sides and roof of which had been rendered bullet-proof. It was connected with the ravine by a trench covered with logs and planks. The second stockade was in the bed of the ravine. It consisted of a hole about six or nine feet square from which a trench ran down the ravine a short distance. The trench and the hole were also covered with logs and planks. All the Chins (10 or 12) found inside the upper stockade were killed, the logs having to be pulled up from the trench to get at them.

Meanwhile a dropping fire was coming from the lower stockade. Captain Mayne, who had been slightly injured at the commencement, was now severely wounded, and Surgeon Le Quesne while dressing his wound, was also severely wounded himself.

The second stockade was not taken, and the force retired to Tātan, which was then burnt. The troops reached Fort White at 9-30 P.M., having been seventeen hours under arms.

The enemy's loss was estimated at 30 and our casualties were—

Killed and died of wounds.
Second Lieutenant W. G. Michel and 2 men of the Norfolk Regiment: 1 Naick 42nd Gurkhas. ... 4

Severely Wounded.
Captain O. Mayne, Surgeon Le Quesne, M. S., 4 men 42nd Gurkhas, 1 Kahar. ... 7

Slightly wounded (by Panjies).
Three men 42nd Gurkhas 3

Total 14

All the Siyin and Sagyilain villages with eighteen of those of Kahows had now been captured, but their former inhabitants, although wandering houseless in the jungles, were still unsubdued, and so far the objects of the expedition had been only partially fulfilled.

COUNTRY TRAVERSED BY THE CHIN FIELD FORCE OF 1889-90.

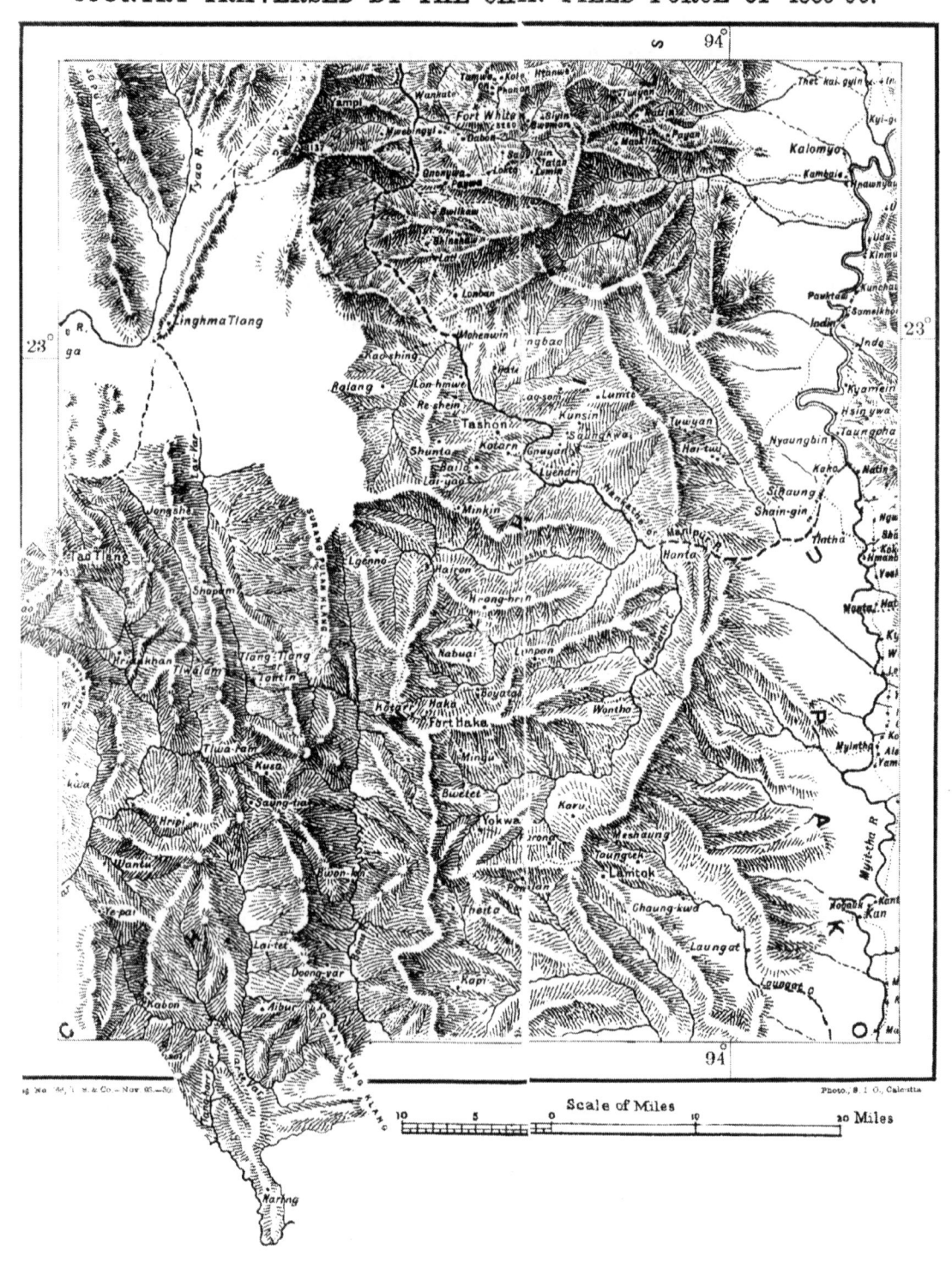

CHAPTER VII.

THE CHIN-LUSHAI EXPEDITION OF 1889-90.

On the March with the 2nd Battalion, 4th Gurkha Rifles.

BEFORE entering into the history of the next expedition, and continuing the narration of successive events appertaining thereto, which, from their similarity, is liable to become monotonous, I propose now to devote a few lines to the description of another hill race, hailing from a country not unlike that of the Chins and Lushais, who had taken a prominent part in the previous expeditions and who were to form a considerable portion of the force which it had been decided upon to send into the interior of the Chin-Lushai Hills when the return of the cold weather should render the resumption of military operations practicable.

I allude to the Gurkhas who constitute a most important element in the Native Army of India, but more on account of their general excellent military qualities and special unrivalled aptitude for hill fighting than on that of their numbers, the present strength amounting to only thirteen battalions and between eleven and twelve thousand rank and file. This small force is, I venture to say, allowed to be among the cream of the Bengal Infantry and unsurpassed for mountain and jungle warfare, as the East India Company found to its cost in the campaign of 1814-15, a struggle which, it is said, was brought to a conclusion favourable to the British interests partly through the treachery of the Gurkha Commanders to their own ruler.

The term Gurkha is now applied to the Nepalese generally, but originally it was restricted to the inhabitants of the district around the town of Gorkha,—the ancient capital—which is about forty miles west of Kâthmandu, the modern metropolis.

These formed the dominant race and are considered to be of Rajput origin.

The Magars and Gurungs occupy the country to the west of the Nepal Valley. They are short powerful men, of Mongolian cast of features and are the castes most sought after for enlistment in the British Army. A Magar or Gurung, with his broad flat face, sturdy frame, oblique eyes, and merry honest expression, is the type which the British Officer loves. He is as brave as a lion in the field, light-hearted as a schoolboy and true as steel : war is his profession, fighting his pastime : yet withal as gentle and docile as a lamb, in cantonments : crime in his regiment is at a minimum and the graver phases of it almost unknown.

" As any one may ascertain by consulting a map of

India, the Kingdom of Nepal is a small independent State situated on the North-Eastern frontier of Hindustan. It is a strip of country about five hundred miles long and a hundred and thirty broad, lying between the snowy range of the Himalayas on the north, Sikhim on the east and the provinces of British India on the south and west.

"The name Nepal is restricted by the Natives of the country to the valley surrounding the capital. This is the only part of the kingdom which is open to the investigation of Europeans; and it would be a hopeless task to attempt the description of places which cannot be visited, or the collection of accurate information regarding a country where every enquiry made by a European is viewed with the most jealous suspicion and where the collection of statistics is looked on as a mere folly."

Personally I am of opinion that this objection to the intrusion of strangers does not altogether do discredit to the intelligence of the Nepalese, for instances are not unknown when too intimate an acquaintance by foreigners with the advantages of a country has led to results not conducive to its national independence.

The Gurkha regiment selected for the coming expedition was the young second battalion of the fourth Gurkha Rifles, and, as this was the first experience by the new corps of active service and the first occasion on which the great majority of the men had seen a ship or even the sea, perhaps a description of the journey of the head-quarters of the battalion from their home at Bakloh on a spur of the Himalayas to Pakôkku on the right bank of the Irrawaddy, where the troops for the Southern Column of the Burma Force had been ordered to concentrate, may be of some interest to my readers.

The proverbial fish out of water or the Scriptural pelican in the wilderness might, at first sight, be assumed to be not more out of correspondence with their respective new environments than a Gurkha on board an Indian Marine troopship. It is true that some years previously as a recruit he and his umbrella, then almost the only article of wardrobe, had been conveyed by the "āggharry" (steam-engine), moved at a supernatural speed, by, to him, a mysterious agency, from the recruiting depôt at Gorakhpur to Pathankot near his future home, and that his appreciation of the marvellous had been somewhat further fed by sights and scenes during occasional descents from his little mountain home He had gazed with wonder, while at the Camp of Exercise, at the Mian Mir Artillery horses, which appeared to him, measured by a Nepalese standard, like the mammoths of a former age. Wheeled vehicles had been a mode of transport perhaps heard of but hitherto unseen.

The streets of Lahore, compared with his native villages, formed a city of fairy palaces. Still, such experiences had all occurred on *terra firma*, while he was now called upon to traverse an unknown element and by a method of which he could form only the most vague conception.

With the sanguine imagination of youth, which loves to paint the possibilities of the future, in rosier lines than the realities of the past, he started down hill on the 23rd October 1889 with hopes high burning and anticipated Naickships*, Havildarships†, and perhaps even Orders of Merit, forming a confused but pleasing mental vision. He had heard the beheading of Chins and Lushais described, and, while on the march, saw the operation pantomimed by an older and more travelled companion, a transfer from the first battalion, and at the time registered a vow as fervid as that of any scalp-hunting Redskin that he would establish a record of his own should opportunity offer.

The mighty " Sirkari Jehaz " (troop-ship) had, however, never come within his ken and an occasional voyage in a dug-out across one of his native streams formed hardly a sufficient unclens from which to envole even an approximate idea.

The duty of selecting the required number of men to remain at the depôt had been rather a painful one, and the medical officer, although not naturally of an aggressive disposition, felt, that in the short space of an hour he had made more personal enemies than during the previous course of his chequered existence.

---

* Naick=Corporal. * Havildar=Sergeant.

The march from Bakloh to Pathankot (40 miles), the terminus of the branch line, was uneventful, the most pleasing incident to my mind being the capture of a good basket of " Mahseer" at Shahpur, a picturesque spot on the left bank of the Ravi which separates it from Cashmere territory. From the verandah of the little bungalow in the bastion of the fort which figured in the mutiny, we descried a number of fairly sized fish in a deep pool some hundreds of feet below and it was not long before several were paying their last debt to nature on the shingle.

From Pathankot to Howrah we halted during the day at Umballa, Bareilly, Fyzabad, Dinapur and Muddapur, being hospitably treated at all these stations by our military brethren who received us with open arms. The skirl of the bagpipes generally attracted a crowd at the hour of departure, and the farewell cheers on both sides were not unworthy of more western lungs and throats.

Calcutta was reached without a hitch or casualty of any kind, and the first to great us on the platform was our permanent Commandant Colonel King-Harman who had just arrived from Bombay by the mail train. Up to this point the head-quarters of the battalion had been commanded by Major Sir Charles Leslie, Bart, who now returned to take the left wing to Chittagong.

Our progress into Calcutta was more like that of a regiment returning from, than (as we fondly hoped) marching to, victory. Headed by two bands, in addition to our own pipes and trumpets, and accompanied by an admiring crowd on either side, each little Magar Thapa felt "a prood man that day." I watched with amused interest the expression of wondering astonishment as the waters of the Hooghly, with its stately forest of masts, broke upon his view, and I saw that the untutored mind within was undergoing a sudden process of development and expansion—marvel upon marvel succeeded each other with kaleidoscopic rapidity. No sooner was the bridge left behind than he saw "Sahibs" riding on wheels without carriages, and carriages moving silently without horses. The steam engine had by this time become a familiar object, but here it was concealed from view, all apparent motive power being absent and progress could only be attributed to magic. The streets of Lahore vanished from memory as suddenly as Cinderella's carriage from sight and even the Artillery horses were forgotten: so much are our ideas governed by comparison.

After three most enjoyable days spent in the rest camp, or rather out of it, for we were lost in choice of hospitality, the right wing of the battalion embarked on the Indian Marine Ship "*Clive*" at 6 A.M. of the 5th November. The left wing sailed at a later date to serve under General Tregear on the Lushai side.

All speed had to be made in order to get out of the river before the tide fell. Soon the *Liverpool*, the largest of British sailing ships was passed, craft of all shapes and nationalities divided attention with the wonders on board; but I could see that the latter claimed precedence. The engine-room appeared to have a magnetic influence, and around it could always be seen a crowd of little figures in khaki, peering in at the port holes on tip-toe, for it was only in this position that a Gurkha was able, like the peri at the gates of Paradise, to obtain a view of the scene. I asked some of them, with what object the pistons moved up and down but could elicit no replies further than "*khabber*" (who knows?) "*chalanaki waste*" (to make it go) or "*Sirkar ka hukum se*" (by the order of Government).

Their understanding was subsequently enlightened by one of the Marine Officers, who kindly set a small model of a steam ship in motion for their instruction.

But now we are past the Sandheads, and why has the *jehaz* begun to roll about in this erratic manner? They can remember a similar personal experience during the "holi" week, but they could account for that, for rum was then flowing freely. And what again is this no less mysterious sinking sensation which a little warrior feels in a particular region and is soon followed by an objective and objectionable symptom?

"*Bokhar*" (fever) he is unfortunately too familiar with in all its stages, but it resembles none of these: rheumatism may have racked his limbs, but now they are free from pain, although rather unsteady. He turns enquiringly to a comrade but sees similar phenomena in progress: I fear the answer again must be "*khabber*."

We arrived at Rangoon on the evening of the 8th November, but too late to land that night, and were obliged to do penance for our sins by being devoured by mosquitos, while sleeping on deck, the cabins being unbearably hot. I was aroused at an unearthly hour by language loud and strong proceeding from an officer who seemed to have had rather a bad time of it, for I heard him afterwards declare that "his feet were so swelled that he could not get them into his boots, and that he had to send them to the engine room:" this irritability was not allayed by his listener mildly enquiring "which he had sent, his feet or the boots."

By night, Rangoon, with a full moon rising among a mass of black clouds above the twinkling lights on the banks, presented a most striking scene, but oh! the heat and mosquitos. I sympathised with my irascible companion, and thought that the recording angel might have blotted out the entry of words he had heard with a pitying tear.

Daylight saw the troops landed and the remainder of the day was spent principally in hunting up Staff Officers, who appeared to be as plentiful in Rangoon as swallows in May, although quite as difficult to catch. The result was that we were told "to reduce our number of fighting-men to 400, get on to service scale, depart at 4-30 P.M., for Pakôkku and there await further orders."

The appearance of the town and cantonments of Rangoon impressed me very favourably, but I cannot say as much for the climate, and as the latter is supposed, in the process of evolution, to have the greatest influence in determining the ultimate psychological and physiological characters of a people, I can quite understand the *dolce far niente* air which permeated the place; although it was not equally easy to account for the general appearance of prosperity, which, contrary to the precepts impressed in text and half-text on our childish memories, accompanied it. As we heard it put by a Milesian Officer "they were sleeping in Bombay, they were snoring in Madras, but, begorra! they were dead in Rangoon."

The strains of the pipes collected a crowd which accompanied us to the station at 4 o'clock. By 4-30 we were off, packed rather tightly in small narrow-gauge carriages. The journey to Prome, a distance of 161 miles, takes twelve hours, and hot ones they were, so that the men were standing on the left bank of the Irrawaddy ready for embarkation before day broke.

As the sun rose the scene which greeted our eyes was indescribably beautiful: before us a broad and swiftly flowing expanse of water, unbroken save by the craft of all kinds which plied on its bosom; the banks rising into low and fantastic hills clothed with dense green vegetation, among which towered stately palms like sentinels of the forest, with here and there a golden pagoda flashing in the morning rays and relieving the prevailing hue.

Our first run was to Thayetmyo (48 miles) near which is the boundary which used to divide Upper from Lower Burma. Night had closed in about an hour before we reached the halting place, and it was a puzzle to understand how the pilot found his way. That, however, he did without any diminution of speed, and shortly after seven o'clock the camp fires on the bank told that the men were preparing their creature comforts such as they were. It might appear hard to make merry over a half-cooked *chapatti* (cake of unleavened bread) and a handful of *dhall* (lentils), but even this feat the Gurkhas seemed to accomplish, judging from the sounds of laughter which reached us.

After a night spent on deck, where we were glad to draw a blanket over us as morning approached, daybreak again saw the *Irrawaddy* under way: but to describe each day's progress would weary my readers.

Suffice it to say that we reached Yuathil without let or hindrance. Minhla was passed on the port-side next morning soon after starting.

Here, as may be remembered, took place (in November 1885) the second fight in the recent campaign, the first having occurred at Sinboungweh, a few miles lower down. The remembrance was rendered the more interesting to us by the fact, that our ship, the *Irrawaddy*, had taken a leading part in the affair, and a corner of the fort still showed where her guns had left their mark.

What changes had taken place in the country since that time! One could hardly imagine that the pretty and peaceful-looking towns with their graceful pagodas and rapidly extending houses had been scenes of dacoity and bloodshed little more than two years before.

I believe that almost the whole trade of the Irrawaddy is in the hands of Chinamen, the Burmese being too indolent and indifferent to make any effort to retain it.

Higher up the river the banks became less rugged than at Prome, but detached mountain spurs in the distance more than compensated for this change in the foreground.

"Popa" an extinct volcanic mountain 3,400 feet high, stood distinctly in sight with a cloud resting on its summit. It is densely wooded to the top, from which, I was told, the adventurous climber can look down into a chasm of 1,200 feet of perpendicular descent, the arena of subterranean forces in a former age.

As the sun was sinking we passed that city of deserted temples—old Pagān—the soft evening light lending an additional air of melancholy to the graceful but now crumbling pagodas, from which, some two hundred years ago, thousands of worshippers had been wont to offer their tributes of homage and devotion to the great Buddha.

I was informed by one of the ship's officers, and have since then heard the statement confirmed, that Pagān contains nine thousand, nine hundred and ninety-nine pagodas, and I confess that when I was first told of the fact it reminded me of the story of the Yankee who said that he had killed ninety-nine duck with one shot, and who, when asked why he did not at once make it a hundred replied that "he guessed he was not going to imperil his immortal soul for the sake of one darned duck." Whether the number I have given is absolutely correct or not, it is an undisputed fact that about eighteen square miles are densely covered with pagodas in various stages of decay, although some are still in a wonderful state of preservation considering the total absence of any care. They were made out by the late Dr. Forchhammer, Professor of Pāli and Curator of the Bernard Free Museum at Rangoon, to have been built between the middle of the fifteenth and seventeenth centuries. The city has long been uninhabited, all traces of even the dwellings of its former residents having disappeared.

It must now be a paradise to an archæologist and I believe the progress of destruction is being materially hastened by the inquisitive and acquisitive Briton.

The inscriptions on the temples are in Pāli, now almost a dead and archaic language. Pagān at one time was the capital of a kingdom.

With the pipes on deck playing "The Campbells are coming" we reached Pakôkku, which was to form the first base of operations, on the 14th November.

CHAPTER VIII.

THE CHIN-LUSHAI EXPEDITION, OF 1889-90.

Concentration of the Southern Chin Column at Pakôkku and Advance to Kān.

AT Pakôkku we found the remainder of the troops which were to form the Southern column of the Chin Field Force, or, as it was at first called, the Gangaw column from the original intention of making Gangaw the immediate base of operations, already assembled. The column consisted of the following troops:—Half battalion, King's Own Scottish Borderers; half battalion, Second Fourth Gurkha Rifles; two guns, No. 1 Bengal Mountain Battery; No. 6 Company, Madras Sappers; and the Second Regiment, Madras Infantry. Colonel W. P. Symons, of the South Wales Borderers, with the temporary rank of Brigadier-General, had been invested by the Governor-General in Council with supreme political as well as military authority of this and the Northern or Fort White column in which Colonel Skene held the immediate command.

Field service was ruled to commence from the 15th November, and the interval between that date and the

23rd November, when the first detachment started for Kān, was employed by the General Officer in inspecting the troops under his command, issuing orders regarding transport supplies, and making other necessary arrangements; while the regimental commanding officers took the opportunity of giving their men a few route marches to prepare them for the journey.

A month's travelling by rail and steamer and halting at Pakôkku in a temperature only suited for a Strasbourg goose had not been a good preparation for such a task as we had before us, namely fifteen days' marching, without a halt, over an execrable road.

The distance from Pakôkku to Kān is stated as 165 miles, but we all agreed that the official who measured it could not have been drawing travelling allowance.

Before dissmissing Pakôkku from the narrative, it may be worth mentioning that we experienced a severe shock of earthquake there on the 23rd November, at 2-30 P.M. It lasted about four seconds, proceeding from north to south, and being sufficiently violent to injure several of the pagodas.

The movement of the troops was arranged as follows :—

(1) No. 6 Company, Madras Sappers and Miners, to start on the 23rd November.

(2) General Symons and his staff on the 24th.

(3) One detachment K. O. S. Bs. on the 25th.

(4) Another on the 26th.

(5) One detachment, 2-4th Gurkha Rifles, on the 27th.

(6) A second on the 28th.

(7) One detachment, 2nd Madras Infantry, on the 29th.

(8) No. 1 Bengal Mountain Battery, two guns, with an escort of the 2nd Madras Infantry, on the 30th.

Each detachment was fully and independently equipped as regards medical and transport arrangements, the carriage up to Kān consisting principally of mules, which experience has taught are the best form of transport where the roads are passable for animals.

The scale of baggage allowed was as follows :—

Officers	80 lbs.	each.
Regimental Mess	163	,,
Warrant Officers	40	,,
Native Officers	25	,,
British Troops	25	,,
,, Cooking Pots	160	per company.
Native Troops	20	each.
,, Cooking Pots	80	per company.
Followers	15	each.

No tents were taken, as temporary mat huts had been erected at the different halting places, and it was intended that the troops should construct shelters for themselves after they entered the enemy's country, the difficulty of transpost precluding any other arrangement.

As regards ammunition, each man carried 40 rounds in pouch; 60 rounds per man were carried on mules; and 100 rounds per man taken to the base at Kān as a second reserve.

In describing the march from Pakôkku to Kān the experiences of one detachment will suffice for all and I take those of the head-quarters of the 2-4th Gurkha

Rifles, which started on the 27th November, and of which I happened to be in medical charge.

Up to Pauk, which is put down as forty-five miles from Pakôkku, the route is over heavy sand in which walking, decked out like a Christmas tree as one is now-a-days, with Sam Browne belt, sword, revolver, ammunition-pouch, binoculars, compass, water-bottle, pocket-filter, haversack (containing plate, cup, fork, knife, spoon, &c.), note-book and a few smaller sundries, while a Burman sun blazes overhead, is no picnic.

The march into Pauk is the worst of the lot, including as it does, two fords of the Yaw river in which the water comes well up to the waist, while the current is very strong.

The Gurkhas, however, appeared to think this the pleasantest feature of the march, and as they had to undress before crossing, the greater portion of the detachment was soon represented by a number of round black objects bobbing about in the stream, from which they emerged with evident reluctance. Pauk is the capital of Yaw, and, including its large suburbs, contains about 1,000 houses. It is at an elevation of 628 feet. The post was garrisoned by 100 men of the 2nd Madras Infantry under a British officer, and from the latter we received a most hospitable welcome.

Up to Tilin the line of march runs west by north- and from Pauk to that post, 48 miles, the road crosses two ranges, the "Pondaung" and "Ponya," the former about two and the latter three thousand feet above sea-level.

After crossing the second range the Chin Hills come in sight.

Tilin is on the right bank of the "Maw," the watershed of which is formed by a spur of the Chin Hills, which curves round and joins the Pondaung. It was garrisoned by a detachment of the 3nd Madras Infantry similar in strength to that at Pauk. At the time of our visit Tilin rejoiced in two imposing institutions, a post office and a telegraph office, with their respective establishments complete, but here the arrangement ended; for they neither received nor despatched letters or telegrams. I believe that the telegraph wire had been fastened to trees without the intervention of insulators, a method which did not suit a moist climate, sappy stem, and weak batteries.

Opposite to Tilin for some miles the Chin Hills are uninhabited, but beyond that they are occupied by the Chin-Bôks, the most southern of the tribes, and even more primitive in dress and customs than their northern neighbours. The word "bôk" is to smell or stink in Burmese, but whether the Burmans thus name the Chin-Bôks on account of their offensive customs or dirty personal habits is not known. The Chin name for the tribe is "Yo-ôn."

The Chin-Bôk and Chin-Mai (black Chins, a section of the Bôks) women tattoo their faces, which gives them a peculiarly repulsive appearance, with the object, it is said, of rendering them less attractive to the Burmans, and therefore less liable to abduction.

From Tilin to Kān, the route which, at the time of our march, was over a mule path and impassable for carts, runs due north through the Myittha valley, first on the left and then on the right bank of the river, distance 72 miles. This was by far the pleasantest part of the march, the country being more open and the road better for walking.

The nights began to get a little cooler and the air drier: previously the dews had been so heavy that in the early morning the dripping from the trees resembled rain.

Gangaw, where there was another post with 100 of the 2nd Madras Infantry, was reached on the 9th December. This is a remarkably pretty place. The stockade, within which the Officer Commanding lived, was on the top of a high cliff overhanging the Myittha, and at the base of which there was a deep pool from which I managed to extract one fish of about 5lbs.

About six miles from Gangaw, on the Pakôkku side, we passed a small Burmese village called Kaukka, which was afterwards raided on the 26th December by a party of about twenty-five Chins, one man and one woman being killed. Opposite and close to the village of Kaukka there is a very peculiarly-shaped hill—Nètoung—which, from the direction we approached, had a striking resemblance to a man's face in the supine position. A small white cloud rested on the upper lip and another round the cheek making an excellent imitation of moustache and whiskers.

The temporary huts erected at the different halting places had been built by Burmese contractors under the direction of the civil authorities and were fairly comfortable, being constructed to accommodate a detachment of two hundred men with followers. The roofs consisted of screens of leaves supported on poles, and the floor, which was raised two feet from the ground, was formed from split bamboo laid in close contact. A nail did not enter into the structure, the joints being united by sockets and fastened with bamboo fibre.

The forest vegetation on the line of march consisted principally of bamboo, "sal," and palm jungle, around the stems of the latter of which, in many instances, peepuls had twisted themselves, while the interspaces were filled up with creeping and climbing plants. We also passed fine specimens of the tamarind, the leaves of which, in the absence of the fruit, are an excellent antiscorbutic. Orchids flourished luxuriantly. The only fruits or vegetables we were able to obtain were watermelons, plantains, sweet limes and pumpkins.

Rice, maize, gram, dhall and "patwas" grew in the cultivated patches.

The country seemed to be the natural habitat of indigo, for we noticed the wild variety growing by the roadside.

There was almost no sickness among the men on the march, and all the transport animals arrived at Kān in good condition and with wonderfully few sore backs considering the work they had been put to.

The Burmese village of Kān is situated on the right bank of the Myittha river, lying in the middle of a valley of the same name, bounded by a range of hills on either side. The plain at the time of our arrival presented large fields of rice, then yellow and nearly ripe. Numbers of palms, tamarinds and other trees were dotted about. The climate was pleasant but damp, and before sunrise heavy fogs hung over the valley. The elevation is 500 feet above sea-level.

In addition to the Burmese inhabitants numbers of Chins, refugees from their own country, had settled in Kān and formed a colony of what were called " tame Chins."

The post or fort, which was stockaded, had been built immediately on the river's bank, the camp for the remainder of the troops lying farther north.

Accommodation was provided for nine hundred men, and consisted of temporary huts similar to those described as having been constructed on the route from Pakôkku. The officers were congregated in an old poongyi Kyaung. The ford of the Myittha was at this time thirty-eight inches deep, and the current very strong. The river was subsequently spanned by a gabion bridge 142 yards long, built principally by the men of the

Scottish Borderers, and in the construction of which Private James Wilson was accidentally drowned.

By the time the troops arrived at Kān about a thousand tons of stores had been collected there, chiefly through the instrumentality of Mr. Holland, of the Indian Marine Service, who, under difficulties that would have been insuperable to most men, had managed to work country-boats up from Kalewa, where the Myittha joins the Chindwin, a distance of 120 miles. The former is a most uncertain river, rising and subsiding so rapidly with each fall of rain that it is impossible to tell for three successive days what the depth of water or the force of the current may be.

It is, moreover, full of snags and rapids which, in many places, except for the small dug-outs called "lôndwins," render navigation impossible.

Beginning at the end of August and contending with rain, sickness, desertions, and accidents, Mr. Holland, before handing over the duty to the Commissariat Department, had conveyed 551 tons to Kān for the southern column and 638 to Kalemyo for the northern column.

His report submitted at the end of the undertaking is a most interesting one, and shows what a man who apparently did not include the word "impossible" in his vocabulary can do.

Having now arrived on the border of the enemy's country it will be well to place succintly before the reader the precise plan and object set for the Chin Field Force.

HAKA WOMEN.

As has been already stated, for some years the tribes had been in the habit of descending from their wilds and carrying off men, women, children and cattle from the Burmese villages. Those persons whom they could not carry off were slain, and their heads taken to adorn the villages as trophies.

The captives were held to ransom, and if not redeemed, were kept and treated as slaves. At the time of which I write, two thousand such unfortunates were believed to be still in the possession of the Chins. To set these free and put a stop for further raiding was the primary object of the Expedition.

It was also proposed to expose, open out, and subjugate the unknown country which lay between Burma and Eastern Bengal.

We have seen that during the preceding season operations had been undertaken against the Siyins and Kanhows by a force under General Faunce, and that our troops now occupied Fort White in the centre of the Siyin country.

The broken remnants of these two tribes still obstinately resisted us, and to further punish or conciliate them into an acknowledgment of the supremacy of the British power was one of the tasks before the northern column. Next to the Siyins came the Tāshôns, the most numerous of all the Chin tribes, and reported to number from 80,000 to 100,000 souls, with 8,000 to 10,000 fighting men and guns. They were, however, of more peaceful character than their northern and southern neighbours, and were not such confirmed raiders, nor had they so many captives.

To the south of the Tāshôns lay the Baungshès, so nick-named by the Burmans from their wearing long turbans. This was the tribe with which the southern column proceeding west from Kān would first come into contact. Hāka and Yokwā are the head villages of the two most powerful sections of the Baungshè tribe, and after penetrating to the former, it was intended that a further advance should be made to the north against the Tāshôns, while the northern column from Fort White co-operated simultaneously in the movement.

After the Tāshôns had been dealt with, the troops were to return to Hāka, and thence, having replenished, start west to meet the Bengal column from Chittagong, coercing the tribes and compelling submission to our authority on both sides of the line of advance.

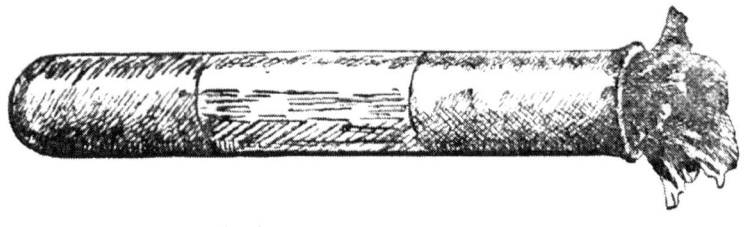

A CHIN POWDER MEASURE.

CHAPTER IX.

THE CHIN-LUSHAI EXPEDITION OF 1889-90.—(*Contd.*)

*Advance of the Southern Chin Column to Hāka.
Rawvan.*

THE advance on Hāka from Kān commenced on the 9th December with the despatch of a working party consisting of 127 Sappers and 103 Punjabi coolies, under Major Henry, Commanding the Royal Engineers, and guarded by an escort of the 2nd Madras Infantry. This detachment with convoy monopolised the whole of the transport with the Commissariat Department then available at Kān. Owing to the depth of water and strength of current in the Myittha river all stores had to be hand-ported across, the operation occupying four hours and a half.

The immediate task that Major Henry and his party had placed before them was to proceed to Kabè hill, an eminence of 2,050 feet, distant about ten miles from Kān, and to construct a mule road backwards to the base, this being the beginning of the path which was intended to unite with a corresponding one from Bengal, and thus form a through route to India. They were instructed, however, to make the road at first only just passable for laden mules, and to reconnoitre and fix the trace well ahead. The work up to Kyauk-pyo-daung at the foot of the Kabè hill, the first post formed, but afterwards abandoned on account of the scarcity of water, was comparatively easy, but beyond that point greater difficulties were encountered than had been anticipated. From Kyauk-pyo-daung the path rose to within fifty feet of the summit of the Kabè hill, where a signalling station was established, and then descended very abruptly to the Laungat stream (a tributary of the Myittha, and taking its rise by two heads near Mèshaung and Lamtôk), having to be zig-zagged down the whole way. From the latter point to Taung-wadet, six miles from Kyauk-pyo-daung, the road ran along the bed of the river, the rugged nature of the banks and surrounding hills putting an alternative route out of the question. The Sappers took three hours and some dynamite getting their own party through the last three miles.

On the 13th December, 98 rank and file of the 2-4th Gurkha Rifles under a British Officer were sent out to relieve the detachment of the 2nd Madras Infantry and to assist the Sappers in road-making. On the same date Mr. D. Ross, Assistant Commissioner, arrived from Gangaw, having been recalled by the General Officer Commanding to act as political officer to the column, in consequence of Major Raikes having been invalided to England. Next day Lieutenant-Colonel

King-Harman, with two native officers and ninety-six men of the 2-4th Gurkha Rifles, left Kān for the front, with instructions to proceed direct to Chaung-kwa, the third post on the way to Yôkwa, distant 23 miles, to make the road good backwards to Taung-wadet, and to reconnoitre forwards to Taung-tek. He was further directed to report as to whether he could employ British troops on road-making. Coolie transport only was taken, namely, 190 Khasia and Naga coolies, and fourteen days' rations for the whole party. I accompanied this detachment.

We crossed the Myittha in dug-outs at daybreak and marched from the Chin bank at 7 A.M., all our baggage being carried by Naga coolies, who were the best with the force for this purpose. They belonged to the Taung-kool tribe under the Rajah of Manipur, by whom they had been impressed for service, and had been sent up the Myittha from Kalèmyo under Major Elliston, who, up to that point, had marched them round from Manipur, north of the Chin Hills. The men were perfect savages in appearance, and, beyond a blanket which they had received from Government and which they discarded when any work was to be done, were in a state of nudity as far as the *convenances* of society were concerned. In addition to his rations each coolie received Rs. 10 monthly, half of which he had to hand over to the Manipur State.

Our route was in a north-westerly direction through

sal jungle, with a mixture of bamboo and other trees; the last three miles being a gentle ascent round the right shoulder of the Kabè hill. The first halt was at Kyauk-pyo-daung (white stone hill) where we found a detachment of our Battalion which had been left there by Lieutenant Hamilton, relieving the same of the 2nd Madras Infantry. At Kyauk-pyo-daung huts were being constructed by Burmese contractors for the accommodation of the troops. Our next march was to Thayetbin (mango tree), a most unhealthy spot in the gorge of the Laungat stream, 8¼ miles from Kyauk-pyo-daung. After a short descent from the latter post we ascended the Kabè hill, rising 1,000 feet in about two miles. We then descended still more abruptly to the bed of the Laungat, and along the course of which the path proceeded to Chaung-kwa. This part of the march was extremely trying. In a distance of eleven miles the river had to be crossed and re-crossed forty-three times, large boulders and a depth of two feet and a half of water in some places impeding progress. There was no accommodation for troops at Thayetbin, and here, for the first time, I had an opportunity of seeing with what celerity Gurkhas can hut themselves. Within an hour from arrival in camp, and that after an uncommonly fatiguing march, they had cleared the ground and constructed excellent shelter for themselves and their officers. Under the *kookerie* the bamboos came down like autumn leaves in Valhambrosa, and were immediately transformed into comfortable "lean-tos." At Thayetbin we found Major Henry with the Sappers. He and Lieutenant Hamilton with their men had been out from 7 A.M. to 5 P.M. clearing the road, which they had made passable up to the next post, Chaung-kwa, distant $5\frac{1}{4}$ miles. We continued next day in the bed of the Laungat, which we crossed and re-crossed twenty-nine times, rather to the detriment of our boots—no light matter in a country where ammunitions cannot be replaced. Our next halt was at Chaung-kwa (two rivers) at the end of a spur where two streams join to form the Laungat. The ground on which we had to encamp was densely covered with bamboo jungle, but in an incredibly short space of time the latter gave place to comfortable huts.

In this march we were accompanied by Major Henry with 35 Sappers and 16 mules laden with engineering equipment.

As the primary object for which Colonel King-Harman's detachment had been sent was already accomplished, we proceeded, on the 17th December, six miles farther on to a place called Taung-tek, or more correctly Taopi-Sakān, the former name being applied to a high hill immediately above, and almost to the summit of which we had to ascend. As the route had not yet been explored, we were furnished with two Chin guides—one Shwè Hlaing, a deposed and refugee chief of Yôkwa; the other a Chinmé whom, for want of a better designation, we nicknamed "Chôk," a word which he was constantly using, and which we afterwards discovered to mean a rat, this animal being his favourite article of diet. Taung-tek is 4,500 feet above sea-level, so that we had to ascend a height of nearly 4,000 feet, this rise taking place in about five miles. The path was a mere Chin foot track, parts of which were quite impassable for laden mules, and so narrow that the detachment had to march in single file, not a desirable formation where the enemy was expected to oppose us at any moment. About a mile from Chaung-kwa we came on the pine zone, the species there being the *pinus khasiensis* that which grows on the Khasia hills, and a little further on we found that the Chins had cut down large trees and thrown them across the path, scarping the latter in places to oppose our advance, but all in a half-hearted and futile manner. These obstructions we afterwards ascertained to have been made during the preceding October. From where the path began to descend to Taopi Sakān it was laid with "pānjis" or pointed pieces of bamboo which are stuck among the grass with the intention of wounding the unwary intruder. During the excitement of a charge serious and even fatal wounds have been received in this way. On the present occasion the only person victimised was old "Chôk," and he was probably thinking of rats at the time.

Taopi-Sakān, or Taung-tek as it was afterwards called,

is on a saddle-back on the north side of the hill, six miles from Chaung-kwa, and at an elevation of 3,900 feet. On arrival we found a Chin grass thatched hut on the saddle-back which would account for the name of the place, "Sakān" in Burmese signifying resting-place, while "Taung-tek" in the same language means high summit. The ground on which we had to encamp was covered with stunted fir trees, scrub, and long grass, which it took some little time and trouble to get rid of. Lower down the sides of the hill there was dense bamboo jungle, so that we had lots of material wherewith to hut ourselves. The nearest water-supply was on the west slope, about three hundred yards away.

As can be easily imagined, the sudden change from the close low-lying gorge of the Laungat to an elevation of nearly 4,000 feet on an exposed ridge was accompanied by an equally sudden and trying change of climate. A cold bracing atmosphere is the best for a man in robust health, but it is well known to residents in eastern countries that this very condition frequently developes the effects of malaria hitherto latent in the system. The Gurkhas had, up to their arrival at Taung-tek, been remarkably free from sickness, but, soon after, they began to show signs of malarial poisoning, contracted, I believe, in the unhealthy valleys which they were obliged to traverse on their way to Kān, and the still more fatal terai in which they had been exposed since leaving that place. The rains had been unusually late, and the season was consequently fully six weeks behind its proper time. At no time, however, did the Gurkhas exhibit a mortality or amount of sickness anything approaching that of some of the other components of the force.

On the 19th December, Colonel King-Harman with a party of his men reconnoitred the road to Yôkwa as far as the site of an old Chinmé village, Mèshaung, the inhabitants of which had deserted it ten years before and now formed part of the tame Chin settlement at Kān. The place is five miles from Taung-tek. Trees had been felled as obstacles by the Chins in dozens of places across the path, which, however, presented no great difficulties. Water was not found at Mèshaung, but was known to exist near.

At 5 P.M. on the 22nd our camp at Taung-tek was fired into—six or seven shots altogether. No one was hit, and the fire of the Chins was not returned, as the Gurkhas could see no one to aim at, owing to the very dense jungle which extended to within a few yards of our encampment and which there had not yet been time to clear away. Signal shots were fired by the enemy during the evening, beacon fires were lighted, and Chins could be seen moving with torches over the hills. There was, however, no further active manifestation of hostilities until Christmas Day, when one of our most senior and best havildars, Fateh Sing Newar, was shot through the right chest, and died the same evening. He had been engaged with a fatigue party in the forenoon making a path to the water-supply, and while stooping to pick up his rifle, on the alarm that Chins had been seen, was hit in the back, the bullet emerging at the right arm-pit. The enemy had crept up unseen to within twenty paces of the covering picket. They got clear away from two small parties which were sent out at once to intercept them, and were afterwards heard shouting at the bottom of the ravine. Lieutenant Hamilton arrived in the afternoon with a detachment of his regiment, the 2-4th Gurkha Rifles, which had been engaged in road-making in the rear. Between us we managed to raise a pretty good dinner, but never, even in India where the day is generally a melancholy affair, do I remember having passed a more miserable Christmas. A Scotch mist had prevailed all day, but at night it passed into a regular downpour which continued without intermission until the following evening, soaking our kits and making us feel rather out of harmony with the supposed festive season. The depression was further added to by the intimation that poor Fateh Sing had died as we were rising from dinner. All road-making had to be stopped for a time on account of the rain.

General Symons who had left Kān on the 17th December, and had since then been superintending the work on the line of communications, arrived at Taung-tek on the 27th accompanied by Mr. Ross, Political Officer, and

Lieutenant Stewart, Orderly Officer. A few minutes before daybreak of the following morning, the Gurkha sentry of the north picket heard a rustling in the grass some yards below him. Thinking that the sound was caused by some animal, he threw a stick at the spot, and was answered by a shot, which was the signal for a pretty sharp fusilade into camp. The men first seen were coming round the north-east shoulder of the north hill, apparently in ignorance of the presence of the picket, and when discovered, bolted to join their comrades who were on a ridge to the north-west. From the latter position they were soon dislodged by a party of Gurkhas headed by General Symons, and fled beating a gong and shouting lustily. After a hasty breakfast the General, Mr. Ross and Lieutenant Norie with 70 Gurkhas under their Adjutant, Lieutenant Hamilton, advanced on the Yôkwa road. Three miles from camp they met with two stockades, strengthened by an earthwork, thrown across the road in a very strong position, and behind which a large body of Chins were posted. A few volleys from a commanding spur changed the aspect of affairs, and we soon heard the gong and some other musical instruments beating a retreat. The Chin commander, when we subsequently came into more amicable relations with him, informed us that his army had numbered 500, and that it had been the greatest battle and defeat ever recorded in the military annals of his country. Small as the affair appeared at the time, we afterwards had the best grounds for believing that it had exercised considerable influence upon the political attitude and submission of the tribes. On our way home old "Chôk" caused some amusement by asking for a personal guard while he dug for his favourite prey, some burrows of which he had come across. On the same day a Punjab coolie wandering about by himself on the Taung-tek hill was shot in seven places by the Chins and his head taken.

At Kān two Chins had arrived from Wunhla, a village on the road from Myintha to Hāka, who stated that nine more of their party were in the jungle but afraid to come in. These men added that the Chins of Wunhla and Hāka were anxious to make friends with the English. Oone of them was at once despatched to General Symons at Chaung-kwa.

Mules got into Taung-tek for the first time on the 3rd January, the Sappers and coolies having taken seventeen days to make the six and a half miles of road from Chaung-kwa.

On the 1st January 1890, three officers and 70 men of the King's Own Scottish Borderers, under the command of Major Stoney, left Kān, with orders to pick up Captain Johnstone and 25 men of the same regiment at Kyauk-pyo-daung, and proceed to join the advanced party at Taung-tek, which they reached on the 4th.

Meanwhile things, from a sanitary point of view, had been going badly with the force at the front, on the line of communications, and at the base, as will be seen from the following notes :—

On the 16th December there were sick at Kān, 7 British officers, 14 British and 23 Native soldiers, 18 followers, 107 Punjab coolies and 25 hill coolies.

On the 18th, 15 sick Punjab coolies were returned from the front to Kān, and on the 19th, 7 more. On the latter date 10 per cent. of the Gurkhas at Taung-tek were on the sick list. On the 20th, of the Sappers, 3 officers and 38 men were sick, with 40 per cent. of Punjab coolies, leaving not more than 100 men of Sappers and coolies combined to work on the road. The Survey party had been delayed at Chaung-kwa by fever among the subordinates.

On the 21st, 5 officers, 8 out of 12 British signallers, 11 out of 50 Borderers, 39 out of 120 Sappers and Miners, 10 per cent. of the Gurkhas and 52 per cent. of the Punjab coolies with the advanced troops, were down, principally with fever.

In Kān, 5 British officers, 27 British soldiers, 34 Native soldiers, 31 public followers, and 33 Punjab and hill coolies were shown on the sick list, to which number may be added about 50 British soldiers and 50 native followers and coolies that attended hospital daily and were quite unfit for duty.

On the 22nd, Private Rafferty, King's Own Scottish Borderers, died at Kān of ague.

On the 23rd, the state of sick at Kān was as follows :—

Five British officers, 31 British soldiers, 39 native soldiers, 38 public followers, 29 Punjab coolies. At Gangaw there were 24 men in hospital.

On the 24th, Private Dixon and Private Knowles died at Kān of ague.

On Taung-tek hill, Captain Swayne, R.E., and Lieutenant Hutton, R.E., were both seriously ill, and Captain Oldfield was also in bed with fever.

ADVANCE TO HAKA.

The state of health at the advanced posts was as follows:—

At Chaung-kwa.

	Strength.	Sick.
King's Own Scottish Borderers...	11	10
2-4th Gurkhas	100	25
Sappers and Miners...	143	46
Punjab coolies	370	77
Public followers	21	3
Hill coolies	307	35
Private followers	20	12

At Taung-tek.

2-4th Gurkha Rifles	100	10
Followers	50 per cent.	

On the 27th, there were sick at Kān 7 British officers, 83 Borderers, 7 of the Mountain Battery, 9 Gurkhas, 23 Madrasis, 44 public followers, and 11 Punjab and hill coolies.

On the 28th, Private Whitehouse, King's Own Scottish Borderers, died of remittent fever at Kān.

On the 29th, the state of sick at Kān was as follows:—

British Officers	5
King's Own Scottish Borderers...	86
No. 1, Bengal Mountain Battery	7
2-4th Gurkhas	8
2nd Madras Infantry	23
Public followers	52
Punjab and hill coolies	11

On the same day Captain Oldfield, R.E., was ordered back to Kān on account of ill-health.

On the 30th the state of the coolies at Kān was—

	Fit.	Sick.
Punjabis	15	32
Khasias	24	30
Nagas	5	49
Total	44	111

On that date there died at Kān Lance-Corporal Kilbeck, King's Own Scottish Borderers, and a sepoy of the 2-4th Gurkhas, both of remittent fever.

On the 31st, of 7 Sapper officers, 6 were in bed.

On the 1st January 1890, Lance-Corporal Goodwin, King's Own Scottish Borderers, died of remittent fever at Kān.

On the 2nd the distressing news was received from Kān that there were only 187 men of the King's Own Scottish Borderers fit for duty out of 400 present; also that 62 men of the 2nd Madras Infantry were in hospital at Kān.

On the 3rd January, there being no sound officer present with the advanced three companies of the 2-4th Gurkhas, Lieutenant J. Stewart, 5th Gurkhas, Orderly Officer to General Symons, was appointed to do duty temporarily with them.

On the 5th January 120 Kasia and 95 Naga coolies under a Lance-Naick of the 44th Gurkha Light Infantry were left on the Taung-tek hill, all more or less sick, and some in a dying condition.

The above tale is dismal enough, and it has to be remembered that only the severe cases were shewn. Had every man who would have been formally admitted into hospital in cantonments been similarly treated in this Expedition, the latter would simply have come to a standstill.

The cause of all this sickness was malaria acting upon the systems of men rendered susceptible to its influence by the exposure and hardships incidental to field service, and to a greater extent by the want of suitable food, which, up to this period, had been unobtainable.

On the 5th January, General Symons and his staff, with 90 men of the King's Own Scottish Borderers and 100 Rifles of the 2-4th Gurkhas, left Taung-tek for the Chinmé village of Rawvan, nine miles distant on the road to Yôkwa.

The advance at first proceeded through the Sapper Camp, which had been pushed on two miles, and to which the road had been nearly completed. Further on, the track ran along the ridge held by the Chins on the 28th December, and, leaving the site of Mè-shaung village to the north, went slightly to the south of west along a high ridge. The path for four miles was heavily staked with *panjis*, one Gurkha being severely, and one coolie slightly, wounded. No resistance was met with, although the guides expected some to be offered at a high bare peak called Forsong Klang, which was reached about six miles from Taung-tek. From this point a magnificent view was obtained. Kān could be distinctly seen to the east, while a vast extent of new country, consisting of range upon range of high mountains, stretched away south-west and north-west. Below, about two miles off, was Rawvan village, and a few people could be seen running away from their houses into the jungle.

The only passive obstruction found was in the form of felled trees, many of which lay across the path and seemed intended more as a formal protest against our entry than in the hope of resisting the advance. For the rest of the march the path descended gradually. The village was found unoccupied except by a few goats, pigs and fowls, which were soon disposed of by the Borderers and Gurkhas. It consisted of forty-five houses, some of them substantially built of planks for floors and walls, and well roofed with thatch. The houses were much on the same plan as those of the Siyin Chins, although inferior in construction and finish. Each dwelling consisted of three or four rooms, in all 40 to 60 feet long, the latter being connected by a single round hole $2\frac{1}{2}$ feet in diameter which led from the one to the other. Every house was decorated with skulls of bison, buffalo, deer of all kinds, pigs, dogs and birds; also with bright-coloured birds' feathers; and the residences of the Chiefs were marked by superior size and construction. Aqueducts made of bamboo led a good water-supply to each house. The village was situated on the northern side of a steep hill, and, as each house stood on a terrace formed by cutting into the slope, the area occupied was considerable. The only point furnished with defences was the approach, which consisted of a sort of tunnel formed of logs and rocks and roofed above with logs. The inhabitants of Rawvan consist almost entirely of Chinmés who acknowledge Yôkwa as their head, and who are looked down upon and lorded over by the Baungshès. Quantities of beans and some grain were found in and near the village; also an excellent forge with feather piston bellows such as is generally used in Burma, from which country the Chins obtain nearly all their iron.

On the following day, the 6th, the General and Mr. Ross, with an escort of Borderers and Gurkhas, reconnoitred five miles towards Yôkwa. The first two miles were found easy-going, through thin forest jungle and tall grass; then a steep descent into a deep valley and corresponding rise to a ridge, on the top of which, among numbers of pine trees, was a stone-faced platform with a large pointed stone $7\frac{1}{2}$ feet high in the centre. This was said to be a rest and eating-place. Across another ravine there was a ridge supposed to be only one mile from Yôkwa. In the Yôkwa fields the party placed a notice written in Burmese, in the hope that some of the captives might be able to read and translate it to the Chins, to the effect that the Yôkwa Chiefs had been foolish and permitted their young men to attack and oppose us; but that we should think little of this provided they came in and submitted, &c.

The policy pursued by General Symons was to be very careful not to threaten what he could not enforce, not to drive the Chins to despair by burning their villages and wrecking their property, and to lose no opportunity of trying to get into touch with those singularly shy and wild people.

In the return to camp a better trace for another road was looked for through the small Baungshè village of Farôn. The latter was quite deserted, nor, with the exception of a few scouts on the hill-tops, were any Chins seen during the day.

Next day the covering party of the men engaged on road-making was fired into by three Chins, but without a casualty. An attempt was made to induce some of the Chinmés to come in by calling to them from the hill-tops through the Chin guides, but without success. Reports were received that the escort to the hill coolies who had accompanied the force into Rawvan, had been fired on while returning to Taung-tek.

On the 8th two men came into camp who stated that they were delegates from the Yôkwa Chiefs and had been sent to enquire what was our object in coming into their country. Both were young, one, called Naw Lôn, being the adopted son of Lyan Sôn, the Head Chief of Yôkwa, and the other, Lai Huet, who had lived at Shon-shè, near Gangaw, for three years and spoke Burmese well. They said : "We do not want to fight, but wish to receive you as friends ; we have not received any of your notices, and have no one who could read them." They also added that one of the chief reasons why they had come in to talk, was to save their villages from being burnt. The General replied : " (1) If you build us a camp near Yôkwa, to hold 50 officers and 4,000 men, we will not occupy the village ; (2) that we should be in Yôkwa in seven or eight days, as soon as we had finished the mule path ; (3) that we would make no treaty nor discuss terms with any but the headmen ; (4) that we were going on from Yôkwa to Hāka, there to meet another army from the west, and then all go on to the Tashôn Ywama; (5) that they had opposed us and fired on our people, but that we had not burnt their villages in reprisal, as we wished to give them a chance of making terms; (6) that if they submitted quietly, they would get much better terms than if they persisted in resisting us and then came in afterwards.

On the 9th January General Symons was visited by six more Chins. One was Ko-ôk, the Chief of Pômlan, a small village of twenty houses, ten miles south-west of Rawvan. He wore a plume of feathers stuck straight up in his hair, said he was of Hāka Chiefs' blood, and was quite independent. He had come in to submit and save his village. He was told that his submission would be accepted, and that he would be treated well for coming in soon. At the same time the General Officer declined to discuss any terms with him until he had seen the Yôkwa Chiefs, and asked him to come in with them. Ko-ôk objected to the latter condition on the grounds that he owed no allegiance to Yôkwa, and wished terms made separately with himself, thus confirming previous information about the Baungshès, namely, that they are sub-divided into numerous independent septs without any responsible head.

The Chins informed us that (*a*) the Chinmés of Rawvan had spiked the path leading to their village by order of the Yôkwas; (*b*) that when the Yôkwas heard of our advance into their hills, they sent to Tantin (Tlan Tlang) and other Chins for assistance, but received a reply to the effect that another army was coming from the west, and that in consequence they, the Tantins, had their own hands full; (c) that on the 28th December, near Taung-tek the Chins had had 500 men engaged, and that they looked on it as a great battle and defeat; that Yôkwa, Thetta and Bondwa Chins had been engaged on that occasion; (d) that the Gurkha Havildar had been killed on the 25th December by Thetta Chins, and the Punjab coolie on the 20th by Tinam people.

Next day the following deputation was received from Yôkwa: Ratiaw, a representative Head Chief of Yôkwa; Tèhet, a smaller Chief; Ranwè, son of Nitin, a Chief; and six followers. They said that they had come to meet us and wished to be friends. On being asked if they were responsible messengers, and whether the Yôkwa people would accept and hold to any terms they agreed to, they replied in the affirmative, and said that they could make their people do anything they wished. They gave the following as the list of villages over which the Yôkwa Chiefs exercised control, and from which they took revenue:—Yôkwa, Rawvan, Tinam, Hrôngwin, Farôn, Kawa and Lawtôk, seven in all.

The General then explained that we had come into the Chin Hills to stop raiding all down the border, that we were going to make a good road from Burma to the sea on the west, that we were going to meet another force at Hāka and go north into the Tashôn country and compel all villages to submit to us. Then, the terms on which we would accept their submission were read out, and each item carefully explained. They were as follows :—

(I) To recognise the supremacy of the British Government by (*a*) paying an annual tribute, the amount of which was to be fixed, after our arrival at Yôkwa, in money or in kind at the head-quarters of the Civil Officer, North Yaw, on or before the full moon in Nadaw in each year (about 1st December); (*b*) giving friendly reception at all times to British officers, and being responsible for their safety whilst in Yôkwa territory.

(II) As a punishment for having resisted our advance, and also for having murdered two messengers sent up with Shwè Hlaing to ask them to come down to a friendly conference, they must now pay a fine, amount to be afterwards fixed, in cash or kind; an amount, to be afterwards fixed, to be paid to the family of the Gurkha Havildar shot by them on Christmas Day.

(III) To restore all Burmese captives at once.

(IV) To entirely cease from raiding anywhere in Burma or other British territory.

(V) To assist us in our advance through their country.

(VI) To be responsible that no damage was done to the road or telegraph wire.

(VII) To give up the head of the Punjab coolie taken on the 28th December, for burial.

After this we explained what we would allow them to do if they accepted our terms, namely, on our side we promised—

(I) That we would not annex their country, but would leave the administration of it in their hands as heretofore.

This promise was afterwards modified at Yôkwa on the 25th January, and the following substituted "that we would annex their country, but, as long as they behaved well, we would not interfere with their villages or tribal organisation."

(II) That we would allow them to keep all their guns.

(III) That we would do no damage to life, houses, or property. If any damage were accidentally done, that we would pay compensation.

(IV) That we would pay a fair price for all labour and supplies.

(V) That we would allow them to go down and trade in Burma, at times and places to be settled hereafter.

(VI) These terms were subject to the confirmation of the Chief Commissioner, to hold good for three years, when they would be liable to revision.

The penalties held forth for not submitting to the above terms were, that we would burn every village in the Yôkwa circle, lay waste the country, destroy all grain and crops, and hunt and shoot the people like wild beasts; also that, if after that date our people were fired at in camp or on the road, we would burn the nearest village without further warning.

In reply to the above, the delegates said that they understood and would accept all our conditions because we were all-powerful, and they could not resist us. They were then further told to have all their Burmese captives ready for us the day we entered Yôkwa, and to build a camp for us at Yôkwa, or that we should occupy their village. Ratiaw requested that when we advanced we should only bring a very few troops, as a large number might possibly alarm the women and children, but he was informed that we would bring what we chose, and that, as troops would be quartered at Yôkwa for several months to come, the sooner the women and children got accustomed to them the better. The representatives acknowledged their inability to call in Thetta (300 houses) or any other villages, adding that they were not on very cordial terms with Thetta, although they had assisted them in trying to resist us. Finally, on learning that we were going to leave posts everywhere along the road, Ratiaw exclaimed: "It is your country now, you can do what you like. The road will be good enough for us to go down to trade."

Throughout the parley the envoy sipped tobacco-juice which is collected by the women, the sex to which smoking is almost entirely confined in this part of the country. In this way the Chin woman has to do double work. Her pipe consists of a receptacle into the top of which the stem and bowl of the pipe are let in separately, so that in smoking all the tobacco-juice, &c., collects at the bottom. This fluid, composed of a mixture of nicotine and the saliva of their better halves, the men carry about in little gourds, using it as a liqueur and offering it to their friends on social or State occasions.

In consequence of the apparent satisfactory result of the negotiations with the Yôkwa delegates, General Symons on the next day sent the following message along the line of communications:—"Yôkwa has submitted, and has agreed to all our terms. They have guaranteed that no more shots will be fired at posts or convoys. If another shot be fired, please burn at once the nearest village, except Rawvan, which is not to be destroyed except under the General's special instructions, without further warning. Rawvan villages are working for us. We are reducing guards and sentries to low limits. Escorts should be reduced to only half previous strength."

Relying on the above, at Taung-tek on the following day Lieutenant Foster of the King's Own Scottish Borderers accompanied by two other officers proceeded for a short walk. When a mile and-a-half from camp they were fired on, and poor Foster was shot through the head, his body being carried in by his companions. In retaliation the nearest village, Lamtôk, was burnt on the 13th, but, as the houses were of the most wretched description, the punishment was not a severe one. It was afterwards ascertained that the men implicated in the deed came from Thetta, although it is most probable that they had rested at Lamtôk on their way.

On the 11th January messengers were sent to the former village to call in the Chiefs. They returned on the fourth day, and said that three Chiefs had accompanied them as far as Pômlan on their way to come in when they were met near there by the three men who had shot Lieutenant Foster, and who persuaded the Chiefs to go back on the grounds that it would not be safe for them to approach our camp after what had happened. The Chiefs were then recalled with a message that they would not be held responsible for the act, and that safe conduct would be guaranteed them. Two minor Chiefs named Shain Byik and Van Duin responded to the invitation and came in on the 16th January, asking to be allowed to make submission on behalf of their village. We explained our terms, the same as offered to the Yôkwas, when they said they were sorry that they had resisted us, and that now, hearing that we were not injuring people or property, they wished to surrender. They promised that no more shooting should take place, either by Thetta people or in their circle, and understood that Thetta village would be burnt if any more resistance were offered to us. The delegates were desired to tell their Head Chiefs to come into Yôkwa on the 19th January with all their Burmese captives.

This was the first occasion on which we received news of the approach of the western column from Chittagong, the Thetta Chiefs informing us that the sound of loud shots had been heard at Saungkya, two days' journey west of Thetta, and I have no doubt that their own conciliatory attitude had been stimulated by the fact.

On the same day that we received the deputation from Thetta (16th January) the telegraph wire was reported open to Taung-tek, and from that post the garrison at Rawvan received a reinforcement of 105

Borderers. On the 17th the force was further augmented by the arrival of 110 Gurkhas.

In spite of a good deal of personal suffering from fever, Lieutenant Renny-Tailyour, R.E., had now managed to complete the survey as far as Rawvan, and Major Henry had made the road passable for mules all the way to Yôkwa. Before, however, describing the further advance of the column, it may be of some interest to take a glance at the health of the troops and followers. This, as far as the Gurkhas were concerned, had improved considerably, for they were now beginning to pull themselves together and throw off the fever they had contracted in the more unhealthy localities in the rear. The Borderers and others of the force, however, still continued to suffer severely as the following details will show :—

Lance-Corporal Hunt, King's Own Scottish Borderers, died of fever on the 6th January on the Myittha River, *en route* to Kalèwa from Kān.

On the 9th, 33 convalescents of the same regiment were sent on elephants from Kān to Myintha for a change. On the 10th, a sick convoy of 10 transport drivers, 10 Punjab coolies, and 8 dooly bearers were sent down the Myittha.

Captain Gramshaw, 5th Battalion (City of London Regiment), Royal Fusiliers, died at Kān of remittent fever on the 9th.

On the 12th there were ill at Rawvan—

    5 British Officers.

    24 men, King's Own Scottish Borderers.

    8 men, 2-4th Gurkhas.

    46 coolies, hill and Punjab.

    5 dooly bearers.

On the same date 2 Engineer Officers, with 52 men of the King's Own Scottish Borderers, and 2 Apothecaries were sent down sick from Kān to Kalèwa—

Private Tanner, King's Own Scottish Borderers, died of remittent fever at Rawvan.

On the 14th there was sent from Kān to Kalèwa a sick convoy consisting of—

        4 British Officers.
        11 men, King's Own Scottish Borderers.
        16 men, Native Troops.
        6 followers.

Before Colonel King-Harman started from Taung-tek on the 17th, he sent back sick 2 men of the Borderers and 20 Gurkhas to Chaung-kwa, and left 21 of the Borderers and 9 Gurkhas in hospital at Taung-tek.

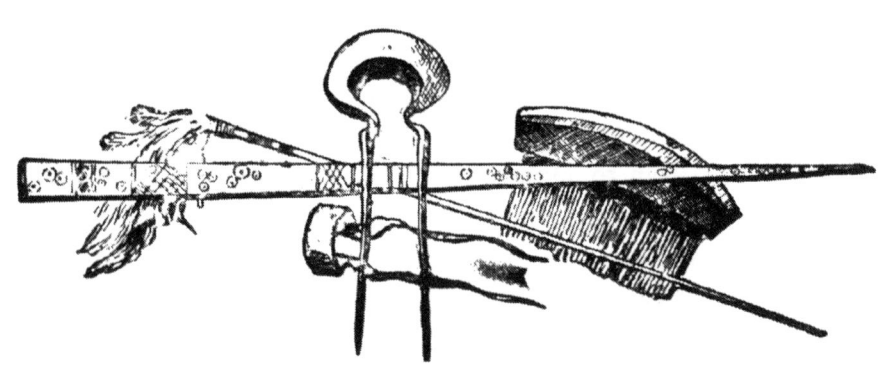

CHIN-LUSHAI HAIR ORNAMENTS.

CHAPTER X.

The Chin-Lushai Expedition of 1889-90.—(*Contd.*)

Advance of the Southern Chin Column to Hāka.

Yôkwa.

From Rawvan an advance was made to Yôkwa on the 18th January, the force moving in two columns, and fifty men of the 2-4th Gurkhas being left to garrison the former post. The first party, which started at 9 A.M., consisted of the General Officer Commanding and Staff, 80 rifles King's Own Scottish Borderers, and 103 rifles 2-4th Gurkhas; the second leaving an hour later was composed of 105 Borderers and 65 Gurkhas under the command of Colonel King-Harman. With the column were 410 hill coolies, 130 Chin coolies and 200 mules.

Although the path had been made passable the whole way, the Engineers had cut their road for only half the distance, and that the easier one. At $3\frac{1}{2}$ miles we passed through the Sapper Camp, and at $1\frac{1}{2}$ miles further crossed the Laivār stream, with a good supply of running water. This is one of the main sources of the Nanpathè River. Thence the path by a steep ascent led up-hill to a well-defined ridge. The Yôkwa hill, representing as it does a rise of 1,100 feet in 1¼ miles, was a hard pull for robust men, but to those who had been weakened by repeated attacks of fever it appeared insurmountable. Although thirteen weak and sickly men of the Borderers had been left behind at Rawvan, a number fell out on the march unable to keep up or carry their rifles. Out of twenty-three officers who arrived at Yôkwa on that day, nineteen had suffered lately, some severely, some several times, from malarial fever.

From the highest point on the route a slight descent led to Yôkwa village, 1½ miles distant. The troops encamped for the night on two ridges east of the village, some distance from an indifferent water-supply; and although the spurs looked cold and cheerless in the dull light of a winter evening, we were glad to reach our sleeping quarters and make the best shelter we could out of the grass and stunted trees which covered the ground, for we had now left the all-useful bamboo behind us. A good many of the Yôkwa Chins, headed by two Chiefs, met the force, in a friendly manner, on its approach. Not far from the village were seen some mythun and cows grazing; and Chins were working in the fields gathering the late crop without fear.

General Symons accompanied by Mr. Ross, Political Officer, visited Yôkwa on the following day. The village fronts north-west on the slope of a hill, and although it was said to consist of from 360 to 380 houses, it did not seem to contain more than from 180 to 200. The houses were of a much superior description to those of Rawvan. Each had a separate courtyard. A great number were deserted, but others were seen to be occupied by men, women, and children, some of the girls being not uncomely. Near the east gate was the tomb of a Chin who had been shot during a recent raid in Burma. The body had been brought all the way home by his comrades for burial. As a rule, the Baungshè Chins bury their dead in the courtyards of the houses, but when a man is killed in a raid or fight he is buried outside the village on one of the paths leading to it. The entrance to the village consisted of a narrow lane, between stone walls, only capable of admitting men in single file, with open rafters overhead. Near it was a large tree with stone platforms at the foot, at which, when returning from a successful raid, the robbers were accustomed to be met by the women of the village, and where they fired off their guns in triumph. Close below there was a small tank, the water of which was considered sacred, and therefore not used for ordinary purposes. At the lower east gate there was a spot where the skulls of all tigers killed were buried. This animal appears to be regarded with some superstition, and its skull is never hung on the walls of the houses like other trophies of the chase. The Head Chief, Po Lyan Sôn, seventy years of age, received the party at his house, which was clean and well-built. The walls of the vestibule were crowded with skulls; in front, those of seven elephants, and behind, closely packed, others of bison, sambhur, mythun, wild boar, buffalo, bear, monkey, &c. The old man said that the whole were of his own shooting, and boasted that he had himself accounted for 1,070 wild animals of different kinds. The village was remarkably clean and free from any insanitary conditions. The walls and floors (the latter well raised) consisted of wooden planks, while the roofs were of thatch. To burn such a village must be a heavy punishment, destroying as it does the work of years.

Later in the day, Po Lyan Sôn with four other Head Chiefs came into Camp to negotiate, some thirty minor Chiefs being absent. They said that they had all agreed to submit, but asked for five days more to deliver up captives; the excuses offered for the delay being that most of the slaves were at a distance, and that the minor Chiefs did not recognise the central authority in such matters. The Chiefs were then told that the tribe would be fined Rs. 500, which would, however, be accepted in the equivalent of cattle and other goods. In the end it was settled that if the captives were not all restored in five days, on the morning of the sixth ten houses would be burnt; on the morning of the seventh fifty houses; and on the morning of the eighth day the whole village, if they were still not forthcoming.

In leaving, the Chiefs promised us their best efforts to have our orders carried out. The fact that there were in Yôkwa itself about thirty minor Chiefs, who all had a following and owned no central authority, rendered negotiation extremely difficult. For instance, those who owned Burmese captives said that they would not give them up at the request of the community, even to save the village, unless they were recompensed for their loss. In the same way with the fine. This had purposely been fixed at a very low figure, for the Chins had no system of assessing a fine or collection, nor means of making each other pay.

Late in the afternoon, a Hāka Chief named Shu-Lut, a brother of Rôn Hmôn of Hāka, rode into camp from Bwètet, and, having presented a pig and a gourd full of liquor, said that he had come to offer submission, and that the Hāka people would not fight or resist us. Shu-Lut was a fine-looking man, of good manners, and lived at the Hāka village of Bwètet to protect it from Yôkwa raids. He slept that night at Yôkwa, and seemed to have no fear in passing from one tribe to the other. The blood feud between the Hākas and Yôkwas is peculiar, and seems to be confined to certain sections or families, the villagers not infrequently intermarrying. The dialects of the two tribes are somewhat different, but undoubtedly the same language. Shu-Lut said that whilst we were in the country they would worship us as spirits or "nats," and he was only afraid that when we went away we should cause them all to die or to be stricken with some fell disease. On the same day some envoys from Thetta also came in, but as they had not brought the Burmese captives with them, they were turned out without a hearing.

On the 20th January General Symons reconnoitred the road onwards towards Hāka. A well-worn path led away from Yôkwa village down and across a deep valley, in which ran a fair-sized stream called the Ein Vār ('vār' being Chin for 'stream'), one of the principal feeders of the Nanpathè or Daung Var, as it is called by the Chins. Then the ascent led in a northerly direction to a ridge about on a level with the camp at Yôkwa. This ridge forms the boundary between Yôkwa and Hāka territory. Bwètet, the first village of the latter tribe, was seen about 1½ miles distant, lying in the bottom of a valley, and, beyond, the course of the path could be traced leading to Mingun village, which lay on the north side of another deep valley. From Mingun the road ascended uninterruptedly to a higher range of hills, behind which lay Hāka, and which shut out all view of the country to the north and west. A good many mythun in a semi-wild state were seen on the hill sides. The path from Bwètet to Yôkwa had been ridden over on the previous day by the Hāka Chief already mentioned, and the sure-footedness and strength of the pony and the nerve of the rider must have been of exceptional quality. Next day the first instalment of captives was brought in by the Yôkwas in the shape of a small Burmese boy of seven, who could not speak the language of his native country, and who cried bitterly at the idea of being separated from his captors, who had probably primed him with tales of the horrible things that would happen to him if he fell into our clutches.

A considerable number of Chin coolies were now employed in bringing commissariat stores into Yôkwa from the supper camp, and seemed much pleased with their daily remuneration of four annas, although many of the Natives who frequented the camps with articles for sale appeared to prefer brass buttons and other commodities to coin of the realm. As in more civilised countries the prices rose rapidly with the demand, and a day or two after our arrival a Chin had hawked round one egg for the modest price of a cardigan jacket, which I need hardly say he was unable to obtain. From the appearance of the egg in question he was probably charging for a chicken as well! The local supplies obtainable were so scanty as not to be worth considering, and the officers and men may be said to have had nothing to depend on but their Government rations.

On this date (21st January) information was received through Tinam headmen that the Bôndwas would not submit, thus repudiating the promise they had made at Rawvan on the 17th. During the next three days a few more Burmese captives began to arrive. On the 22nd two children were brought from Thetta by four

BARGAINING WITH CHINS.

headmen, who swore that only one other remained in their possession. In the evening, however, one of the men confessed that they had two more captives, but begged that his name might not be given as the source of information, as he had only told to save his house from being burnt. This punishment seemed the only one that appealed directly to the feelings of the Chins; but experience with the Siyins and Sagyilains had shewn that when their villages have been destroyed all touch with the people becomes lost, their houses and their guns being their most valued possessions.

Next day the Yôkwa Chiefs brought in three captives (two children and a girl about eighteen), saying that there was one more in their hands, but that she was at Thetta, and could not be delivered up until the following day. They also brought one hundred rupees as the first instalment of the fine, and promised the balance at the time they were to give up the remaining captive. As a precautionary measure sentries had been placed on a herd of cattle grazing below the camp, and three of these were now converted into beef. Soon afterwards the remaining captive, making five in all, was given up, and the fine paid in full. The latter had, as we have seen, been assessed at Rs. 500; but as the headmen, after bringing in Rs. 150, had declared that they could not possibly raise any more cash, the remainder of the sum was accepted in kind, *viz.*, one fine bull mythun (Rs. 100), and five smaller animals (valued at Rs. 50 each).

This day, the 24th January, was an eventful one in the history of Yôkwa, and the proceedings caused an amount of excitement among the villagers proportionate to the gravity and importance of the occasion. For us a further interest was added by information received that on the 17th East Sihaung village had been raided by the Hanta Chins and eighteen captives taken, a bold outrage considering that our troops were already in the country. Permission was sent to the Officer commanding at Sihaung to burn Hānta village, and he was at the same time requested to try to rescue the prisoners, if he could with any hope of success undertake the task.

Permission was given to the Pômlan headmen, who had asked for it, to go down to Burma and trade. Accordingly, the Chief and five men, without guns, were to proceed by the new road to Kān, Gangaw and Shônshè. It will be remembered that this village had no captives, and that the headman had come in readily and given assistance in calling in other villages. The day was further marked by a reconnaissance towards Thetta, performed by General Symons and one or two of his staff. The path for the first hour and three-quarters led up-hill to a ridge, probably 2,000 feet above Yôkwa. After a further march of one hour and ten minutes along a narrow crest, a point was reached, from which Thetta was seen some 1,800 feet below, pleasantly situated in a basin surrounded by hills. Near the village ran, towards the south, a well-defined stream,—the main source of the Zabaw Creek, which joins the Myittha near Gangaw.

Another and final diplomatic interview was held by the General and Mr. Ross with the Yôkwa headmen on the 25th January, in which the terms and promises made at Rawvan on the 10th were again gone over. The Chiefs were told that nothing now remained for them to do but show their fealty to the British Government by always receiving its officials in a friendly manner and by paying annually Rs. 100 or two mythun. On being informed that the Hākas, Tantins, and Tashôns would all also have to pay an annual tribute, they appeared to be perfectly satisfied with their bargain, and agreed to the terms imposed, promising to cease from all raids on British territory and to preserve uninjured the roads and telegraph wire. The Chiefs then asked if the troops would assist them in compelling those to return to their village, who might elect to live elsewhere in order to evade the obligations, and were told that, as all Chin tribes would be compelled to submit, it did not matter where the people lived. Before the interview closed, Po Lyan Sôn requested that the murderer of his son, a Rawvan villager, then a refugee at Kān, might be handed over to his tender mercies, and it was only after it had been pointed out to him that the British Government had not asked for the surrender of any Chins who had of late years killed its subjects, and, under the persuasion of the other Chiefs present, that the old man waived his claim. It turned out afterwards on inquiry that the alleged murderer's father and another relative had already been killed in retaliation for the deed—a fact which did not, however, appear to satisfy the old Chief's thirst for revenge.

On the 26th the headmen of Seinkwa, a small independent village of 20 houses, lying ten or twelve miles north-east of Yôkwa, came in and offered submission. They said that they had no slaves or captives, had never raided, that they sometimes were obliged to feed Hāka or Yôkwa people passing through their village, and that they only wished to trade with Burma. A delegate also arrived from Thetta to say that the villagers could not agree among themselves regarding our terms, that the majority were for submission and giving up their captives, but that a certain number had one prisoner and would not release him. The messenger asked for a force to be sent to Thetta to compel the unwilling to come in, but was informed that the village as a whole would be held responsible for all its members, and that it must take the consequences of its obstinacy. Under the persuasion of Po Lyan Sôn, the Yôkwa Head Chief, the Thetta Chins gave up three more captives on the 27th January, making five in all, and an expedition against them which had been arranged to start on the following day was accordingly postponed. The fine was settled at Rs. 200, to be paid in five days. One of the restored prisoners, a boy of 14 or 15, had left Thetta under a compulsory oath not to give up the names of any more captives, a promise which, on arrival at Yôkwa, he promptly broke by naming five. One of the Thetta captives stated that he and the four children had been redeemed by the whole village from their owners at Rs. 100 each; that the people fully expected their village to be burnt and had removed all food supplies and articles of value; that they had 70 guns and had been very boastful of their powers before the affair of the 28th December, since which date their valour had cooled considerably.

There is little of interest to record during the rest of the stay of the force at Yôkwa. On the 29th January a survey and exploring party, consisting of 20 men each of the Borderers and Gurkhas, under the command of Lieutenant Norie, Intelligence Officer, left Yôkwa for Gangaw. There are three roads by which the Chins travel,—one the southern, by Thetta and Kapi; a second the central, running between Thetta and Rawvan through Bôndwa; and the third through Rawvan. The Chins said that the last was the best, and Lieutenant Norie had directions to follow it. The party reached Gangaw on the 4th February, and reported the road as much inferior to that from Kān to Yôkwa

On the 31st another party of 70 rifles of the 2-4th Gurkhas, under Captain Carnegy, and accompanied by Mr. Ross, Political Officer, left for Bwètet. A report was received in the evening that Bwètet contained 46 houses, and was situated 200 yards above and on the north-west of a stream called Bwètet Vār, then twenty feet broad and one foot deep. The villagers appeared alarmed, but received the party in a friendly manner. The headmen of Bôndwa came in to surrender, on the 1st February, with two Burmese grown-up captives, who gave the names of twenty more prisoners in that village. The Yôkwa Chief, Po Lyan Sôn, pleaded for the saving of Bôndwa from burning, saying that he would compel the villagers to give up all their captives. Mr. Ross returned from Bwètet on the 3rd February, and reported that on the evening of the 2nd he had had a very satisfactory interview with twelve Hāka Chiefs and a crowd of minor notabilities. The Chiefs were accompanied by 200 armed men who remained 800 yards off during the interview. The discussion of terms was, however, postponed until the head-quarters of the force should arrive at their village. La Byit, a Hāka Chief, the father of Lwè Sin, the leading Hāka headman, after the interview admitted that the late raid on Sihaung had been perpetrated by Hāka Chins. On the 4th February the Thetta headmen paid up Rs. 200, the fine imposed, and were sent back to get Rs. 25 more for being three days behind the time agreed upon. On the same day two Burmese captives, a boy and a girl, were given up from Bôndwa, and handed over to their parents who were in camp, the restoration being rather a touching scene. The headmen of Bwônlôn, a small independent village of 30 houses two days' journey south of Yôkwa, came in on the 6th and tendered their submission which was accepted. Next day Hmaika, another small independent village of 20 houses near Wunhla, followed their example, and the Thettas sent a small mythun, in place of Rs. 25, the balance of fine due, again denying that they had any more captives. In this case Thetta was informed that no one from the village would be allowed to trade with the Burma frontier villages, until such time as all captives were restored.

On the 11th February the Yôkwa Chiefs, having heard that the head-quarters were going to move on to Bwètet on the following day, came into camp and asked that the usual Chin ceremony of swearing an oath to cement friendship, or "thissa" as it is called, might be observed. General Symons and Mr. Ross had agreed not to consent to this, because it was a bond that could only be made between equals. The fact of the Chins asking for the oath to be taken, however, placed them as suitors in inferior rank, and consent was given. After the various points and terms to be observed on both sides had been again explained, and it being pressed on their minds that all captives must be given up, the following interesting ceremony was gone through. The Chins brought a half-grown pig and a fine cock. The former was securely tied and laid on its side. The principal headman then stood with a cup of liquor, which he slowly poured over the pig, and swore an oath that they would all be good friends with the English, that they would cease to raid in British territory, and that they would not injure the road or telegraph wire, &c.; should they fail in any way, might they die as this pig and cock were going to die. After this one of the Chin interpreters, acting on behalf of the General and Mr. Ross, stood over the pig, and going through the same form said that if the Chins kept their oath, they would not be killed or imprisoned, and would be treated in a friendly way. The pig and cock were then killed, the former by being stabbed to the heart with a dagger, and the latter by having its head cut off.

In the evening a most unfortunate occurrence took place by which a Chin slave boy lost his life. A servant cleaning a revolver, and supposing it to be empty, pointed it at the boy, who was looking on, and pulled the trigger. The revolver was loaded in one chamber, and the cartridge being opposite the hammer exploded, the bullet passing through the boy's chest and killing him almost instantaneously. The headmen were immediately sent for, and the accident explained to them. They took it much to heart, refused to be comforted, and demanded the life of the man who fired the shot. They said blood for blood was the Chin custom, and they at once interpreted the incident as an indication that their "nats" or spirits had taken this early opportunity of showing their displeasure of the oath that had been sworn that day. It was explained to the Chiefs that the English people also had customs, and for an accident that compensation could only be given. The Chins, however, refused to take money, saying that they were not in the habit of selling the bodies of their people.

The camps at Yôkwa had been placed on two exposed spurs at an elevation of 4,500 feet, and while we were there the minimum reading of the thermometer varied from 48° to 51°, the effect of the low temperature being accentuated by a strong breeze which usually sprang up about sunset. To men saturated with malaria, as a large proportion of the force were, this condition was a severe test.

Before proceeding with the description of the further advance to Hāka, I shall give a few data indicative of the sanitary condition of the force.

Information was received from Kān that Private Belk, King's Own Scottish Borderers, had died there on the 17th January from dysentery, while at the same post on that date there were 2 officers, 21 British, 31 Native soldiers, and 130 followers remaining in hospital.

On the 21st there were sick at Yôkwa 9 officers, 25 men, King's Own Scottish Borderers, 32 Gurkhas, and 31 hill coolies, with a large number more or less ill attending hospital for treatment.

On the 23rd at Yôkwa there were on the sick list 13 officers, and information was received that on the previous day 1 officer, 42 men, King's Own Scottish Borderers, 5 men, 2nd Madras Infantry, and 8 followers had been transferred from Kān to Kalèwa.

On the 21st, previous to the departure of this convoy, there had been on the sick list at Kān 3 officers, 37 British soldiers, 31 Native troops, and 148 followers.

On the 26th news arrived that out of 100 rifles of the King's Own Scottish Borderers, who were then marching up from Pakôkku to Kān, 12 had been left behind sick at Tilin.

On the previous day there remained in hospital at Kān 2 British officers, 22 British soldiers, 59 Native soldiers, and 174 followers, while the Borderers lost another man in the person of Corporal Boddy at Chaungkwa on the 19th from dysentery.

On the 27th Lieutenant Hildebrand, who was in charge of the Hill Coolie Corps at Kān, Yôkwa and intermediate posts, reported that of his total of 741 men there were 252 sick and only 489 fit for duty, 25 had died since their arrival at Kān, and 97 were pronounced utterly unfit for further service.

On the 28th a sick convoy was despatched from Yôkwa to Kān consisting of 3 British officers, 19 British, 26 Native soldiers, and 18 followers.

On the same day there were sent down the Myittha River from Kān 3 officers, 15 British, 41 Native soldiers, and 14 followers, while there remained in hospital at that post 13 British, 21 Native troops, and 233 followers.

There were 6 officers sick at Yôkwa on the 30th.

The following sick convoy was sent down the Myittha on the 5th February, 3 British officers, 20 men, King's Own Scottish Borderers, 10 Native soldiers, and 81 followers, leaving 1 officer, 33 British soldiers, 49 Native soldiers, and 196 followers in hospital at Kān.

On the 8th February the state was as follows :—

Sick in Hospital.

At Yôkwa, 3 British officers, 18 British troops, 42 Native troops, and 158 followers.

At Kān, 1 British officer, 43 British troops, 49 Native troops, and 186 followers.

At Thayetbin, 4 men, 2nd Madras Infantry.

At Chaungkwa, 6 British troops, 17 Native troops, and 64 followers.

At Taungtek, 6 Native troops and 13 followers.

At Rawvan, 4 British officers, 67 British troops, 125 Native troops, and 6 followers.

Total, 4 British officers, 67 British troops, 125 Native troops, and 427 followers.

On the following day 24 British troops were transferred from Kān to Kalèwa.

A further convoy was despatched on the 12th February, consisting of 10 British soldiers, 20 Native soldiers, and 10 followers, leaving 28 British, 45 Native soldiers, and 203 followers sick at Kān.

The mule path was opened into Yôkwa on the 27th January, the last five miles of road having taken ten days to make.

The telegraph wire was carried in on the same date.

On the 30th the bridge over the Einvār stream was completed.

CHAPTER XI.

The Chin-Lushai Expedition of 1889-90.—(*Contd.*)

Advance of the Southern Chin Column to Hāka.
Hāka.

General Symons left Yôkwa for Bwètet on the 12th February, and on the following day advanced on Hāka with 97 men of the King's Own Scottish Borderers and 117 of the 2-4th Gurkha Rifles.

The road after leaving Bwètet went through the Sapper Camp and then, crossing the Mingun Vār stream by a natural bridge formed by the roots and branches of a banian tree, led steeply up for a mile. Thence bearing more to the west it ran along the side of the hill to Mingun, a village of 45 houses. From Mingun the Chin path led away fairly on the level, until in fifty minutes, a good stream of water was crossed at the foot of a steep rise. From this point the path ran up a long spur in continual ascent to the top of a high ridge 7,420 feet above sea-level, and some 3,500 feet above the Sapper Camp. It was a hard climb for all but very sound men, and took the head of the column one hour and forty-five minutes from the stream. Twenty per cent. of the

ADVANCE TO HAKA.

Borderers fell out on the march. The troops were then halted for an hour while the General went to the highest point of the ridge, and from there obtained a fine view of the hills to the north and west. The Chin guides pointed out a number of these by name, but none of them could be recognised by the Hāka designations. Leaving the ridge the track descended for a mile through forests which bore signs of exposure to much rain and mist. On leaving the wood, in fifteen minutes a good stream of water was reached, on the banks of which, on an excellent site, the troops encamped for the night about a quarter of a mile from and above Hāka head village. The Chins came out to meet the column and appeared friendly. The chief points of interest gathered were that the Tashôn Ywama (mother village), which was to be the next objective, was not more than thirty miles or three marches from Hāka, and that Malliam Pui, where the Chittagong column was then supposed to be, was between fifty and sixty miles to the west.

On the following day, the 14th, a number of Chins were in camp from early morning, and later an assembly of all the head Hāka Chiefs was held, at which the British terms, intentions, and movements were explained. The first were as offered to the Yôkwas, except that as the Hākas had not resisted our advance they would not be fined. In reply, the Chiefs asked for three or four days to consider, and at the same time requested that the Chin slaves, who had run away from them and taken refuge in Burma, might be given up. They also wished to know whether such Burmese captives as did not wish to return to their own country would be compelled to do so. The Chiefs then retired, drank heavily all the rest of the day, and consulted.

No better site than the one first occupied by the troops could be found for a permanent post, and it was therefore finally selected for that purpose.

During the afternoon of the 15th February three Tantin, or, as they, call themselves, Tlan-Tlang, Chiefs presented themselves, and in the usual terms asked to be permitted to live as brothers and sisters with the white strangers. This was graciously accorded, and the following information gathered. The Tantins have the same customs, wear the same peculiar head-dress, and speak the same language as other Baungshè tribes; they live on good terms with the Hākas and Tashôns; they claim the following villages, but it is more probable that a large number, particularly those lying to the west of the Ti Pi river, are only so far subservient that they have occasionally to pay blackmail. On the east of the Tui Pui or Ti Pi (Tui or Ti being Chin for water) as the Hākas and Tantins called part of the course of the Koladyne, the latter tribe claimed—

	Houses.
Tantin or Tlan-Tlang Ywama	130
Shopum	30

ADVANCE TO HAKA.

	Houses.
Shihmu	10
Farôn	30
Lôndein	10
Lôn-ler	100
Dôn	100
Tang-Zang	100
Bûnkwa	30
Tùnka	20
Ruakwa	30
Tao	100
Hriankan	50
Bwè or Buil	20
Sa-len or Sang-kal	30
Hmûnlipi	60
Tlwa-lam	50
Lông-sao	80
Tlanrwa	80
Tlangpi	100
Tlangbwè	30
Twong-Fyin	80
Kwa-hai	10
Hmunhai	80

On the west of the Ti Pi river, Ramvi, Lakarr, Ainet, Yaunglein, Taungmwa, Ngaipia, Lônswè and Sabaung, the sizes of which were not given. The head Tantin Chief was called "Ya Hút," or "Ya Hwit," an individual who was afterwards ascertained to be identical with the Jahuta implicated in the attack on Lieutenant Stewart's party. Tao is the most westerly village belonging to the Tantins on the east of the Ti Pi. They called the people who lived to the west of them Tlaikwin, and said that they wore large earrings. The Hākas called

Howsata's village, which had been burnt the previous year, Wunlaipai, and Lyan Mo a Hāka Chief averred that the village had belonged to him, and that he used to get revenue from it.

Accompanied by a strong escort, taken for effect, the General and staff, with many other officers, visited Hāka Ywama on the 16th. They found the village to consist of about two hundred fine well-built houses lying sheltered under the Rông-Klang, and, like the other Chin villages already inspected, in a remarkably clean and sanitary condition. The women and children were in the houses and courtyards. The new village called Hāka Kotarr is about one mile from the present Ywama and to the west. During the day representatives from three Hāka villages lying to the north of the circle came in to submit. They stated that they had been greatly harassed by the Tashôns, who had recently killed eight of the tribesmen, and asked for our protection. Arrangements were completed for a reconnaissance to start on the following day (17th) to explore the roads leading north to the Tashôn Ywama, but at the last moment the expedition was postponed at the very earnest entreaty of the Hāka Chiefs, who, unknown to the General or the Political Officer, had sent a guarantee to the Tashôns that no movements would be made against them, pending an answer to a communication that had been sent to the headmen of Minkin, the most southern Tashôn village. The Hākas also said, judging, I suppose,

THE POST AT HAKA.

from past experience, that their messengers would be murdered if faith were broken. Instead therefore of going to the north on the day fixed, General Symons with Mr. Ross, Major Ind, 50 rifles King's Own Scottish Borderers, 50 rifles 2-4th Gurkhas, and 100 hill coolies, all that could be spared from the work of carrying provisions to the advanced troops at Hāka, with four days' rations, started to the west to explore as far as possible towards Malliam Pui and General Tregear's Camp on the Koladyne river.

The party marched on the first day to Tantin Ywama, sixteen miles from Hāka, on the second to Tlwalam, six miles further on, and on the third to Hmuntipi, thirty-three from Hāka, to which they returned on the 21st February. In describing the route taken, I shall quote the report made at the time by the late Major Ind, Staff Officer.

"The road on leaving the post at Hāka runs nearly level in a W. N. W. direction for about 5 miles, and is good for transport animals. A short descent is then made into the Boinu Valley. The Boinu stream, the most easterly tributary of the Koladyne river, flows south from the Tashôn country, and is crossed at the sixth mile. The banks of the stream are steep, the water, now 30 feet broad and 6 inches deep, flowing over a rocky bottom. Hence the path follows for $4\frac{1}{2}$ miles the valley of Sa or Tsa stream which flows into the Boinu. The valley is open, and the path, which is excellent, crosses the stream several times. It then turns more west, and ascends a spur of the Sarangpulôn range some 2,000 feet above the valley. From the highest point crossed, the Rông Klang above Hāka bears 103°, and the highest point on the Tiriang Klang 274°. Passing over the crest of this range at the 12th mile a long descent for 3 miles, steep in places, is made to a small stream, when, after a slight ascent one mile further on, the Tantin Ywama is reached. The read throughout, with slight improvement in a few places, is passable for laden transport animals.

"The village, as all the other Tantin villages that have been seen, is built on a minor spur running down the centre of a broad valley between the main ranges; it contains 130 houses. The water-supply is from two wells, one to the north-west, the other to the south-west of the village. It is not sufficient for more than 200 men, nor for transport animals. An unlimited supply is from the Lavār stream in the valley to the west of Tantin, and by the path 1½ miles from the village. The name of the headman is Ya Hút or Ya Hwit.

"From Tantin the path descends easily to the Lavār stream 1½ miles. The Lavār flows from south to north, then joins the Tya-o stream, and the two flow into the Ti-Pi river, near the Mer Chin village of Fanai (500 houses). From this stream the path ascends, very steeply at first, then easier, until the top of the Wishwip range, some 1,500 feet above the valley, is reached at 4 miles from the Ywama. From the point where the path crosses the crest of this range, the Rông Klang (about Hāka) bears 116°, the Pupi Taung (hill) 136°, and Tlwalam village 260°. The road then steadily descends for 1½ miles to a small stream (running south to the La-aw river, and thence into the Ti-Pi) where there is a fair camping ground in tree jungle with a good water-supply. The village of Tlwalam, situated on a low spur, is reached ½ mile further on. The road would require making for about 3 miles for transport animals. Tlwalam contains 50 houses, and the villagers get their water from two small springs near the village. The name of the headman is Win Karr. From a stone platform on the spur immediately above the village the Sangal Klang Peak bears 243°, the north point of the double peak on the Tiriang Klang 247°, and the highest point of the same range 252½°.

ADVANCE TO HAKA. 147

"Ducks, fowls, goats, pigs, mythun, and cattle were seen in the village.

"The road ascends steeply to the spur above Tlwalam village, then goes down into a deep narrow valley, thence ascends very sharply to a ridge named Chin Klang, 3½ miles above, and from, the village of Tlwalam. It then descends gradually to a small stream with a good water-supply over a fair track for 3½ miles. Thence for 3 miles the road is good through open pine forest, with but slight ascents and descents, for 2½ miles till the Boorr-pai stream is crossed. The Boorr-pai runs from north to south, and flows into the La-aw, and then away south-west into the Ti-Pi river. There is a good camping ground to west of the Boorr-pai stream, and an excellent water-supply for a large force of men and animals. The village of Hmûnlipi is situated on a minor spur 1½ miles from the Boorr-pai; it contains 60 houses. Water is obtainable from a well and a stream to the north of the village.

"The general direction of the whole road from Hāka is W. N. W. Considerable work would be required to make the ascent of the Chin Klang passable for transport animals. From the furthest point of the road reached at Hmûnlipi, the Sangal Klang bears 185°, the highest point of the Tiriang Klang 222°, and the Tao Klang 286°. Tao village was said to bear 277°, and Malliam Pui 265°. From Hmûnlipi onwards the road was said to run W. N. W. through a gorge at the north end of the Tiriang Klang, and to the south of the Tao Klang, to the village of Tao, 11 miles, which contains 30 houses. Then from Tao village to the Ti-Pi river, a long day's journey for a Chin, say 14 or 15 miles.

"The true Sangal Klang is also called the Salen Klang from the village of Salen which lies on the eastern slope of the hill. The Tao Klang has been well ascertained to be the Sangal Klang of the maps. The latter being a minor feature and much lower, could not have been observed from the north or west."

The Tantin people received the party well and accepted the terms, under which they might live in subjection to the British Government, very readily. During the march representatives from many Tantin villages, indeed from all those within reach, came in and made submission, and both the General and the Political Officer formed the opinion that the Tantin or Tlan-Tlang tribe would give no further trouble, an anticipation, which more recent events have shewn, was not realised. The Tantins said that they had not been accustomed to trade with Burma, but would like to be permitted to do so, as well as in the western bazaars. In their houses were seen china-plates, tumblers, bottles, lanterns, &c., which they said they had obtained from the West. They also professed themselves much afraid of the Chittagong column, who, they had heard, were arresting and locking up certain Chiefs. This no doubt hastened their wishes to submit and save their persons and their villages.

In collecting information in the Tantin circle regarding the country to the west, much confusion was caused on account of the Chins and Lushais pronouncing names and words somewhat differently, and thus rendering connection uncertain. For instance there seemed reason to believe that the chief "Jahuta" of the Lushais, was "Ya Hwit" or "Ya Hút," the premier Chief of Tantin Ywama. For record it was noted that he and his four sons, Van Hmôn, Yair Lein, Rông Suom and Ken

Suit lived, and said they always had lived, in Tantin Ywama.

At Tlwalam, Win Karr, the headman, told Mr. Ross that General Tregear had arrested Vantura, Howsata's brother, but that another brother, Do Kwè, had run away; also that Vantura was a cousin of Ya Hwit of Tantin, and that Howsata was married to Win Karr's sister, by name Ngwin Daung. According to Chin custom when a man dies the next unmarried brother takes his widow to wife. (For a similar Jewish custom see Genesis, Chap. xxxviii.)

On the 22nd February, the day after the return of the party from the Tantin country, information was received from Fort White that the Tashôns had withdrawn their offer of assistance with coolies, and intended to oppose the advances of the British troops. Also that the Tashôns had given the Hānta Chiefs a guard, and had assisted them to build huts on the site of their village, recently burnt by Captain Hunter, 10th Bengal Infantry, from Sihaung. A reconnoitring party was sent out from Hāka at daybreak to explore and report upon the road to the north leading to the Tashôn country. It returned in the evening, and Major Stoney, King's Own Scotish Borderers, who was in command, reported that they had gone eleven miles out, and that with very little doing the road could be made passable for laden mules as far as they had gone. On the same day the headman of Hāka reported that a man in their village who had four grown-up sons and two Burman captives, refused to give the latter up and threatened, if force were applied to him, to shoot one of the English officers, and thus cause Hāka to be burnt. They were informed by the Political Officer that at any cost captives must be given up, and in a few days, or that measures would be taken to compel them to do so.

Laden mules being now able to get into Hāka and thus free the coolies from bringing up the food for the troops, General Symons was enabled to despatch on the 23rd a party consisting of—

    25 rifles, King's Own Scottish Borderers.
    25 rifles, 2-4th Gurkhas.
    105 hill coolies.
    Small plane-table party with Officers.
    Captain Rundall, 2-4th Gurkhas in Command.
    Lieutenant Stevenson, King's Own Scottish Borderers.
    Lieutenant Norie, Intelligence Officer.

They were furnished with 12 days' rations and received instructions to proceed, through Tantin, Shopôn and Tao, to the west until they reached General Tregear's camp on the Koladyne, or got into touch with his troops. The route directed for the party to take lay a little to the north of the line taken by General Symons in the former reconnaissance. This Expedition returned to Hāka on the 3rd March, having done excellent work and added much to the knowledge previously gleaned of the country between Hāka and the Koladyne river. From information received, Captain Rundall, whilst in the Tantin country, was enabled to recover the heads of Lieutenant Stewart, of the Leinster Regiment, and of the two British soldiers who had been killed with him by the Lushais on the 3rd February 1888. The heads were buried on the 5th March 1890 at Hāka in a spot selected as a cemetery. They had been in the village of Tang-zang (Tinyin.) Captain Rundall also recovered, and brought into Hāka, Lieutenant Stewart's aneroid and field-glasses, two sniders and one Martini rifle, all of which had been lost on the occasion. The aneroid and field-glasses were given up by Lalwè, a very handsome fine-looking young Tantin Chief. One rifle was got from the same village, one from Tlwalam, and one from Tang-zang. All were given up at once when demanded, as well as a Burmese captive woman from the Tantin (Tlan-Tlang) Ywama. The party was met at Tao on the 26th February by Captain Hall and 60 rifles of the 2-2nd Gurkhas, with Captain Shakespear, Intelligence Officer, and 30 Chakma coolies, from General Tregear's forces, all of whom accompanied Captain Rundall on his return to Hāka, where they remained until the 6th, when they started to rejoin General Tregear.

On the afternoon of the day on which the above party started for Tao, two Burmans came up through Kān and Yôkwa from Sihaung, without any escort, to look for their relations lately raided by Hāka Chins, and this was accepted as a very satisfactory sign of the acknowledgment by the Burmans of our power to protect them and reduce the Chins to order. A Burmese female taken in the late raid alluded to was given up on the following day, but as seventeen more captives belonging to Sihaung were known to be still in the hands of the Hāka Chiefs, the latter were told that if all these were not restored by noon of the 25th, the tribe would be fined Rs. 300. They, accordingly, brought in fifteen on the date specified, leaving two to be accounted for, who, however, were given up on the 1st March.

On the 24th February at Hāka the first opportunity was offered of witnessing the obsequies of a Chin hunter. In the afternoon the camp was aroused by a number of shots to the south-west, and it was at first thought that the Chins had broken through the terms of peace entered into by them. About eighty men were seen firing away as quickly as they could load; but it was soon ascertained that a mighty hunter having died in Hāka, these Chins had been out to slay a wild animal, in order that the spirit of the dead man might rest in peace. They had killed a fine sambur, and the shots were being fired to announce the success of their efforts.

A second reconnaissance towards the Tashôn Ywama was made on the 26th February by the General Officer Commanding and staff, with Mr. Ross and an escort of 75 rifles, King's Own Scottish Borderers, and 110 rifles, 2-4th Gurkhas. Their object was to explore the road

ADVANCE TO HAKA.

from Hāka to the Tashôn capital, and ascertain the intentions of that tribe of Chins. For some days attempts had been made to get into communication with the outlying and southern border Tashôn villages through the medium of two minor Hāka Chiefs, who had relations living in the Tashôn village of Minkin. These negotiations were very successful, and were chiefly instrumental in gaining a peaceful and complete result, in spite of repeated warnings given to the General that the Tashôns were prepared to resist and defend the approaches to their capital in large force. It is probable also that the sudden and quick advance paralysed the action of the Tashôns for resistance. In the four days out the bulk of the troops did severe work. In three days they marched 47 miles over steep hills and deep valleys, besides building themselves shelters. On the fourth day large escorts attended the survey and plane-table parties, by whom a good portion of a totally unknown country was plotted out and mapped. The river Pao divides the Hāka from the Tashôn lands. As soon as it was crossed a change was at once apparent in the greatly increased areas of cultivation, and larger and more populous villages sighted on the hill sides. It is certain that the eager desire shown by these villagers to submit arose from the fear of having their villages destroyed. Instead of opposition and flight and hiding, as was expected, the people, including women and children, advised and encouraged by the

Hāka emissaries, remained quietly in the villages, nor had any food-stuffs been removed from the houses or granaries in the fields. The behaviour of the people and appearance of their fields inspired the belief that they were peace-loving and industrious. It is matter of congratulation that the Tashôns did not oppose us on this occasion, as, although the reconnaissance was only intended to gather information, if hostilities had commenced they must have been pushed through. Any movement savouring of a retreat, or that might have been constructed so by the Chins, would have been an error. The road right into the Ywama was now well known. Throughout its length no positions capable of a strong defence were observed by the party, and, with many populous villages on the line which had nearly all expressed a desire for peace, it was anticipated by General Symons that the warlike party known to exist would be suppressed by the majority. The Expedition returned to Hāka on the 1st March. On the same date orders were given for a mule path to be made from Hāka to Hairôn, $15\frac{1}{2}$ miles on the Tashôn-Ywama road, to take on supplies.

The through road had been completed to Hāka on the 24th February, and was by this time two miles further on towards Tantin. The Sappers and Punjabi coolies worked under the very able instructions of Major Henry, Commanding Royal Engineer, who had devoted himself with untiring energy to the work. The 55 miles from

Kyauk-pya-daung to Hāka had taken 77 days, or at an average rate of 1,234 yards a day. The natural obstacles had been great, but the further difficulties of the undertaking, involved by the excessive amount of inefficiency due to sickness among the men engaged in the work, may be estimated by the following statement :—

The greatest number of Sappers working on any one day was ...	81
The least number of Sappers working on any one day was ...	46
The greatest number of coolies working on any one day was ...	327
The least number of coolies working on any one day was ...	43
The daily average of working men was { Sappers ...	60·9
{ Coolies ...	187·5

The question of the performance of "thissa" or swearing the oath of friendship between the British representatives and the Hāka Chiefs had been urgently pressed by the latter for some time and duly considered. All requisitions for coolies, building materials, or supplies had been met by refusal pending the performance of the ceremony. Chiefly on account of the " oath of friendship" implying equality of the contracting parties, the General Officer Commanding had been at first adverse to its being taken, but the obstinacy of the Chins gained their desire. Pains were taken to explain to them that this method of ratifying the treaty was adopted only as a great favour to them, and that the supremacy of the British authority over them must not be questioned. As the ceremony on this occasion differed considerably from that performed at Yôkwa, it may be worth describing. By 3 P.M. representatives from all the villages of the Hāka circle, in number some 2,000 men, with a few women and children, had assembled, and sat in an orderly manner in the form of a square, round which the Pipers of the 2-4th Gurkhas marched to the great delight of the Chins. A large number were armed with guns and spears. The Chiefs were desired to sit under the British standard, which had been erected for the occasion, and the conditions of their submission to the Government were again read out to them. They swore to accept the terms. The paper on which these were written was then burnt, and the ashes thrown into a large basket-made vessel full of rice-beer. A large bull mythun was brought into the square, and being held by representatives of the Government and Hāka Chiefs, a libation of beer was poured over its head and horns. The oath of submission and obedience was now sworn by the Head Chief, and the promise given that, as long as the Hākas abided by the terms, they would neither be killed nor imprisoned, nor have harm done to their persons or property; also that they would be allowed to trade in Burma when they had given up all captives. After two or three slight thrusts in the skin, to see whether the bull would bellow or not—the best omen, as happened on this occasion, being the sacrifice without even a groan—the animal was killed by a Chin with a spear. Its tail was then cut off, and all the principal performers in the ceremony were brushed with it. Finally the rice-beer and paper ashes were drunk, and the assemblage dispersed.

The detachment of No. 1 Bengal Mountain Battery, under command of Lieutenant Pasley, R.E., arrived at Hāka from Kān on the following day. The reasons why the guns had not been advanced sooner were, that there was no service for them to perform, that the feeding of such a large number of additional animals as necessarily accompanied them would have added considerably to the difficulty of transport, and that the presence of the guns might have had a disturbing influence upon the Chins, an effect which it was desirable to avoid as far as possible.

During the stay of the advanced troops at Hāka, their strength was increased by the arrival of further reinforcements from the rear. Lieutenant Renny-Tailyour, R.E., Survey Officer, Lieutenant Norie, Intelligence Officer, Lieutenants Hamilton, Stevenson and 20 rifles, King's Own Scottish Borderers, Captain Rundall, Lieutenant Battye, and 25 rifles, 2-4th Gurkhas, arrived on the 18th February from Bwètet. These were followed by Lieutenant Malcolm with one Native Officer and 42 rifles, 2-4th Gurkhas, on the 21st. The Gurkhas had garrisoned Taungtek until relieved by 50 rifles of the 2nd Madras Infantry. On the next day No. 6 Company, Madras Sappers and Miners, marched into Hāka, strength, 5 British officers and 96 of other ranks.

Captain McArthur and 52 rifles, King's Own Scottish Borderers, arrived at Hāka from Kān on the 4th March, being the remnant of the detachment of that regiment which had last been despatched from Kān, strength, two officers and 100 men. On the same day one Native Officer and 46 rifles of the 2-4th Gurkhas marched in from Rawvan, where they had been relieved by a detachment of the 2nd Madras Infantry. Such additions were sorely needed to compensate for the numerous curtailments which had taken place.

The health of the troops at the front was by this time considerably improved, but a good deal of sickness still prevailed at the more unhealthy posts along the line of communications and at the base.

On the 15th February Lieutenant Pratt, King's Own Scottish Borderers, and three hill coolies were the only sick at Hāka.

The list at Kān on the 17th was represented by 2 officers, 27 British troops, 35 Native troops and 94 followers.

On the 18th the number at Hāka had increased to 1 officer and 2 men of the King's Own Scottish Borderers, 1 man of the 2-4th Gurkhas and 10 followers; while, on the same day, 11 sick Borderers, who had been left behind at Bwètet, were sent back to the second medical rest depôt at Yôkwa.

Reports were received that there were sick at Kān on the 20th February, 5 officers, including 2 of the King's Own Scottish Borderers and 1 Surgeon, all three fresh admissions.

Lieutenant Denne was also reported seriously ill at Chaungkwa.

Eleven sick Gurkhas of Lieutenant Malcolm's detachment were left behind at Taungtek. There were sick at Hāka, on the 22nd February, 2 King's Own Scottish Borderers, 10 Gurkhas and 36 fol-

ADVANCE TO HAKA. 159

lowers, and at Kān, 6 British officers, 53 British soldiers, 42 Native soldiers and 203 followers.

Lieutenant Malcolm, 2-4th Gurkhas, 5 King's Own Scottish Borderers, 5 Sappers, 19 Punjabi coolies and 3 men of the Survey Department, were sent down sick from Hāka on the 23rd, and on the following day a report was received from Kān that Lieutenant Dickson, Commissariat Department, and 45 British soldiers had been invalided to Kalèwa, and that there were still sick at Kān, 3 British officers, 11 British soldiers, 22 Native soldiers, and 113 followers.

On the 26th these numbers had increased to 5 British officers, 16 British soldiers, 36 Native soldiers and 131 followers; 40 followers were next day transferred to Kalèwa.

On the 4th March there were sick at Kān, 4 British officers, 32 British soldiers, 67 Native soldiers and 275 followers (including 156 Punjabi coolies); also in the Yôkwa medical rest depôt, 2 British soldiers, 2 Madras Sappers, 2 Gurkhas, 12 Second Madras Infantry, 5 public followers, 51 Punjabi coolies and 19 hill coolies.

On the 5th March Lieutenant Malcolm, 2-4th Gurkhas, Lieutenant Denne, 2nd Madras Infantry, Surgeon Marder, Medical Staff, with 25 British, 9 Native troops and 49 followers, were transferred from Kān to the base hospital at Kalèwa, a further convoy of 99 sick Punjabi coolies following them on the 6th.

On the 7th there were in hospital at Kān, 1 British officer (Lieutenant Norman, 2nd Madras Infantry), 9 British, 50 Native troops and 137 followers.

Private Bowman, King's Own Scottish Borderers, died at Hāka on the 8th March of remittent fever.

On reading the above numbers, when the original strength of the Southern Column is remembered, and further, that all men sent down the Myittha river to Kalèwa were thenceforward absolutely lost to the Expedition, it becomes a matter of some doubt and speculation as to how the remaining work of the undertaking was to be accomplished.

The telegraph wire had been brought into Hāka on the 15th February, and an office opened there.

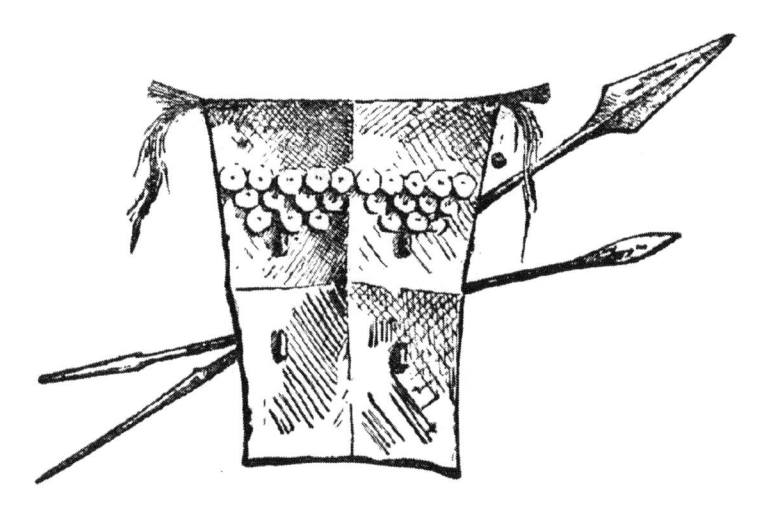

CHIN-LUSHAI SHIELD AND SPEARS.

CHAPTER XII.

THE CHIN-LUSHAI EXPEDITION OF 1889-90.—*Contd.*

Advance of the Southern Chin Column to the Tashôn Capital and close of the operations.

THE first objective of the Southern Column had now been accomplished, and it only remained to carry out the second, namely, the advance on the capital of the Tashôns, in which was to be simultaneously associated the Fort White Force under the command of Colonel Skene, D. S. O.

The Sappers had made the road passable for mules for a distance of nineteen miles, and, accordingly, on the 9th March, General Symons marched to Hairôn fifteen and a half miles north of Hāka with the following force:—

    100 men King's Own Scottish Borderers.
    164 ,, 2-4th Gurkha Rifles.
    2 Guns No. 1 B. M. Battery.

Karôn, 9½ miles further on, was reached on the 10th, and on the 11th the force advanced on the Ywama. The people appeared friendly everywhere and were not frightened. Two of the Head Chiefs of the tribe, Man

Lôn and Sônpek, met the column, and, having tried to persuade the General not to advance as far as the Biluma ridge, which lies south of and overlooks the Ywama, pointed out various grounds suitable for a camp. Their wishes were not acceded to, and the ridge was reached at 9 A.M. The northern column was at once discovered near the village of Patè, about 8,000 yards off, on the slopes of the hills on the north of the Manipur River. Signal communication was soon established. The southern column halted itself on the northern slopes of the above-mentioned ridge, 1,000 yards north-west of the Ywama. A meeting of the Chiefs was called, and the following attended: Sônpek, Man Lôn, Ka Lyan, Boimôn, Wûn Sè-ao, and a minor official called Shin Lay. When asked if they agreed to our terms, namely, to pay the fine of Rs. 10,000 and an annual subsidy of two elephant tusks and ten silk sheets, or their equivalent, namely, Rs. 500, they said plainly that they would not pay an annual tribute, nor were they sure whether they would pay the fine, or any portion of it, or not. Their arguments were—that they had not got the money; that they could not make rupees; that they had got the few they had from Burma; that they were asked to pay silk sheets, which they had to purchase in Burma, and that we had prevented them from trading, and so they could not get any; that they were not raiders or bad people like the Siyins or the Hākas and Yôkwas, and yet they were being punished more severely than these last two tribes; finally, that the Chiefs got their sustenance from the villages, and if they paid it all away in a fine or tribute, that they would have nothing to live on. Greatly astonished at the refusal of the Chiefs to accede to terms which they had long known, and up to this had not objected to, General Symons, having cautioned them to think again well over their refusal and the consequences it would entail, dismissed them. Their decision and straightforward boldness in giving it, when their capital was at the mercy of the united columns of the British troops, whom they had permitted and assisted to march on it, was a remarkable one. After long consideration it was decided to adopt an expectant policy which, as will be seen, was favoured by fortune.

On the following day, the 12th March, the Brigadier-General, accompanied by Major Henry, Commanding Royal Engineer, left camp early with an escort of 25 King's Own Scottish Borderers to meet Colonel Skene, D. S. O., Commanding the Northern or Fort White Column at the Nankathè or Manipur River. Immediately after leaving camp numbers of armed Chins ran towards the party from the Ywama and did all they could short of using force to prevent the General proceeding. Their object was soon made apparent, as, after ascending the steep ravine side for a little, stone, earth and wooden breastworks were discovered, as well as wooden stockades, blocking in reverse and in all directions the paths of approach to the Ywama from the north. Every point of vantage was protected with crow's-nests and masked stockades. These continued in increasing numbers to the river bank, across which, from the feet of rocky precipices to the water's edge, stone walls and barricades had been built. At the ford leading away to Patè village the river was 55 yards wide, 2 feet 10 inches deep, and flowing evenly over a bed of shingle from west to east. The aneroids showed a descent of 3,400 feet from camp, a distance of 3 miles. Colonel Skene with an escort of 50 rifles of the Cheshire Regiment and 50 rifles 42nd Gurkha Light Infantry, soon arrived. He had experienced the same emphatic protests of the Chins against his descent to the river; and their protective works, the whole way from Patè to the river, were even in greater profusion than on the southern side. The march of the Northern Column from Fort White had been perfectly peaceful, Chin coolies having been furnished daily. The health of the men had also been very satisfactory. Colonel Skene, who had had much experience of the Chins and their ways, was greatly astonished at the decision of the Chiefs and agreed with General Symons that it was probable that the Chiefs themselves were responsible for the opposition, and that the mass of the people were for peace and surrender.

Before returning to the Southern Camp Major Ind made a very useful reconnaissance along the ridges lying to the west, south, and east of the Ywama. Good drawings of the village and its approaches were obtained. All the ridges were stockaded and some of the works were well constructed, whilst all were well placed. In front of some of the breastworks were driven, in a broad band, large numbers of stakes, the size of tent-pegs and a foot out of the ground. Their tops were not sharpened, but they would have acted as an entanglement. The descent from Patè to the river was 3,300 feet and the distance $3\frac{1}{2}$ miles. The valley of the Nankathè is deep and bold, and can only be ascended and descended in certain places. The river itself, as far as could be seen, flows in a succession of rapids and shallows. At the time of our visit it was fordable once at least in every 200 yards or so.

Negotiations with some of the Chiefs went on in the afternoon. It was explained to them—

(i) that the English Government asked for a yearly tribute as an acknowledgment of British supremacy, and as a yearly guarantee that the tribe would keep faithfully their promises to the Government;

(ii) that all the Chin tribes would have to pay an annual tribute;

(iii) that in consideration of their not having opposed the advances of the troops, the terms would not now be enforced, but whether they agreed to pay an annual tribute, or any portion of the latter, or not, the columns would return to Hāka and Fort White without injuring them or their villages, but that the Government would be advised to occupy posts in their country until they submitted;

(iv) they were asked to consider whether it was not better to pay a small annual sum rather than have troops permanently quartered in their country as those at Hāka and Fort White.

The advantages of submitting peaceably were—

(a) that their country would not be occupied;

(b) that they would be allowed to trade in the Myittha Valley.

The assembly was then dismissed.

At 1 P.M. of the 13th the four Chiefs, including Boimôn and Wûn Sè-ao, and some 20 minor men (all perfectly sober, not a constant condition on such occasions), the leaders of the war party, were received in durbar by the General Officer Commanding, Mr. Ross, and Mr. Carey (Political Officer with the Northern Column). They said: " We acknowledge that you have beaten us, that you are the conquerors; but, as you are strong be merciful and reduce the fine which we cannot pay, and the amount of tribute which we ask to be allowed to pay once in three years; we wish to accept your terms and be friends." They were told that the tribute must be paid annually; nothing else would be accepted. After consultation they asked if five full-grown mythun or in default Rs. 500 would be accepted. Being answered in the affirmative, they all promised to pay this and deliver the cattle or money yearly to the Political Officer at Hāka. This unexpected surrender and turn in the situation disposed most satisfactorily of the question of the annual tribute.

Regarding the fine the Chiefs asked for a reduction—

(a) because they had not the money and could not collect it in the tribe; (b) because it was excessive. They also said that they did not possess any elephant tusks. The point was carefully considered. General Symons, Mr. Ross, and Mr. Carey were all of opinion that the tribe could not find the amount in cash. The Chins were asked what they had collected and what they could pay. They replied that up to that period they had not been able to collect Rs. 200 in money, and that they had 40 mythun ready to give up. Feeling certain that it would not be the wish of the Government to despoil the people of all their cattle, and taking into consideration that two very great points had been gained, namely, the unopposed advance on the Ywama and the submission of the people manifested in their agreeing to pay an annual tribute, the General agreed to reduce the fine to Rs. 5,000 on the condition that this amount was paid before the Hāka Column left the Ywama, or within four clear days. If not then paid the whole Rs. 10,000 was to be insisted upon. The concession was immediately and gratefully accepted with its conditions, minor points were reserved for future discussion, and the meeting broke up.

Next morning General Symons and a party of officers

from both camps, with an escort, inspected the surroundings of the Ywama. The Chiefs asked for the party not to go into the village, and, as there was no particular object in doing so, it was foregone. Certain rock figures that had been mentioned by Major Raikes as being near the Ywama were visited and proved to be merely natural conglomerate stains on dark grey perpendicular rocks, without any shape or meaning. The modern capital of the Tashôns, known in Burma as the Tashôn Ywama, though the tribe calls itself and the capital "Falam," lies on the northern slopes of the Biluma range and 2,000 feet below its crest. Two long spurs, running down to the Nankathè River, protect it on the east and west, whilst its northern approaches are defended by the river itself (called "Rrun" by the Chins) which flows in a deep valley 2,500 feet below the Ywama. Some six miles to the west the Manipur or Nankathè River makes a very bold sweep from north to east. Except from the north, the town cannot be seen until closely approached. On its southern side, a few hundred feet below the crest of the Biluma range, an excellent bird's-eye view of the whole of the houses is obtained. Nestling among the hills at the foot of precipitous slopes lies the town. It has some 450 houses. The general appearance resembles Siyin rather than Baungshè villages. A curious custom, different from that of all other Chin tribes, is that the houses of the Chiefs do not exceed in size those of the rest of the people. Consequently, the

ADVANCE TO THE TASHON CAPITAL.

Ywama, which is built on three minor spurs of fairly even slope, has a uniform appearance, with the houses all standing at regular intervals. The present town, never before visited or violated by an armed force, has only existed for a hundred years. The original capital stood on the west of the present Ywama, and the reason for its abandonment, as given by the Falam, is that a beautiful Burmese maiden, finely dressed in silks and jewels, appeared in a cave in the rocks above the Ywama. Whoever looked on this Burmese Medusa, however, quickly perished; hence the transfer of the town.

In the afternoon three or four of the Chiefs again came to talk, and, being sober, a good deal of business was done. The tribute due at the commencement of the last cold season was paid in five fine mythun. They agreed to pay the fine as follows:—

	Rs.
16 goats	100
70 mythun, at Rs. 65 each	4,550
Cash	200
1 elephant tusk	200
Total	5,050

They further agreed and promised never again to raid in Burma. They promised to be security for Hānta village that it should behave properly in future. They promised to provide 50 coolies to take a small party of troops from the Ywama to Sihaung, to be paid at the rate of Rs. 3 for each man for the three days. They agreed to send representative men back with the northern column to try and get the Siyins and Kanhows to surrender. The question of how the English Government was to communicate in future with the Tashôn Chiefs was discussed, but no satisfactory decision could be arrived at, as the Chiefs stated that they had no one who could read or write Burmese. They were then given permission to trade anywhere in the Kalè Valley, provided that they did not sell to our enemies. They asked leave to trade all the way down the Myittha Valley, but it was ruled that for a time they were not to go outside the Kalè Valley.

The northern column started on its return march to Fort White on the 15th March, taking two Tashôn headmen with them, and, on the same day, the Division of Mountain Guns and Detachment of Sappers under Major Henry left Tashôn Ywama for Hāka. At noon some of the Chiefs came again, and, after paying in the Rs. 200 in cash, which they were very loth indeed to part with, "thissa" or the "oath of friendship" was performed over a bull mythun under circumstances similar to those observed at Hāka. The Chiefs said that if the Hākas had offered any resistance they would have fought also, that the defences around the Ywama had been all constructed against the English, and that since they had put the headmen of Mwebingyi and other northern villages in the stocks, to make them deliver up captives, they—the Tashôns—had never seen, nor had communication with, these men. It will be for the future to decide whether this submission of the Tashôns, wrung from them only with extreme reluctance and sacrifice of pride, will be binding on them or lasting. The policy of accepting their surrender only at the capital was without doubt the most advisable. All previous treaties made with them were worthless, and, believing themselves invincible and their country safe from invasion, would have been disowned on any requiring occasion. Before leaving the Ywama, the Chief, Boimôn, and the Kweshein thugyi said that they would not give up the Shwegyobyu Mintha, nor say where he was, because they had sworn the oath of friendship with him; but they promised that if any Burman dacoits came into their villages, they would arrest and give them up.

On the 16th March a party of 50 rifles, 2-4th Gurkhas, under Captain Rundall, with Lieutenant Norie, Intelligence Officer, a plane-table section, and 40 Chin coolies, left the Ywama for Sihaung, and, on the same day, the Brigadier Commanding with the remainder of the column started on the return march to Hāka. The rainy season sets in early in the Chin Hills, and already a few premonitory bursts had given warning that soon all military operations would have to be brought to a close. On the day the troops reached Hāka, the rear-guard did not get into camp until 7 P.M., having taken 13 hours doing the 16 miles, so steep and slippery was the path. Some of the hill coolies were very much exhausted.

Two havildars and 38 sappers of the Burma Company Sappers and Miners had arrived at Hāka on the 13th, and on the next day the following sick convoy had been despatched to Kān:—

    Major Stoney, King's Own Scottish Borderers.
    Surgeon Maidment, Indian Medical Service.
    21 men, King's Own Scottish Borderers.
    2 ,, 2-4th Gurkhas.
    2 ,, Queen's Own Sappers and Miners.
    24 Naga and 43 Punjabi coolies.

The detachment No. 1 Bengal Mountain Battery, under command of Lieutenant Pasley, R.A., also left Hāka for Mandalay.

The independent village of Rum Tlao, 300 houses, lying between the Tashôn and Tlan-Tlang circles, surrendered on the 19th March. As nothing was known against this village, it was assessed to pay an annual tribute of one mythun, to which the villagers agreed.

The transport being able to only just ration the garrison and followers then at Hāka and on the line of communications, it had become necessary to reduce the force on the hills to enable supplies for the rains to be got up. In consequence, on the 21st March,

    60 Rifles, King's Own Scottish Borderers, under Captain Woolcombe and Lieutenant Hamilton;
    3 Rifles, 2-4th Gurkhas;
    6 Punjabi coolies
    128 Hill coolies and 3 other followers } under Lieutenant Reynolds;

all of whom were weakly and more or less unfit for further hard work, left Hāka for Kān.

On the same day the Hāka Chins brought into camp sixteen so-called Burmese captives. Of these, five were men and eleven women. All were dressed as Chins, and none had been raided less than fourteen years before. The men had all married Chin women, had their liberty, and wished to remain in the hills. They were allowed to please themselves. Of the women, four wished to return to their villages in Burma, and were, accordingly, subsequently sent down. The remaining seven women, who could not even speak Burmese, said that they did not wish to leave the hills unless their children were allowed to go with them. The Chin fathers of the children did not care one way or the other, but the owners of the women, who are all slaves, in whose houses the children had been born and then lived, objected to the children being taken away. The women, although slaves, were not kept in durance of any kind. They were not married to Chin husbands, and were only allowed to receive visits from their men at night. They were all sent away, and told that if they claimed our protection with or without their children they would receive it.

Meanwhile good progress was being made on the new post at Hāka. Buildings were springing up and thatching grass being brought in by the Chins, who did not seem in the least put out at the knowledge that we were going to remain permanently at Hāka. A garden had been fenced off and started. Heavy rain accompanied by high winds and thunder was now of frequent occurrence, and the final arrangements had to be hurried.

Of the operations of the Southern or Kān Chin force little remains for me to add. On the 24th March, Lieutenant Hildebrand, with 240 hill coolies and escort, left Hāka to proceed to Tao village, to meet the left wing of the 2-4th Gurkhas from the Chittagong column, and provide them with transport to join General Symon's force at Hāka. This wing was selected to garrison Hāka under the command of Captain Drury, with Mr. Ross as Political Officer, while the right wing and head-quarters of the battalion under the command of Major Sir Chas. Leslie, Bart., was to proceed *viâ* Kān and Kalémyo to Fort White for a like purpose. The Chins were restoring captives, and faithfully fulfilling their obligations. A Pôngyi (Burmese-Buddhist monk) arrived at Hāka on the 24th March to look for his small brother who had been raided by Hāka Chins from Minywa village in North Yaw two years previously. The Pôngyi arrived safely without an escort. Three other Burmans had been taken off at the same time. One escaped, whilst two were ransomed at a total cost of Rs. 800. The fourth, a lad of twelve, was brought into camp and handed over to the Pôngyi. On the 31st the Tlan-Tlang (Tantin) Chins paid in, their tribute for the previous year, three mythun; and in mythun and paddy the value of Rs. 500 that they had been fined for the raid in February 1888 on Lieutenant Stewart and his party.

The Chiefs also said that they had ready to give up the six captives taken from Lal Seva's village. They were ordered to deliver these captives to General Tregear at Fort Tregear. The Hāka Chiefs paid up Rs. 300 that they had been fined for the raid on Sihaung in the preceding February. They also gave in two mythun that the head village had been fined on account of one of the villagers threatening a Burman with a knife and beating a coolie. The whole Hāka tribe, as a community, were purchasing from the owners the Burmese captives who were being given up. Three female captives were given up by the Hāka village of Faron on the 13th April. On the same date Brigadier-General Tregear, with his staff officer, Captain Gwatkin, and the force as below, arrived at Hāka from Fort Tregear.

No. 2 Company Bengal Sappers and Miners—10 officers and 33 men.

28th Bombay Pioneers—1 officer and 32 men.

Signalling party—1 officer and 5 men.

A survey party and medical establishment.

Transport—1 officer, 89 mules and 3 ponies.

45 public and 8 private followers.

With the exception of General Tregear and staff, 20 rifles, 28th Bombay Pioneers, and survey party, they left on the 14th to rejoin the Chittagong Column.

The active operations of the Chin Column were brought to a close by a reconnaissance made by General Symons to the south and south-west of Hāka.

The party under him consisted of:—

37 Rifles, King's Own Scottish Borderers, commanded by Lieutenant Stevenson.
50 Rifles, 2-4th Gurkhas, under Lieutenant Grant.
Lieutenants Renny-Tailyour and Bythell, R.E., Survey Officers.
Lieutenant Norie, Intelligence Department.
Captain Burton, Staff Officer.
Surgeon McGill, M.S.
185 Naga coolies.

As the report is of interest I shall quote it.

Reconnaissance from Hāka, 5th to 15th April 1890.

Objects.—To explore the line of the Boinu River, south and west; to visit and obtain the submission of numerous Chin villages lying in the loop of that river; and to prospect the country for a possibly better track for a road between Burma and Bengal.

5th April.—The party under the command of Brigadier-General Symons left Hāka, and marching south-west passed in succession the "Népar," "Ooti" and "Sorell" streams, all flowing west into the Boinu River. At the end of 6½ hours' marching and halting, or at 12 miles, the Boinu river itself was met, flowing south through a fine open valley. Where touched, the path crosses, with water at this season 15 inches deep and 30 yards wide, the banks 12 to 20 feet high and 55 yards across, thence, following the right bank over low spurs running down to the river, Bwônlôn village, 70 houses, was reached at 2 P.M.; total distance, 16 miles. The troops encamped close to, and south of, the village. From Bwônlôn a path runs east to Thetta, which is said to be a little nearer than Hāka.

6th.—The march was continued in a S.-S.-W. direction, still on the right bank of the Boinu. The path crossed in succession he "Kookvār," "Shûrlavār" and "Silashivār" streams, all running into the Boinu, and which were separated by somewhat steep pine-clad spurs. At the end of 9½ miles the village of Doongvār was arrived at, and the camp was formed above the village at an elevation of 1,300 feet above the Boinu river, which from this point was seen flowing away a little east of south. The water-supply at this camp was only sufficient for drinking, and for this purpose it had to be cut off from the village. Doongvār had 110 houses. It was known that there were three Burmese captives in this village, and after some pressing they were given up,—a man, woman and a child. From information furnished by the headmen, the original idea of tracing out the Boinu had to be abandoned. From Doongvār it was said to be four very hard and difficult marches, or about sixty miles to the most southern village in the loop. The information was that the Boinu river flowed in a southerly direction for this distance, and then turned north. The villagers said that laden coolies could not follow the right bank of the river, and that a path would have to be made most of the way. They gave the names of four villages along the right bank of the Boinu down to its southern reach, the most southern being Lônchin, and also the names of some villages on the left bank, and said that all these could best be got at from Thetta by paths along and above the left bank. After giving up the three captives the Doongvār people were given permission to go down to Burma and trade, with which concession they professed themselves well pleased.

7th.—At daylight, 12 rifles of the King's Own Scottish Borderers, who said they were weak and unable to keep up, were sent back to Hāka with 21 of the weediest of the Naga coolies. As soon as they had gone, the remainder of the party turned west and ascended steadily for 3½ miles to the top of the "Yovailangklang," which is the main ridge running north and south down the inside of the Boinu loop. At the point where the path crossed the ridge the aneroids registered 8,400 feet, or 2,500 feet above Doongvār camp. Unfortunately, the hills were shrouded in thick cloud, and, though the Survey Officers waited till noon, few observations could be taken.

The descent to the west was at first very abrupt through fine big-tree forest, then at an easier gradient for four miles to the flourishing village of Laitat, 100 houses. Passing through the village the path descends, turning south to a stream which at point of crossing was 4,000 feet below the crest of the "Yovailangklang." On the west of the path along this section was a deep valley, down which ran a considerable stream, flowing south into the Boinu, called the Tanghorr. The path from the stream steadily ascended to the village of Aibûr, 110 houses. The troops bivouacked south of the village near good water, the day's march being 14 severe miles.

8th.—Marching at dawn due south, at five miles the large village of Shûrngan, 200 houses, was seen two miles to the east of the path, and at $6\frac{1}{2}$ miles the considerable stream of Tiarrte, flowing south-west into the Tanghorr, was crossed. On the south side of the Tiarrtè the path led up very steeply for 1,600 feet, and continued fairly level for nine miles south to the large independent village Naring, containing 300 houses. Naring is built on a spur round the foot of which runs the Boinu, here flowing in a general direction from south to north. Duration of march, 16 miles. The Naga coolies all got in before night, but were very tired. In the four days from Hāka $55\frac{1}{2}$ miles had been covered. During this last march at many places along the road-side were considerable heaps of stones, explained to have been erected, some in honour and remembrance of a marriage, others to mark the number of pots of liquor drunk by a man, or the number of mythun or pigs killed by a Chief, a stone for each. The Naring villagers were frightened at first, but gradually became friendly and more confident. Two hours were spent in looking for water, the village supply being insufficient and exhausted for the day. At last in a deep gully half a mile from, and north-west of, the village, sufficient water was found, and the troops and coolies soon settled down.

9th.—Halted to rest coolies, whilst the Survey Officers went out on hill tops, and the General and Captain Burton descended 2,000

CLOSE OF THE OPERATIONS.

feet west to the Boinu and explored the river as far as possible. At the point touched the bed was 2,275 feet above sea-level, the river having fallen 2,725 feet below the point where the Hāka Tlan-Tlang road crosses it at six miles west from Haka, and 10 miles from its source. The river at Naring is from 30 to 60 yards broad, flowing through pools and over shallows. It had three times the volume of water as when left at Doongvār. The banks were from 120 to 200 yards wide. Four miles north of Naring the Tanghorr joins the Boinu, and from this point the Chins call the river "Tipi" meaning "great water" or "big river," whilst "Boi" means chief and "nu" wife. It is now absolutely certain that the Boinu and Tipi are one and the same and are the upper waters of the Koladyne river. From the junction of the Tanghorr and Boinu the river flows in a great bend to the south-west, and then trends away round to the north. Having returned to camp, the General and Mr. Ross had a long talk with the Naring headmen. They said it was the first time that any of them had seen any "Marang Boi" or "White Chiefs;" that they never travelled nor traded to the east nor west; that they made their own salt and clothes and had no wants; that they had large herds of cattle; that they had no money, did not know the value of it, did not want any, and refused payment for goats, pigs, fowls and eggs, which they hospitably supplied; that formerly they paid a yearly tribute to Hāka, but had discontinued it for twelve years and were independent. Certain young Hāka Chiefs that had accompanied the General professedly as guides and to see that no harm happened to the party were anxious for the "Marang Boi" to pass orders that the tribute should be re-imposed. This was refused, as a matter of course, to the great delight of the Naring people, who in the next breath begged that the troops might go with them and compel some six villages lying on both sides of the Boinu to pay up old debts of a like nature. Naring village was assessed to pay the British Government one mythun in each year. The Chiefs agreed at once to the terms, and said that they were astonished that they were so light.

10*th*.—The return march commenced. The line to be taken lay north and west of the outward route. The Aibûr road was followed for 7 miles, when the path turned off to the north-west, and for 5½ miles ran down a spur to the Tanghorr stream, up the valley of which for another 4½ miles the troops plodded through the water and over boulders, and lay in bivouac for the night at the junction of the Tanghorr and Hlampè streams. Distance of march, 17 miles.

11*th*.—The valley of the Hlampè was followed for half a mile, when the path left the right bank and ascended almost precipitously in places, in others steeply, for 6½ miles to the crest of the Kwèpiklang (Honey Hill) 6,000 feet above the sea, and 3,000 feet above the last bivouac. The Kwèpi range runs nearly parallel to, and is lower than, the Yovailangklang on the east (the meaning of Yovailangklang is " Klang " the hill, " Lang " from which can be seen, " Vai " the north, and " Yo " the south Hāka districts). After crossing Honey Hill the path descended through the centre of the village of Kabôn, below which a halt for the day was made. Length of march, 7¼ miles. Kabôn is a well-to-do village of 100 houses. Excellent Chin beer, pigs for the Nagas, hill rice, eggs and fowls were obtained. The afternoon was spent in gathering much information about neighbouring villages and the surrounding country from the intelligent thugyi of this village.

12*th*.—Starting at 5·30 A.M., the path was followed down a sharp descent almost to the foot of the valley of the Pai stream, when it turned north, and led at an easy gradient up a beautiful open valley, containing open glades and park-like bits of pasture land and clumps of trees, for 7½ miles to the poor village of Yèpai, 65 houses. From Yèpai the path led up a spur still going north to a point 5,850 feet, where it descended gradually 1,900 feet to a village called Wantu. Many well-built and large houses were noticed in this village of 100 or so houses, but as no water could be found, a halt was not called till the Nuit-Vār stream was reached, 1,500 feet below and north of the village. Total distance this day, 13½ miles.

13*th.*—The day's march commenced by a stiff toil for 2½ hours up a hill north-east with a rise of 3,000 feet. From the top a very good path led at the end of 4 miles into an amphitheatre of hills with a delightfully green level and meadow-like central area of some 350 acres. From this oasis a very good road ascended gradually, to the well-situated village Hripi, 70 houses, facing northeast and standing at an elevation of 5,700 feet. Water was found in a ravine ½ mile south of the village. Distance marched 9 miles. At Wantu and Hripi, on commanding spots above the villages, small pagoda-like structures had been built of stone. Questioned, the villagers said that they were built in imitation of Burmese pagodas, but had no reference to religion. At Hripi a Burman captive known to be in the village was demanded. He was given up late in the evening and proved to be a Burman who had been many years with the Chins. He arrived in a state of great excitement and drew a dagger, with which he said he would rather kill himself than be taken back to Burma. As he was married to a Chin woman, he was allowed to go in peace.

14*th.*—The march to-day was in a general direction of N.-N.-E. After 8 miles of up and down hills the village of Saungtia was reached. It contains about 90 houses. Beyond the village the path ran fairly level for 3⅓ miles, and then steeply up-hill for 1½ miles to the village Kusa, 35 houses. Water was found and a rest made close to, and on east of, this village.

15*th.*—The path from Kusa led very steeply up for 1 mile east from the village, and then descended to the Lawtehna stream, which flows into the Boinu. Distance from Kusa, 9½ miles. At the point of crossing, the bed of the Boinu is 4,900 feet above the sea. The nature of the stream and appearance of the valley are as before met with and described. From this point on the Boinu to Hāka is 6 miles.

"The attitude of the Chins throughout the march was very friendly and their hospitality marked. With the exception of Naring, every village visited was tributary to Hāka. A Hāka Chief is said to "eat" a village, that is, he demands, and usually receives, certain food supplies yearly. An appeal to force to exact this tribute is rarely resorted to; but there are no fixed laws on the subject. The tax, such as it is, is paid to the Chiefs as the original owners of the land. The general nature of the country marched through was very hilly with the systems running nearly north and south. The hill sides were covered, where not cleared for cultivation, with pine and open tree and bush jungle, except in a few places where fine woods and forests were passed through. It is doubtful whether the country would support a much larger population under the present wasteful vogue of cultivation. As far as could be seen no better trace for an east and west road than the present Kān-Yôkwa-Hāka-Fort Tregear line will be found anywhere within 80 or 90 miles south of Hāka. The hill sides are more precipitous, and the whole country more broken up and tumbled than near, or north of, Hāka. Careful observations with the aneroid record that, on an average, nearly 9,000 feet a day were climbed by the exploring party and an equal descent made. The total length of the march made was 132 miles in 10 days. The plan was followed throughout the march of the advance-guard laying a trail of torn-up paper at every point where roads crossed, or the path might be missed. By this means, with one guide only, survey and detached parties and rear-guards were enabled to follow on often at many hours of interval."

The villages of Thetta, Bondwa and Kapi were subsequently visited by Captain Jones, of the 2nd Madras Infantry, with a detachment of the 2-4th Gurkha Rifles from Yôkwa.

Thus ended the operations of the Chin Force, in which, although we all recognized that the work of subjugating the whole of the Chin tribes had not been completed, the primary objects of the expedition had been carried out successfully with singular exactness in detail. As will have been gathered from the particulars given, the most formidable enemy which the Southern Column had to contend with was the excessive amount of sickness which dogged troops and followers from beginning to end. Out of sixty-nine officers in the column only seven managed to keep off the sick list entirely, while over thirty were invalided during the expedition, and the remainder, with few exceptions, had to be sent to England on medical certificate, soon afterwards. One officer died at Kān, and two (Major Stoney and Major Ind), shortly after the close of the operations, from disease contracted in the Chin Hills.

The medical arrangements, which had apparently been based on the anticipation of a small percentage of sick, were as follows:—

A general hospital at Myingyan and a field station hospital at Kalèwa. These two received the sick from the Northern as well as the Southern Column. With the Southern Column there were further a section of a field hospital at Kān and one also later on at Haka, with rest depôts at Chaung-Kwa and Yôkwa, while at the intermediate posts between Kān and Hāka there were hospital assistants or apothecaries with a supply of medicines.

CHAPTER XIII.

THE CHIN-LUSHAI EXPEDITION OF 1889-90—(*Contd.*)

Operations of the Southern Lushai Column.

While the force from the Burma side was pushing its way into the Chin country, another, with one of the objects in common, namely, the construction of a road from India to Burma, was working from the former frontier, and termed the Lushai or Chittagong Field Force.

It, too, consisted of two columns, a Southern and a Northern, augmented by a body of Military Police which was to co-operate with the latter from Cachar. The force was under the command of Brigadier-General V. W. Tregear, and was composed of the following troops :—

Corps.	Total strength in Officers and men.
No. 2 Co. Bengal Sappers and Miners	177
3rd Bengal Infantry	821
Detachment 9th Bengal Infantry	301
2-2nd (P. W. O.) Gurkha Rifles	779
Half Battalion 2-4th Gurkha Rifles	369
28th Bombay Infantry (Pioneers)	731
Chittagong Frontier Police	202
Total	3,380

COUNTRY TRAVERSED BY THE LUSHAI FIELD FORCE OF 1889-90.

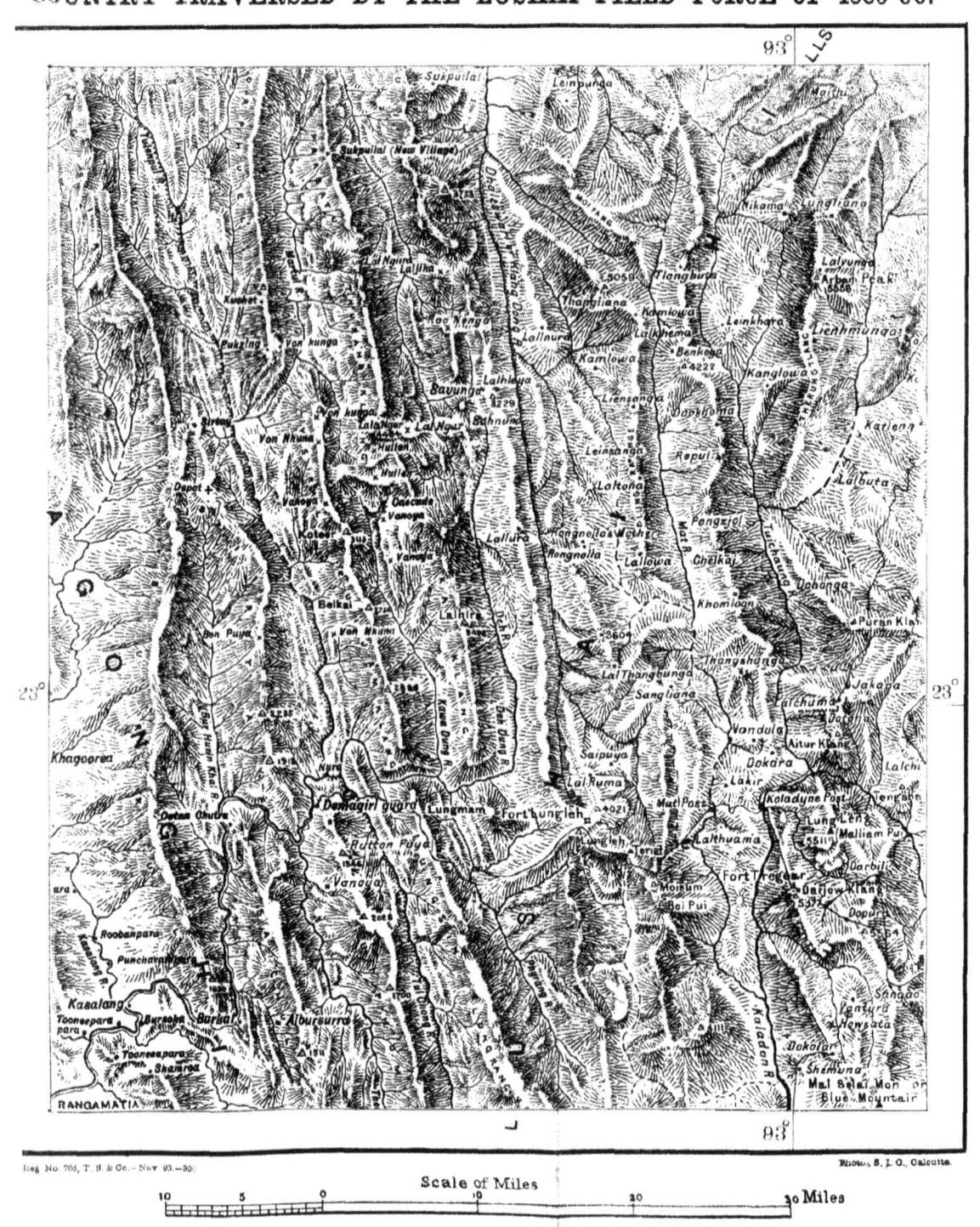

The Cachar Column consisted of 400 men of the Cachar Military Police.

The above were distributed as follows :—The 3rd Bengal Infantry to garrison Rangamatti, Demagiri, and the line of communications up to Fort Lungleh. The Northern Column (with which the Cachar column was to co-operate) to consist of—

    250 men, 3rd Bengal Infantry.
    300 men, 2-2nd Gurkha Rifles.
    100 men, 28th Bombay Pioneers.
  Half Co. (80 men), Bengal Sappers and Miners.
    50 men, Chittagong Frontier Police.

This column was placed under the command of Col. G. J. Skinner, 3rd Bengal Infantry.

The remainder of the troops, namely, half company, Bengal Sappers and Miners ; detachment, 9th Bengal Infantry; half battalion, 2-2nd Gurkha Rifles; half battalion, 2-4th Gurkha Rifles ; 28th Bombay Pioneers, and 100 men of the Frontier Police formed the Southern, or Hāka Column as it was sometimes called, which was under the personal command of Brigadier-General V. W. Tregear, and also garrisoned the line of communications beyond Fort Lungleh.

The specific work assigned to the Northern Column was—

(1) To punish Lienpunga for the raid on the Chengri Valley.

(2) To punish the sons of Vutai for their raid on the Pakuma Rani's village.

(3) To establish a permanent post in the vicinity of Lienpunga's village, to be garrisoned during the summer.

The main task to be undertaken by the Southern Column consisted of—

1. The construction of a mule path to Hāka which would there unite with that being carried on from Kān, and thus form a through communication between India and Burma.

2. The establishment of posts on the route so as to secure complete pacification and recognition of British power.

3. The subjugation of tribes as yet neutral, but now by force of circumstances brought within the sphere of British dominion.

The troops were to be considered on field service from the date they left Demagiri. As on the Chin side, no tents were to be taken, and baggage was to be reduced to a similar scale. With the exception of a break of about two miles at the Burkal rapids the troops and stores were conveyed by water to Demagiri, and thence pushed on by land to Lungleh, the most advanced post. Subsequently the transference of goods from Peshgiserra, the point of disembarkation, to Burkal was much facilitated by the construction of a tramway on the right bank of the Kurnafulee for the distance alluded to. This line was opened on the 12th December, and was worked by a coolie corps of 500 men, who ran twenty-five trucks, each carrying twenty maunds (1,600lbs).

The transport of the force consisted of 2,511 Punjabi coolies, 782 local coolies, 2,196 mules, and 71 elephants.

Major Leach, R.E., Commanding Royal Engineers, accompanied by Captain Mulaly, R. E., Field Engineer, arrived at Fort Lungleh on the 29th November, and, after reconnoitring the country, started the trace for the road which was to go on to Hāka on the 6th December; a detachment of the 2-2nd Gurkhas and the Frontier Police clearing the jungle in the direction of Teriat, on the southern slope of which the path was commenced by the 2nd Company Bengal Sappers and Miners, who arrived at Lungleh on the 12th December. Owing to a deep ravine in which the upper branch of the Dhaleswari or Klang Dong river takes its rise, the road had to be taken by a detour of several miles in a south-easterly direction, although the increase in distance was compensated for by the easier gradients that were thus obtained. The jungle was not so dense as that met with in the former expedition; but the trees were bigger, compelling the Gurkhas to lay aside their national weapon the *kookerie*, and take to the less familiar axe.

Up to this time the health of the troops had been good, but that of the followers indifferent; great numbers of coolies of the Transport Department coming into hospital suffering principally from malarial fever and bowel complaints, while a considerable proportion of the admissions were also due to ulcers of the feet, said to be produced by wet mud. Four cases of cholera were reported as having occurred in the Rangamatti Bazar about the 11th December, but there was reason to suppose that the seizures had been simply due to diet excesses. The disease, however, soon after undoubtedly made its appearance among the coolies working on the Burkal-Demagiri Road and the boatmen on the river. Twenty-two cases, all fatal, were reported at Burkal between the 14th and 17th December, and five deaths amongst Captain Du Moulin's corps of coolies; while five seizures with one death were said to have occurred among the boatmen at Rangamatti. Special precautions were taken to guard against the spread of the outbreak, and, with the exception of two or three cases in the 28th Bombay Pioneers and one in the 2-2nd Gurkhas, this disease did not spread to the troops, and had died out among the followers by the end of January. The Bengali coolies were supposed to have afforded a *nidus* for the development of the disease; and as they were as useless for practical purposes as they were filthy in their habits, the men were paid up and disbanded. The elephants supplied to the force for transport purposes suffered severely, a disease having appeared among them called by the natives *Lurza*; and by the 11th December twenty-one of these animals had died, and others were daily being attacked. Among the troops the 3rd Regiment of Bengal Infantry was the most unhealthy.

General Tregear with some of his staff arrived at Fort Lungleh on the 24th December, and, two days after, the submission of Dokola and Vantura, brothers of the late Chief Howsata, who had been concerned in Lieutenant Stewart's murder, was tendered through Lal Ruma, with a request that they might be informed of the terms which would be granted to them. They were told that these were unconditional surrender, release of all captives, the return of guns and heads taken from our people, and the giving up of Chiefs implicated in the murder of Lieutenant Stewart and of the man who had shot a Police bugler. They also professed their willingness to help in cutting jungle on the road to Hāka, and then returned to their village, having been given a fortnight to think the matter over. The villages of these two Chiefs lay near the site of Howsata's which had been burnt the previous season; and as the mule path, which was now being steadily pushed on, would pass close by, they probably pictured for them a fate similar to that which had overtaken the village of their brother. The time allowed, however, expired without the appearance of the Chiefs, whom doubtless a consciousness of guilt had inspired with a fear of personal retribution.

Meanwhile, the Howlong Chiefs were cutting a path for the Northern Column, which was to march due north from Lungleh, following the course of the Dhaleswari or Klang river. This rises by two heads, called the

Lower and the Upper Klang, which unite about ten miles from Lungleh. The former springs from the ridge of that name, and the latter takes its rise further east from the northern slope of the Teriat Hill. Mr. Murray, who was to accompany the Northern Column as Political Officer, left Lungleh on the 28th December with a reconnoitring party to explore the proposed route, but I think it will be better to postpone a description of the operations of that part of the force until I have finished that of the Southern Column.

On the 8th January, 1890, an interpreter and two guides were despatched to the Malliam Pui Chiefs, who, it will be remembered, occupy the district enclosed by the loop of the Koladyne, which, by a sudden bend, reverses its direction from north to south. The purpose of the party was to prepare the Chiefs for a visit from Mr. Murray, Political Officer, and from our recent negotiations with Howsata's brothers it was not anticipated that any opposition would be offered to their advance. The men, however, returned on the evening of the 11th January, with a report that, on reaching the banks of the Lower Koladyne, as the nearer arm of the river is called, they were threatened and turned back by an armed picket belonging to the brothers of Howsata. They also added that they had ascertained that Lalthuama, son of the Howlong Chief Vandula eldest brother of our friend Saipuya, was in league with the Shendús and had received Paona, in whose possession the heads taken in the raid on Lieutenant Stewart's party were supposed to be, at his village. On the following day a reconnoitring party of 50 rank-and-file of the 2-2nd Gurkhas under Captain Hall, and the same number of the Frontier Police under Mr. Murray, Political Officer, was ordered to proceed to explore the country between the Mat River and the Tuichaung (another tributary of the Koladyne which joins it at the apex of the bend) to find out the real disposition of the Chiefs of that region towards us, and also to determine the best direction for the road to take after it crossed the former stream. Captain Shakespear, Intelligence Officer, accompanied the party which was further ordered to bring in, if possible, all Chiefs who had neglected or refused to make submission to Government when ordered to do so by Mr. Murray, and among these was included Lalthuama. The adventures of this small expedition were described in the *Englishman* as follows :—

"Lalthuama is the youngest son of the late Vandula who was the head of all the Southern Howlongs, and is therefore a nephew of our near neighbour and ally Saipuya. He had already started a village of his own before his father's death, and after that event his importance in the eyes of the Howlongs was considerably increased. His village is the nearest of all the Howlong villages and the Shendús, and contains many pure Shendús. In fact the first village visited by us was purely Shendú, though it acknowledged Lalthuama's supremacy. Mr. Murray had suspected the loyalty of this Chief for some time, and though he had always returned polite messages the Chief had never come in. Sometimes a rumour reached us that the party of Shendús, who killed the bugler in April last, was supplied with guides by Lalthuama, and in fact Saipuya admitted it, but explained that the men had been taken by force; but as the Shendús were known only to have numbered fifteen, this was absurd, as Lalthuama's two villages number about 150 houses. We were therefore not very sorry to hear that matters had been brought to a crisis by our messengers to the Malliam Puis being stopped on Lalthuama's territory. On their return the messengers reported that they met, in Lalthuama's dependent village, men from the village still known by the name of the late Howsata, our old enemy; and that there were Shendú pickets close to the village, evidently on the best of terms with the inhabitants, and that these pickets threatened to shoot them if they went on. Furthermore, that Paona, the Chief who was reported to have the heads taken in the raid on Lieutenant Stewart's party, was actually in Lalthuama's village at the time, and that Lalthuama refused to come in to Lungleh. As our road-making party was on the point of crossing the River Mat and entering the territory of this Chief, it was evidently very necessary to place things on a more satisfactory footing. The General therefore decided to send 100 men to give force to Mr. Murray's persuasive eloquence and to assist in bringing the true state of affairs before the Chief in an intelligible manner. Accordingly, on the 13th, 50 men of the 2nd Gurkhas and 50 men of the Frontier Police started from Fort Lungleh, and duly reached the Mat River about 1 P.M. on the 14th. As we passed the various working parties along the road, they all wished us luck, somewhat enviously, and anxiously enquired if there was any chance of our being in need of reinforcements. On the far side of the Mat we found some look-out men, who took themselves away very quickly. Presently a deputation came down to see what we wanted, but these gentlemen were told that we would talk to no one except the Chief. Our interpreter described the next day's march as two steep hills and the rest all level; we were therefore disappointed to find it mostly steep hill, with two bits steeper than the rest. As each sepoy was carrying his kit and five days' rations, in addition to his 50 rounds of ammunition, rifle, and accoutrements, our progress was not very rapid. We passed through a number of this year's 'jooms,' and noticed that in each was a granary well-stocked with 'dhan' (unhusked rice). About 10 o'clock we reached a village which is dependent on Lalthuama. This we found almost deserted, as the people were moving into a new village about four miles off. Here we halted, and Captain Browne soon had his helio out. In a moment, three helios from different stations were 'tempestuously at play.' As occasionally the morning mist hangs about one hill later than another, our careful Signalling Superintendent had warned every station within sight to be on the look-out; and he now had his hands full, for each station refused to stop till it had received what it thought its fair share of news. While the natives were being much exercised in their minds by the strange light on the hills, the Chief was quietly sitting outside the village trying to summon up courage to come in. This he eventually did, and was at once taken in charge of by two little Gurkhas, who looked very pleased, and evidently thought it would be capital fun if he tried to escape, and gave them a chance of shooting him. In order to prevent this accident, the monarch was bound by a rope and led along by one of his guards, and in this manner, somewhat suggestive of an organ-grinder's monkey, he returned to his village. This we found only half-built, the people in the meantime living in shanties near. We got in about 2 P.M., and were all precious glad to get into the shade; for the last two miles had been up a bare hill as steep as the side of a house, with the sun shining down on our backs. The terms of the fine were then announced to the Chief, and the fact intimated to him that until it was paid he would have to partake of our hospitality at Lungleh. The fine consisted of 30 guns, 1 gyal, 10 pigs, 10 goats, 20 fowls, and 100 maunds of rice. The portion of the fine destined for the consumption of the troops and coolies was rather long in coming in, as the villagers expressed themselves quite incapable of catching the pigs or goats. When, however, three pigs had been shot, the other animals suddenly became possessed of a self-sacrificing spirit, and the requisite number soon allowed themselves to be captured. The people did not seem to resent our occupation of their village, and were eager to look through our field glasses and examine our weapons ; in fact, they did not seem to believe that we meant our visit to be an unpleasant one for them. The levying of the fine somewhat undeceived them, and when the Chief was marched away there was much weeping."

Lalthuama, who appeared to be about 21 years of age, was married to a daughter of Lienpunga, so that he was connected with our enemies on both sides. He arrived at Lungleh on the 19th January, and was so impressed with the manner in which we had constructed the road, that he said we were gods and not men! The 30 guns which Lalthuama had been fined were brought in on the 21st January, and, as he professed himself unable to produce the rice unless he was allowed to return to his village, he was released on that day under a promise to supply the grain at the Mat River camp, the point which the tracing party had now reached. The fine was paid up in full on the 28th. On the same day Mr. Stotesbury, of the Survey Department, with an escort of ten Frontier Police, marched to the village of Lalthanbunga, and returned on the 31st. He was well received by the Chief; but the curiosity excited among the villagers by the arrival of this, to them, strange specimen of humanity proved rather embarrassing in its results. They submitted him to a most rigid scrutiny, turning up his sleeves and trousers to prove whether the unnatural complexion extended over the rest of his person, and tried to measure the size of his limbs, height, &c. In their endeavours to see what was going on they also knocked against the plane-table, and it was only by the exercise of great forbearance that Mr. Stotesbury was able to complete his sketch of the surrounding country.

Another reconnaissance party, consisting of Captains Browne, Shakespear, Mulaly, Lieutenant Bythell, and Mr. Walker, Assistant Superintendent, Telegraphs, with 50 rifles and seven days' provisions, started on the 2nd February from the bridge camp on the Mat River (22 miles from Lungleh) to visit the Malliam Pui Chieftainess, Darbilli, who had supplied us with guides for the advance on Howsata's village during the expedition of 1889. The old lady was a widow, her husband having been dead for seven years, and lived in a village on the Darjow Klang, at an elevation of 5,100 feet above sea-level. Although the mutual relations between her and the British Government had hitherto been of a most amicable nature, she seemed to have taken alarm at the capture of Lalthuama, and, report said, had fled to the village of one Dopura, situated six miles from her own. The objects of the expedition were to reassure the Chieftainess, obtain the submission of the Malliam Puis, survey the country, and, if possible, open communications with General Symons' column by heliogram.

The party marched on the first day to Lalthuama's village and thence to the Koladyne, on the east bank of which they encamped; the river here being a clear swift stream, about two hundred yards in with, and running between precipitous forest-clad mountains. The second day's march led them up the Darjow Klang, and, after a very steep and tiring ascent from the bed of the Koladyne, an elevation of 4,600 feet was reached, at which spot a camp was formed. Here they were met by messengers from Darbilli with friendly assurances. After another long and tedious march the party arrived at the village of the Chieftainess on the afternoon of the 4th February, and were well received by her, the bond of friendship being subsequently cemented by an oath taken in the usual manner, Captain Shakespear representing the British Government on the occasion. Information was also received through Darbilli that Vantura and Dokola, Howsata's brothers, were anxious to come in and make terms, and that Jahuta wished to tender his submission. She was told that if the Chiefs wanted to treat they must come in, and it was explained to her that Government meant to take over the whole country; that it would treat all as friends who showed a friendly spirit towards us, and would punish those who resisted us. Messengers were at once sent on to Vantura and Dokola to tell them to come in. Heliographic communication with General Symons' column was found impracticable on account of an intervening high range.

As the reconnoitring party were returning on the 7th February they met some of Vantura's men, who said that their Chief was close at hand and wished to give himself up. Finally, Vantura presented himself and gave up Lieutenant Stewart's revolver, which he said he had brought from Jahuta, and in whose possession he averred that the stolen rifles still were. He was immediately made a prisoner of and brought into camp, followed by about two hundred of his clan, who appeared very reluctant to part with their Chief, and who eventually had to be driven out at the point of the bayonet, although not one of them was touched. They were then told that they would be fired on if they attempted to re-enter the camp. It seemed likely that under the cover of darkness an attempt at rescue would be made; but the night passed quietly, and when morning dawned it was found that all the men had disappeared. Vantura pleaded illness as the excuse for the absence of his brother Dokola. He was informed that when Dokola came in terms would be dictated to them. In addition to Darbilli, two other Malliam Puis, Dokapa and Patbia, took the oath of friendship and professed themselves willing to assist us, so that the objects of the visit to Darbilli were almost completely attained. Three Karbaris or councillors accompanied Vantura to the Koladyne, from where one was sent back to summon Dokola. On the 12th February a Karbari arrived from the latter Chief, saying that he was too ill to come and offering himself as a hostage in his stead.

Up to this period the left wing of the 2nd Battalion, 4th Gurkhas, had been kept at Demagiri on account of the difficulties of transport, it being much easier to ration the troops there than at the front, and it being desirable to push on stores for the provisioning of Fort Lungleh. It was now necessary to order the wing to the front, as it was intended that it should march through to Hāka to join the head-quarters of the battalion there. They accordingly received instructions to move from Demagiri on the 13th February. The transport difficulties were further increased by the loss of the service of 700 Chakma coolies, these men having to return to their homes to "joom." To partially replace them, General Tregear arranged with the Commissioner of Chittagong for the supply of 300 Sonthal coolies. The troops themselves tried to lighten the work as much as possible by cheerfully carrying their own kits from camp to camp; but such a burden was hard upon men already heavily laden with arms and ammunition, and I consider that the voluntarily undertaken additional task was a striking testimony of the zeal and devotion to the objects of the expedition with which the sepoys were imbued.

By the 9th February a good mule road, of which the gradients nowhere exceeded 1 in 10, had been completed to the Mat River and was now being carried on to the Koladyne, while the trace was being pushed on ahead up the Darjow Klang. The road reached the Darjow Klang on the 27th, and the upper portion of the site of an old village, which had belonged to Darbilli, about four miles further on, at an elevation of 5,000 feet, and with a good supply of water, was selected as the position of the future advanced post, which, by the general wish of the officers of the force, was called Fort Tregear.

A reconnaissance party composed as under was sent out on the 22nd February to reconnoitre towards Hāka, and with a view to meeting another party from the Burma force a telegram was sent to General Symons that they would probably be on the Tao (or Sangal Klang as the mountain had been called) on the 25th. Strength—Captain Hall, 2-2nd Gurkhas, commanding; Captain Shakespear, Intelligence Officer; Lieutenant Bythell, Survey Officer; 60 men, 2-2nd Gurkhas; 20 men, Frontier Police; rations up to and for 1st March, and carrying 50 rounds ammunition per rifle. The men carried their own kit, in addition to arms, accoutrements, and ammunition, which rendered the labour of climbing up the steep ranges and toiling over the rough path, which lay before them, very great. The party reached

Darbilli's village on the 23rd, where Lieutenant Bythell with three signallers and the twenty men of the Frontier Police remained until the rest should return. About two miles beyond the village they met a messenger bearing a letter from General Symons, which was sent on to General Tregear, the man returning with the party to point out the way. The march was resumed on the 24th, along the top of a ridge running due south to a village called Sangao, where the party met with a hospitable reception; the villagers turning out to build huts for the troops and supplying them with a day's ration of rice on payment. On the next day a very steep path was followed which led to the Koladyne —here a clear stream varying in width from twenty to fifty yards and running due north. It was fordable in places with a depth of two feet and a half. After crossing the river the party encamped at a place called Sé-Si, about eight miles from Sangao. The village of Tao, six miles farther on, was reached on the 26th February, after another very trying march, in which two streams, the Shertak and Pullock, were crossed. During this march Captain Shakespear received a note from General Symons, saying that the Tao Chief, Mapoya, had submitted to him, and that he had accepted his submission.

Just as the usual temporary shelters had been run up after getting into camp, and while the signallers were heliographing back to the detachment which had been left at Darbilli's village, Captain Rundall and his party from Hāka emerged from the jungle. Only those who have themselves, at some period of their lives, wandered far from the confines of civilisation, can realise the warmth of the greeting which followed, heightened by the feeling that a definite task had been accomplished, and that the meeting of the two forces represented, as it were, the laying of the keystone in the arch which now stretched across the wild country separating Burma from India. On comparing notes, Captain Rundall discovered much to his surprise that the village of Tang-Zang, at which he had encamped the previous night, belonged to the Chief Paona, in whose possession the heads of three Europeans taken in the raid on Lieutenant Stewart's party were known to be. He had received strict orders from General Symons to conciliate all the people whose country he passed through, and therefore considered it necessary to try to obtain further instructions from Hāka before taking forcible steps for the recovery of the ghastly trophies. For this purpose a halt was made on the 27th and heliographic communication attempted from the summit of the Tao Klang. In this effort Captain Rundall failed. On the same day Captain Shakespear sent his interpreter to see Mapoya, and to tell the Chief that it would be to his own interest to assist us in the recovery of the heads, guns, &c., as he (Captain Shakespear) was going to Hāka and would explain matters to General Symons, which would certainly lead to his being punished. This message quickly elicited from Mapoya the reply that the heads were in Paona's village (as was already known) and also one gun, and that two other guns were at Tlan-Tlang.

The names by which some of the Chiefs were known on the Chin side differed considerably from those familiar to the officers in General Tregear's force, and hence had arisen some confusion regarding the identity of the several individuals implicated in the raids. For instance, General Symons had heard of the Chief of the Tlan-Tlangs as Ya Hut or Ya Hwit; while he was known to Colonel Tregear as Jahuta, one of the Chiefs whom we wished to punish. To the Burma force Lalleya was Lalwé, and Dokola, Do Kwè. The Chiefs had taken advantage of this fact to make their peace with General Symons, naturally concluding that they would obtain easier terms with a force coming from the east than from one coming from the west, where their identity and guilt were better recognised.

The combined parties proceeded to Hāka by a more southern and easier route than Captain Rundall had come. They left Tao on the 28th February, the first march being to Hmunlipi over an excellent road. Here, again, Captain Shakespear sent a similar message to that delivered to Mapoya, and, before leaving the village on the following morning, a reply was received from the Chief to the effect that he and his people had talked the matter over and had despatched a man to Paona, advising him to give up the loot in his possession. The next halt was at Tlwalam; two streams, the Boiphai and La-aw Var, being crossed in the course of the march. On nearing the village Captain Rundall sent his interpreter to summon the Chief; but the man soon returned, saying that Lalleya was in the village, and that his servant had threatened to shoot him. A slight display of force soon brought Lalleya to his senses, and he confessed that Lieutenant Stewart's aneroid and field glasses were in his possession; that one rifle was in Tlwalam, and that the heads and one other rifle were in Tang-Zang (Jahuta's village); the rifle was produced, but before it arrived the heads and one rifle were brought in from Jahuta to Captain Shakespear. The parties marched for Tlan-Tlang on the 2nd March. Here the aneroid and field glasses were produced and handed to Captain Shakespear, while a Burmese captive was also surrendered to Captain Rundall. At the next halt, in the valley of the Sa, a barrel and lock of a Martini-Henri rifle were brought to Captain Shakespear, said to have been brought by order of Lalleya from Tang-Zang village. The next march took the parties into Hāka on the 3rd March.

East of Tao the country was much more open than any Captain Hall had hitherto traversed, and the change from dense bamboo jungle to open pine forests and grassy valleys, where the violet and daisy bloomed under foot, was a most welcome one to the weary travellers. To the plucky little Gurkhas, who were carrying their own kits in addition to arms, accoutrements, and ammunition, the comparatively easy Kuki paths must have seemed like carriage roads after the precipitous hills and rough boulders they had scrambled over before meeting with Captain Rundall's party. It is very much to the credit of this detachment of sixty men that not one fell out during the double march of about 150 miles—heavily laden as they were.

Captain Hall commenced his return journey on the 6th March. At Tlwalam, which they reached on the 7th, Captain Hall tried to recover a captive Lushai woman, but failed; the Karbaris saying that they would not give her up without Lalleya's (Lalwè) order. As this Chief's submission had already been offered to and accepted by General Symons, Captain Shakespear was debarred from taking any further steps in the matter. While the party halted at Dopura a female captive taken from Lalseva's village was surrendered. Another taken in a raid by Howsata on Lalseva, and who had been sold to Patbia, was given up by that Chief on the 18th March. Seven more captives (two females and five males), obtained by Howsata in the same manner, were surrendered by Vantura on the 26th, and sent to their homes. The latter Chief was still in custody, pending the full payment of a fine of 1,000 maunds of rice and 100 guns which had been imposed upon him and his brother Dokola, and only part of which had yet been delivered.

A marked change took place in the weather on the 13th March, heavy rain setting in and lasting almost uninterruptedly for six days. In consequence of this the work of road-making and constructing the buildings of the permanent post at Fort Tregear was much interfered with and the sudden rise of water in the Mat and Koladyne at one time threatened to sweep away the bridges which had been erected across these streams.

On the 26th March, Lieutenant Bythell, Survey Officer, with an escort of 40 men of the 2-4th Gurkhas left the camp Upper Koladyne to meet Lieutenant Renny-Tailyour from the Burma force at Tao village, and, in conjunction with the latter officer, to complete the survey of the country lying between the former post and Hāka. On the following day the left wing of the 2nd Battalion, 4th Gurkhas, marched for Hāka in compliance with a request from General Symons. The strength marching out was as follows:—Five British officers, seven Gurkha officers, 337 rank and file (including 40 men sent as an escort with Lieutenant Bythell on the 26th). They were provided with mule transport as far as the road was passable for these animals, and beyond that to Tao (where carriage was to be provided by General Symons) with Sonthal coolies who had been engaged for road-making. On the 28th March a force of 43 rank-and-file of No. 2 Company, Bengal Sappers and Miners, with about 50 of the 28th Bombay Pioneers, left the Upper Koladyne camp for the front, their object being to carry on the mule path to Haka with the assistance of the Sonthal coolies who had been sent with the 2-4th Gurkhas and who had been ordered to return from Tao.

General Tregear joined the force on the following day; and on the 13th April after overcoming many physical obstacles in the shape of ravines and mountain ranges, the path was completed to Haka. The telegraph line had been carried as far as the Upper Koladyne, but, in compliance with Government orders, Fort Tregear was now made the terminus. While returning from Haka, General Tregear received four captives (three girls and a boy) from Jahuta, whom the latter had taken from Lalseva; but so attached had they become to their captors that they ran away during the night.

The rationing for eight months of Fort Lungleh and Fort Tregear ended the work which had been assigned to the force. This was finally accomplished on the 2nd and 3rd of May respectively; the former post being garrisoned by the Frontier Police and the latter by 200 men of the 2nd Battalion, 2nd Gurkha Rifles. A good road of easy gradients had been made from Fort Lungleh to Fort Tregear and beyond the advanced post a fair mule path led to Haka 81 miles, completing the connection of India with Burma. Two large rivers, the Mat and Koladyne, had been bridged. These bridges, the former 206 and the latter 304 feet long, had to be very substantially built, and were of the crate and trestle type.

Considering the arduous nature of the duties to which they had been put, there was wonderfully little sickness among the troops,—a marked contrast to the condition which prevailed on the Burma side. This may, I think, to a certain extent be accounted for by the fact that the men did not take the field as early as those belonging to General Symons' force, being comfortably housed at Chittagong and Rangamatti until January, and thus escaping the influences of the unhealthy season which was a late one. Only one officer lost his life in the expedition, Major Barr of the 3rd Bengal Infantry, who died at Rangamatti on the 22nd May from dysentery contracted at Demagiri. The followers, as is usually the case, suffered more severely, and at one time cholera threatened to assume an epidemic form among them.

CHAPTER XIV.

THE CHIN-LUSHAI EXPEDITION OF 1889-90—*Continued.*

Operations of the Northern Lushai Column.

To return to the Northern Lushai Column, to which had been assigned the task of punishing Lienpunga for his raids in the Chengri Valley, and also of calling to account the sons of Vutai for their ferocious attack on the village of the Pakuma Rani, a Chieftainess who had resided within our territory at a distance of only four miles from the frontier post of Demagiri.

Lienpunga, who was known to be the most powerful of the Lushai Chiefs, had rendered himself so obnoxious to the Howlongs by his tyrannical disposition and oppressive acts, that the Chiefs had at once agreed to assist our troops by cutting a path through the jungle for the march of the Column. As already mentioned the route to be followed lay, for most part of the way, along the course of the Dhaleswari or Klang River, which, arising by two heads, runs almost absolutely due north to Cachar. We left Mr. Murray starting from Lungleh, on the 28th December, with a reconnoitring party to explore the proposed line, and to ascertain how far the Klang River could be utilised for the purpose of rafting, a method which, if practicable, would greatly facilitate the conveyance of stores to the front; paucity of transport being the chief difficulty with which the force had to contend. The escort consisted of forty men of the Frontier Police, provided with ten days' rations and fifty rounds of ammunition. In addition to Mr Murray, Captains Chambers and Allen, Lieutenants Petrie and Twyford, and Mr. La Touche of the Geological Survey accompanied the party. They returned to Lungleh on the 4th January, 1890, with a favourable report of the work done by the Howlongs, and the practicability of utilising the river for rafts. The road after starting skirted Lal Ruma's village, and struck the lower Klang about eight miles from Fort Lungleh, and two from its junction with the upper tributary. From the latter point the stream for a distance of sixteen miles was found to be navigable for light rafts carrying four or five maunds, although at first progress was necessarily slow from the delay which took place in removing stones and cutting down fishing dams. The rafts used were constructed in the following manner: first, three large bundles of bamboos were formed by tying together a number of stems with hill creepers or canes. The three bundles were then bound firmly and evenly together at one end which was to form the bow, rattan cane being used for the purpose; while their

RAFTING ON THE KLANG DONG OR DHALESWARI RIVER.

other extremities spread out something in the shape of a broad arrow. Athwart the centre of this structure, and fastened to it, three thick logs were placed, which served the triple object of giving solidity to the framework, supporting a deck made of bamboo matting for the reception of cargo, and raising the latter above the water line. As can be imagined, such a craft required skilful manipulation, the buoyancy of the bamboos being low and there being a great tendency to roll from the high position of the centre of gravity. The crew consisted generally of two men who poled in deep water but had to get out and drag the raft at the numerous rapids which occurred in the course of the stream. In this duty officers, sepoys, and coolies took their share alike, and it was no pleasant work to spend the first two hours, before the sun was up and while a cold dark mist hung over everything, wading to the waist in water over pointed rocks which cut one's bare feet at every step. Fishing dams were found below each considerable village. They consisted of weirs of stone with a close fence of split bamboos stretching across the stream. There was only one opening, and that into a long tube or lane of close bamboo work into which the fish were swept and then captured. The banks of the Klang were covered with dense bamboo jungle, interrupted here and there by an open "joom" or space which had been cleared for cultivation. Although a mere scratch, the path cut by the Howlongs required very little improvement to make it sufficient for laden coolies, who were intended as the only form of transport for the Northern Column. It followed the course of the Klang river, crossing and re-crossing the stream frequently. The party during their absence of eight days had covered 33 miles and back. The furthest point reached was about two miles beyond the fourth camp, at the foot of the ridge on which the village of Savunga stood. Rafts could not be taken beyond the third camp on account of rapids. Sixteen miles of navigable river were, however, a great boon, as each raft meant a saving of eight coolies for that distance.

While at No. 3 Camp, Mr. Murray interviewed four friendly northern Howlong Chiefs,—Mumpunga, Vantonga, Lalthuama and Lallura,—who arrived bearing presents of eggs, vegetables, and rice-beer. A messenger was also sent to two other Chiefs, Lalhleya and Lalburah, requesting them to assist in the road-cutting, and to find out where Lienpunga lived.

On the 8th January 50 men of the Frontier Police were despatched from Lungleh to the first camp on the Klang river for the purpose of constructing rafts under the direction of Captain Allen, the Transport Officer. This party was followed in a few days by a half company (80 men) Bengal Sappers and Miners, with 50 Chakma coolies and 100 men, 28th Bombay Pioneers, who were instructed to improve the road and deepen the rapids, as the water was reported to be falling.

By the 23rd January the river had been rendered passable for rafts carrying two men and a cargo of four maunds, up to Camp No. 2. Major Begbie, with 300 rifles of the 2nd Battalion 2nd Gurkhas, marched on the 25th to the camp at the confluence of the two sources of the Klang, called Junction Camp, and on the same day Colonel Skinner arrived at this spot and took over command of the Column. He found that Lieutenant Twyford had loaded up 105 rafts with four maunds each, to be in readiness to start with the first convoy on the following morning. Owing to the paucity of coolie carriage it had now been determined that the force was to be provisioned for six weeks instead of two months, and that the amount of ammunition to be taken was to be reduced from 200 to 150 rounds per rifle. The first convoy of 50 rafts arrived at a spot about a mile short of No. 3 Camp on the 1st February; and as Captain Petrie had reported that it would take a considerable time to make the river passable beyond this point, it was arranged that coolie transport should be used for the remaining distance, and the place was therefore called " Porterage Camp."

The whole fighting force of the Northern Column were now on their way and were composed of—

    250 men, 3rd Bengal Infantry.
    300 ,, 2nd Battalion 2nd Gurkha Rifles.
    102 ,, 28th Bombay Pioneers.
     50 ,, Frontier Police.

On the 3rd February a reconnaissance party under Captain Chambers, Intelligence Officer, with Lieutenant Drummond in charge of an escort of 25 rifles, 2-2nd Gurkhas, started from "Porterage Camp," with five days' rations, to fix camps on the road ahead. On the following day, Mumpunga, one of the four Howlong Chiefs whom Mr. Murray had interviewed during his reconnaissance down the Klang, came into camp to seal the bond of friendship, then begun, by taking the usual oath or "thissa." The ceremony was rather an impressive one, and the words used by the Chief might well have been taken from a page of classic story: "Until the sun ceases to shine in the heavens, and until yonder stream runs backwards, I will be your true and faithful friend." A somewhat similar vow was sworn by Paris to Œnone, and it remained to be seen whether the besotted savage would keep more faithful to his declared allegiance than the amorous but perfidious son of Priam.

All the supplies had now been pushed on from Junction Camp, and under instructions from General Tregear a small column commanded by Colonel Skinner was equipped at Camp No. 3 for the purpose of advancing on Lienpunga's village. This force consisted of 80 rifles of the 2-2nd Gurkhas under Major Begbie, and 50 men of the Frontier Police. It was supplied with 12 days' rations and 25 rounds per rifle of reserve ammunition, which were conveyed by coolies; the men carrying their own kits, with the exception of the advanced and rear-guards, whom it was considered advisable to keep unencumbered. The Column left Camp No. 3 on the 7th February and arrived at Camp No. 5 on the afternoon of the same day, distance eight miles. Here it was found that Captain Chambers' reconnaissance party had returned, and 20 men of the 2-2nd Gurkhas who had formed part of his escort were added to the force, bringing the total number of fighting men up to 150. Captain Birkbeck with one British non-commissioned officer and seven Native signallers also joined the party. Captain Chambers reported that the road ahead was fairly easy, and that a second section of the river, nearly fifteen miles long, seemed practicable for rafts, an anticipation which was found to be correct. Camp No. 6, which was eleven miles further on at the junction of a considerable stream with the Klang, was reached on the 8th, the road being found more difficult than had been represented. The following day the road got worse, and the coolies did not arrive at camp till dark, although the distance was only nine miles. During the march to No. 8 Camp on the 10th the Column was met on the banks of the Klang by four Howlong Chiefs,—Lalheya, Lalburah, Lal Chema and Lalova,—who had come to meet Mr. Murray, the Political Officer. They reported that Lienpunga's village was only one day's march distant, *i.e.* a Lushai's march, which may be taken as equivalent to two ordinary marches. In the evening, after getting into camp, two messengers arrived bearing a letter from Mr. Daly, who commandedt he Police Contingent of 400 men, which it will be remembered, had been told off to advance from Cachar, informing Colonel Skinner that he had arrived at Lienpunga's village on the 8th February, and that the Chief had surrendered to him on the following day. Before starting from Camp No. 3 a report had reached Colonel Skinner that the greater number of the captives taken in the Chengri Valley raids had been given up and sent down to Changsil. Orders were sent to Mr. Daly not to occupy the village until Colonel Skinner's Column arrived. The march was resumed on the following day, the 11th, and after proceeding for a mile and a half, Lienpunga's fishing dam was met with in a small tributary stream running into the Klang. A mile and a half beyond this point the road left the course of the river and ran up a steep ascent of about 500 feet. For the rest of the distance the gradients were easy and the path itself excellent. The site of Lienpunga's old village was reached at 3 P.M., and from it could be seen his new village containing about 500 houses, which lay for the most part on three separate small hills. About a mile further on the Column came across a piquet of men armed with guns. They had evidently been guarding the approach to the village, but fled without firing a shot, leaving a gun behind in their haste to escape. Several more armed men were seen lurking about, but no active opposition was offered; some of the men who were near laying down their arms, while

SYLU MEN AT LIENPUNGA.

the others disappeared in the jungle. As the force approached the village, numbers of the inhabitants were seen clearing out, carrying their belongings in large baskets strapped on their backs; while others, by their gesticulations, seemed to be offering a protest against the invasion of their homes. Any such demonstration was, however, disregarded, and after passing through the village Colonel Skinner reached a strong defensive position which Mr. Daly had taken up on the north. Here, much to his disappointment, he heard that Lienpunga had absconded that morning. It appeared that the Chief had come to Mr. Daly's camp on the 9th February, but only on solemn promises made by the political jemadar, who had been sent by that officer to summon him, that he would not be detained. Under these circumstances Mr. Daly did not consider that he would be justified in seizing Lienpunga, and he was therefore permitted to return to his village under a promise that he would return when Colonel Skinner arrived. He had previously surrendered 63 captives, all women and children, who had been taken in the Chengri Valley raids, and these had been sent down to Cachar by boat. They were in good condition and apparently had been well taken care of.

Colonel Skinner occupied the higher part of the village with his troops, the houses which the Lushais had vacated offering a welcome shelter after the rough and often uncomfortable quarters in which both officers and men had put up since leaving Lungleh. The day had been a long and trying one, and it was with a sense of relief that every one settled down to his well-earned repose. This was, however, soon disturbed by the crackling and explosions of burning bamboos. On turning out, it was discovered that a hut only a few yards distant from those occupied by the men was in full blaze; and before the fire could be extinguished, it spread rapidly to the adjoining houses. All efforts were now directed to isolating the fire, and after the most strenuous exertions, in which the Gurkhas used their kookeries and the coolies their dhas, this was accomplished as far as the portion of the village occupied by the troops was concerned,—the distant houses being left to their fate. The incendiarism was undoubtedly the work of Lushais, as several were seen creeping up, evidently with the intention of completing the work of destruction, in which, however, they were interrupted by a cordon of sentries which had been placed round the northern knoll on the first appearance of the fire. The greater part of the village was destroyed before morning, two of the four large guest-houses which it had contained fortunately escaping and remaining to form comfortable quarters for the officers. For several days following, foraging parties and coolies were sent out to collect "dhan," or unhusked rice, from the granaries in the neighbouring "jooms;" and on the 15th and 16th February two of these parties were fired on, but without any casualties on our side. On the former date Colonel Skinner visited a site about fourteen miles from Lienpunga in the Changsil direction, which had been strongly recommended by Mr. Daly for the position of the intended permanent post. The spot had once been occupied by Thanruma's old village and appeared desirable in every respect, with the exception of the water-supply which was rather inferior. It was ultimately selected as the best site that could be found, and a stockade was afterwards built on the site and called Fort Aijal.

On the 23rd February a party of about 50 rifles, sent out under the command of Lieutenant Brownrigg, 28th Bombay Infantry, to destroy some huts and grain, came across a force of about thirty or forty Lushais, who had placed a stockade across the path from which they opened fire on our men, one of the first shots wounding Lieutenant Brownrigg severely in the forearm. The Lushais were driven out of their stockade with little difficulty, and their granaries and "joom" houses were destroyed. Several of the enemy were seen to be hit.

Another small encounter took place with the enemy on the 27th February. Hearing that the Lushais had collected a large quantity of grain on a hill in the immediate vicinity, and that they had built strong stockades to guard the approaches, Colonel Skinner, with 120 rifles, made an early march, his object being to reach the spot before daylight and when it was anticipated that the stockades would not have been occupied for the day. In this his hope was realised. The stockades were found unoccupied, and, passing them, a number of "joom" houses were set fire to. While this was being done a volley was suddenly fired by the Lushais on a portion of the force which had halted on an open space, with the result that one sepoy of the 3rd Bengal Infantry and one of the Chittagong Frontier Police were wounded, the latter fatally. The party returned to camp in the afternoon, having burnt 15 huts containing grain, and destroyed the stockades.

It was now time to carry out the second object assigned to the Northern Column, *viz.*, the punishment of Nikama and Lungliena, sons of the late Chief Vutai, for the raid which they had committed on the Pakuma Rani's village on the 13th December 1888. The force selected for this purpose was placed under the command of Major Begbie of the 2nd Battalion 2nd Gurkhas, and consisted of—

- 10 Men, Bengal Sappers and Miners.
- 78 Rifles, 3rd Bengal Infantry.
- 63 Rifles, 2nd Battalion, 2nd Gurkhas.
- 10 Men, 28th Bombay Pioneers.
- 10 Rifles, Chittagong Police.
- 10 Rifles, Cachar Police.
- 3 Signallers.

Total 184 rank-and-file, with eight British officers, one Medical officer, and five Native officers.

Nikama's village lay nearest to Lienpunga at a distance of 32 miles in a south-easterly direction.

The Column started on the 2nd March, having been provided with thirteen days' supplies, ten days of which were carried by coolies and three days by each individual man. In addition to the three days' rations the troops carried their own kits. Colonel Skinner had intended accompanying the expedition, but was debarred from doing so by a severe sprain of the knee-joint, which he had sustained during the night-march on the 27th February. The outward journey to Nikama's village was accomplished in four marches, the Lushai tracks which were followed being fairly easy-going for laden coolies. On the second day the Advance Guard suddenly came upon a piquet of five armed Lushais, one of whom was captured by a jemadar of the Cachar Police. This prisoner was liberated on the following day and sent with two guides conveying a message to the Chiefs that they were required to surrender themselves and their captives on the 5th March. On approaching Nikama's village on the morning of the date mentioned, Major Begbie was met by his late prisoner, who informed him that the headmen were awaiting him further on; and on arriving within half a mile of the village, he found a large party of Lushais who besought him not to enter their village, saying that the headmen would arrive shortly. After waiting for an hour and a half the Column moved towards the village, which it was compelled to enter for the sake of shelter from a heavy thunderstorm which broke just then, accompanied by torrents of rain. Finally a headman from each village arrived, and, in reply to a demand for the surrender of the Chiefs, they said that Lungliena was dead, and that Nikama had gone off with Lienpunga when the latter Chief absconded. They, however, promised to deliver up the captives on the following day, and, accordingly, about mid-day of the 6th March four women and two young girls were sent in. Originally there had been eight captives; but one had died, and another had been made a present of to a Chief called Bhaugtya. As Nikama still absented himself a fine of 60 guns and Rs. 300 was inflicted, one day's grace being allowed for the payment of it. Major Begbie advanced on the morning of the 8th March with 112 rifles against Lungliena, the remainder of the force remaining at Nikama's village. The march, although only five miles, was rather a trying one on account of a long ascent under a very hot sun, but it and the return journey were accomplished cheerfully by the men. No opposition was offered, there being only some forty men about. An hour was given for the payment of the fine, and as it was not brought in at the end of that time the village was set fire to and burnt in half an hour. A similar punishment was dealt out to the village of Nikama on the 9th, and on the 12th March the Column returned to Lienpunga and rejoined head-quarters. A third son of Vutai named Kairuma had also been implicated in the raid, but time did not permit of his being visited. So great, however, was the impression produced by the punishment of his two brothers that on the return march the remaining captive taken from the Pukuma Rani's village was voluntarily sent in by the Chief Bhaugtya.

During the absence of Major Begbie's Column, Mr. Daly, who had gone on the 25th February to the site selected for the stockade near Thanruma's village, entered into negotiations with Lienpunga and his brothers for the surrender of the Chief. They assembled outside Mr. Daly's camp on the 5th March. Chiefs Kalkam, Lienpunga, Silenpui, Thanruma, Tangaola, Mintang, Senkhomga and Tolera were present with a large following, but persistently refused to give up Lienpunga, although threatened with the resentment of the British Government. The perpetrator of the Chengri Valley raids therefore was still at large in his native wilds.

The construction of a stockade on the site which had been selected near Thanruma's village, and which had been christened Fort Aijal, completed the tasks of the Northern Column. This work was carried out by Mr. Daly's Cachar Police, 200 of whom were to garrison the post, while another detachment of 100 were to hold Changsil Bazar.

What remained of Lienpunga's village was burnt on the 17th March, on which date Colonel Skinner began his return march to India *viâ* Cachar ; while Mr. Murray started with an escort of Chittagong Frontier Police for Fort Lungleh.

The health of the troops and followers of the Northern Column was very good indeed, only one of the former (in addition to the sepoy of the Chittagong Frontier Police, who was shot on the 27th February) and two of the latter having died during the operations.

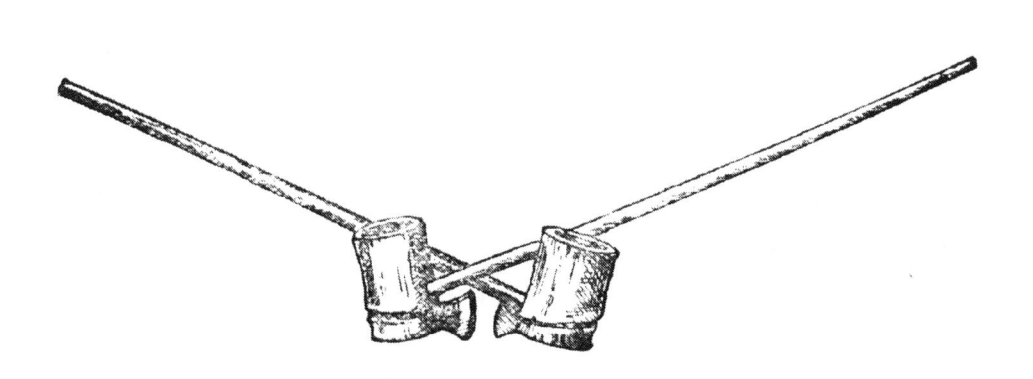

PIPES USED BY CHIN-LUSHAI MEN.

CHAPTER XV.

GENERAL INFORMATION REGARDING THE CHINS.

MANY of the characteristics and customs of the people inhabiting the Chin-Lushai Hills have been incidentally alluded to in the preceding pages; but, before closing this work, I shall endeavour to give some further details regarding the Chins, the result of observations made during the expedition of 1889-90 into the Baungshè Country; and in doing so I wish it to be understood that the majority of the remarks are equally applicable to the Lushais.

As has been stated, the tribes own no central authority but are governed by their Chiefs. The men who claim this position vary in number in different tribes, many of them being little more than village headmen or even leaders of factions or sections of the community Where there is an acknowledged head Chief, his authority, as in all such primitive forms of society, depends to a great extent upon the personal character and qualifications of the individual, especially with regard to his success in war. This was exemplified in the case of Lyan Sôn, Lwè Sin and Jahuta, head Chiefs of Yôkwa, Hāka and the Tantin tribe respectively. The influence of Lyan Sôn and Jahuta was undoubtedly of considerable force with the people and minor Chiefs, while that of Lwè Sin was seen to be merely nominal and often set at defiance. In Tashôn, again, the tribe was split up into numerous factions, the leaders of which, from their jealousy and distrust of each other, hindered the practicability of combined and unanimous action, either in resisting the advance, or in accepting the terms, of a common enemy. When a Chief draws tribute from a village he is said to "eat it," the contribution usually taking the form of food-stuff, baskets of grain, goats, pigs, fowls, &c., and the amount depending upon the pressure brought to bear upon the tributary village or the sense of its obligations to the protecting Chief.

A Chief's house is generally recognised by its superior size and construction, whilst he himself in full dress is distinguished from the common herd by a plume stuck in the turban. This decoration is supposed to be made out of the tail of a particular bird, the "bhimraj," and of which only two feathers can be used. The quills are stripped, leaving only an eye at the end and the whole let into a metal holder, the junction being further ornamented by a circle of bright blue jay feathers. The dress of the Chin men consists of a small loin-cloth and a large sheet or blanket thrown loosely over the shoulders and coming down to the knee, the clothes of the Chiefs being usually worked in coloured patterns and of finer fabric. A haversack, the outer surface of which is covered with hairy skin, rendering it not unlike a Highland sporran, is worn on the right side, being suspended by a strap diagonally across the body from the left shoulder. The women, some of whom are not uncomely, wear a dark cloth skirt and jacket, the former being sometimes woven in patterns like the cloth of a Chief. Their ornaments consist of necklaces, bracelets and earrings.

The men are well-built, with strong limbs and good figures. The average height is about 5 feet 6 inches. Lalwè Jahuta's nephew stood about six feet and was an exceedingly handsome young man.

Like the inhabitants of all uncivilized hill countries, the Chins—both male and female—are extremely dirty in their persons, and rarely wash their bodies, ablution being generally limited to the hands. Abstaining from washing is regarded as a sign of mourning, and after the death of her husband a widow frequently does not wash for two or three years.

Early marriage is uncommon, and I believe that in some of the Lushai tribes the men are not allowed to marry under twenty-five, up to which age the young men are obliged to live together apart from the rest of the community. As in Burma, marriage is a purely civil contract, and the proposal is conveyed to the parents of the young lady through those of the aspiring youth, or, in their absence, some other near relatives, by whom all the further preliminary arrangements are made. The deputation proceed to the house of the intended bride, taking with them the usual present of a pot of liquor and a pig or goat for the parents, with whom the disposal of her hand entirely rests. Should the proposal be accepted the girl's parents next produce their liquor and make a feast, over which the amount of dowry, &c., is arranged. When all the terms have been settled, the bride's parents provide the marriage feast, at which the dowry is paid to them and the nuptial knot tied. The respective parents, who are apparently the contracting parties, being seated opposite each other, those of the man deliver a speech something to the following effect:—" We have given you so much dowry with the object that your daughter shall marry our son," to which the girl's parents make answer: " We have truly received such and such an amount of dowry, and we are willing that our daughter shall marry your son. Let him be kind to her and not divorce her; may they be blessed with many children, &c." A cock is then produced by the girl's parents, who, after pouring some liquor over its head, cut its throat, at the same time declaring the man and girl to be husband and wife. The cock is then given to the head man present, and the young wife goes to live with her husband in his father's house.

Although the bond thus so simply formed can as readily be broken with no penalty further than the forfeiture of the dowry on the part of the one wishing a separation and leaving both free to marry again, this fact is seldom taken advantage of, and it is said that morality among the tribes is strict. Should, however, the wife prove unfaithful to her husband while still united to him, he is at liberty to kill both criminals. The husband, on the other hand, although considered to be properly married to only one woman whose sons become his sole heirs, is allowed to keep lesser wives or concubines who are usually slaves, and whose children have no claim on the estate.

The houses of the Chins are much more substantially built than those of the Lushais, and they and the villages are kept in a wonderfully clean and sanitary condition, considering the dirty personal habits of the people themselves. The floors are raised from three to six feet off the ground, they and the walls being constructed of stout wooden planks cut with great patience and labour out of large fir trees, and generally conveyed from a considerable distance. These planks are from one and a half to two feet broad, up to two inches thick, and sometimes over twenty feet in length. A tree is felled and then split in two, one plank being chopped from each half. As the only tools available for the purpose are *dhas* and rough adzes, some idea can be formed of the time and labour involved, as well as the value set upon their houses by the Chins when finished. The posts and framework are composed of stout timber and the roofs covered with thick thatch.

Each house is generally divided into three rooms, with a platform or courtyard in front of the first. This is the public room where the owner receives his guests, and the walls of which are usually adorned with the skulls of animals, wild or domestic, feathers, birds, eggs, &c. In it are also stored baskets of grain and other commodities. The room beyond is quite dark, and contains a fire-place, but no chimney; the smoke having to find egress as best it may. It is entered by a round hole from the front room about two feet from the ground, and the same in diameter, closed on the inside with a door. A similar opening forms a communication with the third apartment, which has a door at the other end and is therefore not so dark. It also has a fire-place, and appears to be used as a kitchen. In the space beneath the floor are kept the goats and pigs, the latter animal abounding in every village, and by its scavenging propensities materially assisting in the work of sanitation. The villages are generally very straggling and built on the side of a hill, where there is a convenient spring or stream from which timber leads convey the water into wooden troughs at the houses. There are no regular defences, but there is often a pretence of guarding the paths leading into the villages by a gate or door usually at the end of a narrow passage or tunnel.

The method of cultivation practised is that known as the "taungya" or "joom" system. Spaces of jungle

A TASHŌN CHIEF'S HOUSE AT FALAM

are cleared during the dry months by felling the trees and setting fire to them and the undergrowth, the ashes so produced forming a good manure for the intended crops. Thereafter, on the first approach of the rains, holes are dibbled in the ground, into which several seeds are thrown together, with a view to their maturing in regular sequence. In this work both sexes engage, but the greater share of the burden falls on the women and slaves, the latter being kept chiefly for that purpose. A large kind of millet or Job's tears which they call "fang," two sorts of ragi ("si"), a large white bean ("ra," known in Burma as "aunglek"), a black bean ("ooshwè"), smaller varieties ("bai"), maize ("fangwè"), paddy ("fasung"), four sorts of yam ("bar"), sweet potatoes ("korha"), pumpkins and chillies are the principal cereals and vegetables grown by the Chins. Fruit is fairly plentiful in the shape of plantains, oranges and sweet limes; while peach, pear and medlar trees were seen in the villages.

The arms of the Chins, like those of the Lushais, consist of flint-lock "tower" muskets, *dhas* and spears; the use of the bow and arrow being almost entirely confined to the still more primitive Chinboks and other southern tribes. The muskets are obtained from Burma either in the course of trade or by force during raids on the border villages, and as they form the most valued possession of the Chins it is hardly necessary to say that they are kept with great care and in good order. The bullets used are made of hammered iron, lead, or gun-metal.

Each village manufactures its own gunpowder, the three components of which are obtained in the following manner. To produce saltpetre, dung, or the filth which collects under the houses, is placed in a large kind of cradle or basket, and through it water is slowly filtered, the resulting liquor being collected in a pan underneath and afterwards evaporated. The salt thus crystallized out is necessarily a very impure one, but it seems to answer the purpose fairly well. Sulphur is usually procured from Burma, but when not so available it is extracted from the "aunglek" bean, which seems to contain a large quantity of this substance. Charcoal is made from the mango tree and two shrubs, known by the Burmese names of "Salpyalin" and "Mayobin." This home-made gunpowder is, of course, very much inferior to the English article as regards strength, being very dirty and irregular in grain, but its defects in quality are to some extent compensated for by the quantity put into each charge. A carefully-sifted portion is always carried in a small powder horn for the purpose of priming, and so well is this attended to that a miss-fire is of rare occurrence; while the first shots, coming as they always do from a hidden ambush and after a long and steady aim, almost invariably hit their mark. The powder for loading is carried in a large horn made from that of the mythun, and highly ornamented.

From this it is poured into a measure neatly shaped out of a piece of bamboo; to facilitate rapid reloading a number of these ready filled, with the bullet wrapped in a rag acting as a cork, are often carried on the person.

The iron and steel used in making spear-heads and *dhas* are procured from Burma, and, among the Baungshès, fashioned into the desired weapons in the village of Wunhla, which is famed for its iron-workers. Shields are also sometimes carried by the Chins.

In addition to the Burmese captives taken in raids, slavery exists among the Chins themselves as a recognized system and is sometimes entered into voluntarily by persons left without other means of subsistence, and who, by claiming the support and protection of another, generally a Chief or headman, thereby forfeit their own freedom and become his slaves. In the case of one freeman stealing from another, the accused becomes the slave of the injured party, if the latter can catch the criminal and prove the theft. Under both circumstances the slaves, and any children who may be born to them, become, like raided captives, the absolute property of their masters, who are at liberty to beat, kill, marry or sell them at pleasure. Should a freeman wish to marry a slave woman he must first ransom her, or make a feast and publicly declare her free if she belongs to himself; otherwise the children of the union are considered to be born in slavery. Except for a short time, when first taken, the captives are not usually treated harshly, and, as we have seen, several had become so reconciled to their lot, or enamoured of new ties, as to decline the opportunity of returning to their native country. In some cases, with an indulgent master a captive is allowed to work out his own ransom; and an instance of this was seen at Hāka, where a Burman freeman was found living in the village and permitted to go where he liked, who had originally been raided on the frontier. When caught the captives are put in stocks or otherwise confined for about a month, apparently with the idea of taming them, but after that they are granted comparative freedom; the penalty, however, for attempting to escape being death or a very severe beating. As an additional safeguard against such an occurrence the captive is made to take an oath either by eating a little earth and swearing that he has adopted the land as his country, or by drinking some water poured over a spear or *dha* and declaring that he will accept death as a punishment for trying to escape.

There is no order of priesthood among the Chins, although they believe in a future state of existence after death and in the influence of "nats" or spirits over the affairs of this life, considering it politic to propitiate them by sacrifices when misfortunes arise.

Drunkenness is the great curse of the people, the liquor indulged in being a sort of small beer made from millet and often strengthened by the addition of a strong spirit distilled from the same grain. Every occasion of meeting, both private and public, is made an excuse for a debauch, and to such an extent is the vice carried that it is hard to get any political business transacted, as the Chiefs are almost invariably in an advanced state of intoxication before they can be got together for the purpose. When the troops arrived at Hāka, Lwè Sin and the other Chiefs were found to be hopelessly drunk, and remained so for weeks.

Hospitality is one of the few virtues of the tribes, and it is worthy of record and remembrance that the Ta-shôns, teacherous as they are called, persistently refused to surrender the Burmese Pretender, Shwègyobyu Min-tha, with whom they had sworn the oath of friendship, although an overwhelming British force stood at the gates of their capital, and, with this exception, had wrung from them all the terms dictated by a victorious enemy.

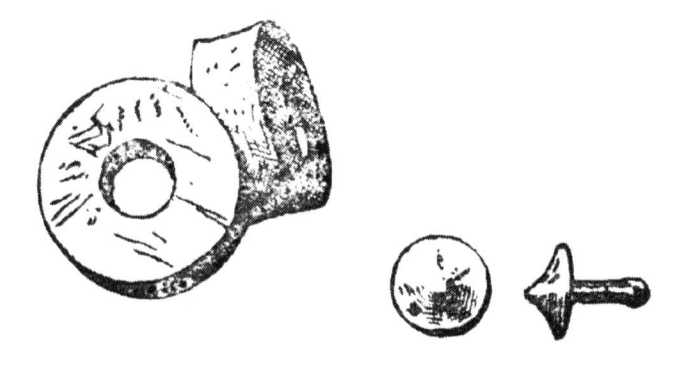

LUSHAI EARRINGS.

Calcutta, Sep. 1893.

THACKER, SPINK AND CO.'S
PUBLICATIONS.

—CONTENTS—

	Page.		Page.
POETRY, FICTION, ETC.	1	NATURAL HISTORY, BOTANY, ETC.	21
HISTORY, CUSTOMS, TRAVELS, ETC.	7	ENGINEERING, SURVEYING, ETC.	23
CAPT. HAYES' WORKS ON HORSES	10	MILITARY WORKS	25
SPORT AND VETERINARY WORKS	12	HINDUSTANI, PERSIAN, ETC.	27
MEDICINE, HYGIENE, ETC.	15	BOOK-KEEPING, &c., MANUALS	30
DOMESTIC BOOKS	17	EDUCATIONAL BOOKS	31
GUIDE BOOKS	19	LAND TENURES AND LAND REVENUE	33
THACKER'S INDIAN DIRECTORIES, MAPS, ETC.	20	LAW BOOKS	36

POETRY, FICTION, ETC.

THE SPOILT CHILD.—A TALE OF HINDU DOMESTIC LIFE. A Translation by G. D. OSWELL, M.A., of the Bengali Novel "*Alaler Gharer Dulal*," by PEARY CHAND MITTER (Tek Chand Thakur). Crown 8vo, cloth, Rs. 3; paper, Rs. 2-8.

"Interesting as throwing a fairly vivid light upon the intimate life of a Hindu household."—*Daily Chronicle.*

"May be heartily commended both for its literary qualities and for the vivid picture it gives of Bengali manners and customs."—*Scotsman.*

SONG OF SHORUNJUNG & OTHER POEMS.—Crown 8vo, cloth. Rs. 2-8.

CONTENTS:—Darjeeling: Summer—The Song of Shorunjung—The Tsari Reed—To the Uplands—A Pastoral—The Jessamine—The Fakir—The Fisher's Supper—A Son—Two Moods—Farewell to Devon—Song—The London Maid—Infancy—A Lullaby—There are Words—Borodino—The Lone Night—The Captive—Cossack Cradle Song—Gifts of the Terek—The Cup of Life—Scenes from Eugene Onyegin.

"Full of tastefully conceived description.... Some of the single verses are very tuneful......A number of translations from the Russian form a noteworthy part of it. The poems have been admirably done into English, the translator having not only retained the sense of the original but the distinctive Russian character of expression and metre."—*Englishman.*

THACKER, SPINK AND CO., CALCUTTA.

RHYMING LEGENDS OF IND.—By H. KIRKWOOD GRACEY, B.A., C.S. Crown 8vo, cloth. Rs. 3-8.

CONTENTS:—The City of Gore—A Mother's Vengeance—The Blue Cow—Famine—A Terrible Tiger—The Legend of Somnath—Treasure Trove—The Idol of Kalinga—Mind vs. Matter—Vultur in partibus.

"A collection of bright little poems. Keen satirical touches are introduced here and there throughout the volume—

Recording the mixture of fact and of fable
In India called evidence which you are able;
To buy as 'twere rice by the pound at a price
That ranges from mohurs to annas and pice.

"The clever little book."—*Morning Post.*

"A charming little book. Of the poems here collected the majority will bear reading several times over. The author writes in lively mirth-provoking fashion."—*Express.*

"The whole volume is, indeed, well worth reading; it is an enjoyable little publication."—*Madras Mail.*

ELSIE ELLERTON.—A NOVELETTE OF ANGLO-INDIAN LIFE. BY MAY EDWOOD, author of "Stray Straws," "Autobiography of a Spin," etc. Crown 8vo. Re. 1-8.

"This novel is amusing, pure in tone, and distinguished by much local colouring."—*Athenæum.*

INDIAN LYRICS.—BY W. TREGO WEBB, M.A., Professor of English Literature, Presidency College. Fcap. 8vo, cloth. Rs. 4.

"Vivacious and clever . . . He presents the various sorts and conditions of humanity that comprise the round of life in Bengal in a series of vivid vignettes .. He writes with scholarly directness and finish."—*Saturday Review.*

"A volume of poems of more than ordinary interest and undoubted ability."—*Oxford and Cambridge Undergraduate's Journal.*

LIGHT AND SHADE.—BY HERBERT SHERRING. A Collection of Tales and Poems. Crown 8vo, cloth. Rs. 3.

"Piquant and humorous—decidedly original—not unworthy of Sterne."—*Spectator* (London).

STRAY STRAWS.—BEING A COLLECTION OF SKETCHES AND STORIES. By MIGNON. Crown 8vo. Re. 1-8.

"It is a capital book to take up when one has a few spare moments on hand."—*Englishman.*

"A very interesting collection of short stories and sketches."—*Morning Post* (Allahabad).

THACKER, SPINK AND CO., CALCUTTA.

BARRACK ROOM BALLADS AND OTHER VERSES.—By RUDYARD KIPLING. Printed by Constable on laid paper, rough edges, bound in buckram, gilt top. Post 8vo. Rs. 4.

"Mr. Kipling's verse is strong, vivid, full of character......unmistakable genius rings in every line."—*Times*.
"The finest things of the kind since Macaulay's 'Lays.'"—*Daily Chronicle*.
"Mr. Kipling is probably our best ballad writer since Scott."—*Daily News*.
"One of the books of the year."—*National Observer*.

POPPIED SLEEP.—A CHRISTMAS STORY OF AN UP-COUNTRY STATION. By Mrs. H. A. FLETCHER, author of "Here's Rue for You." Crown 8vo, sewed. Re. 1-8.

PLAIN TALES FROM THE HILLS.—By RUDYARD KIPLING, author of "Departmental Ditties & other Verses." Third Edition. Crown 8vo. Rs. 4.

"Rattling stories of flirtation and sport . . . . Funny stories of practical jokes and sells . . . . Sad little stories of deeper things told with an affectation of solemnity but rather more throat-lumping for that."—*Sunday Times*.
"Mr. Kipling possesses the art of telling a story. 'Plain Tales from the Hills' sparkle with fun; they are full of life, merriment, and humour, as a rule mirth-provoking. There is at times a pathetic strain; but this soon passes, and laughter—as the Yankees say, side-splitting laughter—is the order of the day. There are spits at persons of note, sly allusions to the mysterious ways of officials in high places, and covert attacks on the peculiarities of a great Government. The mirror of satire reflects all and everything, nothing escapes, and the result is one of the most sparkling, witty, and droll collection of tales which could be well conceived."—*Allen's Indian Mail*.
"Mr. Kipling knows and appreciates the English in India, and is a born story-teller and a man of humour into the bargain. He is also singularly versatile and equally at home in humour and pathos; while neither quality is ever quite absent from his little stories . . . it would be hard to find better reading."—*Saturday Review*.

A ROMANCE OF THAKOTE AND OTHER TALES.—Reprinted from *The World, Civil and Military Gazette*, and other Papers. By F. C. C. Crown 8vo. Re. 1.

INDIAN MELODIES.—By GLYN BARLOW, M.A., Professor, St. George's College, Mussoorie. Fcap. 8vo, cloth. Rs. 2.

"Interesting, pleasant and readable . . . Mr. Barlow's little volume deserves a kindly and favourable reception, and well repays perusal."—*The Morning Post*.

LEVIORA.—BEING THE RHYMES OF A SUCCESSFUL COMPETITOR. By the late T. F. BIGNOLD, Bengal Civil Service. 8vo. Rs. 7-8.

THACKER, SPINK AND CO., CALCUTTA.

INDIAN IDYLLS.—By an Idle Exile. Crown 8vo, cloth. Rs. 2-8.

Contents:—The Maharajah's Guest—The Major's Mess Clothes—In a Haunted Grove—How we got rid of Hunks—My Wedding Day—Mrs. Caramel's Bow-Wow—The Tables Turned—A Polo Smash—After the Wily Boar—In the Rajah's Palace—Two Strings—A Modern Lochinvar—My First Snipe—Mrs. Dimple's Victim—Lizzie; a Shipwreck—How the Convalescent Depôt killed a Tiger—Faithful unto Death—The Haunted Bungalow—Christmas with the Crimson Cuirassiers—In Death they were not Divided.

"A pleasant little book of short stories and sketches, bright and light for the most part, dealing with frays and feasting, polo and pigsticking, with a ghost story thrown in by way of relief."—*Saturday Review.*

"All these are thoroughly Indian in colour and tone, but are not the less amusing and sprightly matter for reading in idle half hours."—*Daily Telegraph.*

"A series of crisp little stories . . . we shall be surprised if it fails to 'fetch' the public who have had nothing better to amuse them since the lamented Aberigh Mackay astonished Anglo-India with his Sir Ali Baba's revelations."—*Express.*

THE TRIBES ON MY FRONTIER.—An Indian Naturalist's Foreign Policy. By EHA. With 50 Illustrations by F. C. Macrae. Imp. 16mo. Uniform with "Lays of Ind." Fourth Edition. Rs. 7.

"We have only to thank our Anglo-Indian naturalist for the delightful book which he has sent home to his countrymen in Britain. May he live to give us another such."—*Chambers' Journal.*

"A most charming series of sprightly and entertaining essays on what may be termed the fauna of the Indian Bungalow. . . . . . We have no doubt that this amusing book will find its way into every Anglo-Indian's library."—*Allen's Indian Mail.*

"This is a delightful book, irresistibly funny in description and illustration, but full of genuine science too. . . . . . There is not a dull or uninstructive page in the whole book."—*Knowledge.*

"It is a pleasantly-written book about the insects and other torments of India which make Anglo-Indian life unpleasant, and which can be read with pleasure even by those beyond the reach of the tormenting things EHA describes."—*Graphic.*

INDIA IN 1983.—A Reprint of this celebrated Prophesy of Native Rule in India. Fcap. 8vo. Re. 1.

"Instructive as well as amusing."—*Indian Daily News.*

"There is not a dull page in the hundred and thirty-seven pages of which it consists."—*Times of India.*

REGIMENTAL RHYMES and Other Verses.—By Kentish Rag. Imp. 16mo. [*In the Press.*

AUTOBIOGRAPHY OF A SPIN.—By May Edwood, author of "Elsie Ellerton," "Stray Straws," &c. Re. 1-8.

THACKER, SPINK AND CO., CALCUTTA.

LALU, THE CHILD-WIDOW.—A Poem in seven parts : Proem—The Zemindar—The Farm—The Betrothal—The Lovers—Widowhood—The Pyre—Rest. By Lt.-Col. W. L. GREENSTREET. Cr. 8vo. Rs. 2.

BEHIND THE BUNGALOW.—BY EHA, author of "THE TRIBES ON MY FRONTIER." With Illustrations by F. C. MACRAE. Fourth Edition. Imp. 16mo. Rs. 5.

"Of this book it may conscientiously be said that it does not contain a dull page, while it contains very many which sparkle with a bright and fascinating humour, refined by the unmistakable evidences of culture."—*Home News.*

"The author of 'Behind the Bungalow' has an excellent sense of humour combined with a kindliness of heart which makes his little book delightful reading."—*Saturday Review.*

"There is plenty of fun in 'Behind the Bungalow.'"—*World.*

"A series of sketches of Indian servants, the humour and acute observation of which will appeal to every Anglo-Indian."—*Englishman.*

"Drawn with delightful humour and keen observation."—*Athenæum.*

"Every variety of native character, the individual as well as the nation, caste, trade, or class, is cleverly pourtrayed in these diverting sketches."—*Illustrated London News.*

INDIAN ENGLISH AND INDIAN CHARACTER.—BY ELLIS UNDERWOOD. Fcap. 8vo. As. 12.

LAYS OF IND.—BY ALIPH CHEEM. Comic, Satirical, and Descriptive Poems illustrative of Anglo-Indian Life. Eighth Edition. Enlarged. With 70 Illustrations. Cloth, elegant gilt edges. Rs. 7-8.

"There is no mistaking the humour, and at times, indeed, the fun is both 'fast and furious.' One can readily imagine the merriment created round the camp fire by the recitation of 'The Two Thumpers,' which is irresistibly droll."—*Liverpool Mercury.*

"The verses are characterised by high animal spirits, great cleverness, and most excellent fooling."—*World.*

THE CAPTAIN'S DAUGHTER.—A NOVEL. BY A. C. POOSHKIN. Literally translated from the Russian by STUART H. GODFREY, Captain Bo. S. C. Crown 8vo. Rs. 2.

"Possesses the charm of giving vividly, in about an hour's reading, a conception of Russian life and manners which many persons desire to possess."—*Englishman.*

"The story will interest keenly any English reader."—*Overland Mail.*

"HERE'S RUE FOR YOU."—NOVELETTES, ENGLISH AND ANGLO-INDIAN. By Mrs. H. A. FLETCHER. Crown 8vo, sewed. Rs. 2.

CONTENTS:—A Summer Madness—Whom the Gods Love—Nemesis—A Gathered Rose—At Sea: a P. and O. Story—Esther: an Episode.

THACKER, SPINK AND CO., CALCUTTA.

ONOOCOOL CHUNDER MOOKERJEE.—A Memoir of the late Justice Onoocool Chunder Mookerjee. By M. Mookerjee. Fourth Edition. 12mo. Re. 1.

"The reader is earnestly advised to procure the life of this gentleman, written by his nephew, and read it."—*The Tribes on my Frontier.*

DEPARTMENTAL DITTIES AND OTHER VERSES.—By Rudyard Kipling. Seventh Edition. With additional Poems. Cloth. Rs. 3.

"This tiny volume will not be undeserving of a place on the bookshelf that holds 'Twenty-one Days in India.' Its contents, indeed, are not unlike the sort of verse we might have expected from poor 'Ali Baba' if he had been spared to give it us. Mr. Kipling resembles him in lightness of touch, quaintness of fancy, and unexpected humour."—*Pioneer.*

"The verses are all written in a light style, which is very attractive, and no one with the slightest appreciation of humour will fail to indulge in many a hearty laugh before turning over the last page."—*Times of India.*

"Mr. Kipling's rhymes are rhymes to some purpose. He calls them Departmental Ditties: but they are in reality social sketches of Indian officialism from a single view point, that of the satirist, though the satire is of the mildest and most delightful sort."—*Indian Planters' Gazette.*

THE INSPECTOR.—A Comedy. By Gogol. Translated from the Russian by T. Hart-Davies, Bombay Civil Service. Crown 8vo. Rs. 2.

"His translation, we may add, is a very good one."—*The Academy.*

ASHES FOR BREAD.—A Romance. By Beaumont Harrington. Crown 8vo, sewed. Re. 1-8.

"A lively appreciation of the trials, intrigues, and capacities of an Indian career."—*Indian Daily News.*

"A very artistic little plot."—*Madras Times.*

A MIDSUMMER NIGHT'S DREAM (Shakespeare).—Adapted to Pastoral Representation. By N. Newnham-Davis. Crown 8vo. Re. 1.

THE SECOND BOMBARDMENT AND CAPTURE OF FORT WILLIAM, Calcutta.—An Account of the Bombardment of Fort William, and the Capture and Occupation of the City of Calcutta, on the 20th June 1891, &c., by a Russian Fleet and Army. Compiled from the Diaries of Prince Serge Woronzoff and General Yagodkin. Translated from the Original Russe by Ivan Batiushka. Crown 8vo, sewed. Re. 1-8.

CÆSAR DE SOUZA, EARL OF WAKEFIELD.—By the Author of "India in 1983." Crown 8vo, cloth. Rs. 2-8.

A NATURALIST ON THE PROWL.—By Eha, author of "Tribes on my Frontier," "Behind the Bungalow." [*In the Press.*

THACKER, SPINK AND CO., CALCUTTA.

HISTORY, CUSTOMS, TRAVELS, ETC.

THE HINDOOS AS THEY ARE.—A Description of the Manners Customs, and Inner Life of Hindoo Society, Bengal. By Shib Chunder Bose. Second Edition, Revised. Crown 8vo, cloth. Rs. 5.

HINDU MYTHOLOGY.—Vedic and Puranic. By W. J. Wilkins, of the London Missionary Society, Calcutta. Profusely Illustrated. Imp. 16mo, cloth, gilt, elegant. Rs. 7-8.

"His aim has been to give a faithful account of the Hindu deities such as an intelligent native would himself give, and he has endeavoured, in order to achieve his purpose, to keep his mind free from prejudice or theological bias. The author has attempted a work of no little ambition and has succeeded in his attempt, the volume being one of great interest and usefulness."—*Home News.*

"Mr. Wilkins has done his work well, with an honest desire to state facts apart from all theological prepossession, and his volume is likely to be a useful book of reference."—*Guardian.*

MODERN HINDUISM.—Being an Account of the Religion and Life of the Hindus in Northern India. By W. J. Wilkins, author of "Hindu Mythology, Vedic and Puranic." Demy 8vo. Rs. 8.

"He writes in a liberal and comprehensive spirit."—*Saturday Review.*

"......volume which is at once a voluminous disquisition upon the Hindu religion, and a most interesting narrative of Hindu life, the habits and customs of the Hindu community and a national Hindu historiette, written with all the nerve of the accomplished littérateur, added to the picturesque word-painting and life-like delineations of a veteran novelist."—*Lucknow Express.*

"A solid addition to our literature."—*Westminster Review.*

"A valuable contribution to knowledge."—*Scotsman.*

THE ETHICS OF ISLAM.—A Lecture by the Hon'ble Ameer Ali, C.I.E., author of "The Spirit of Islam," "The Personal Law of the Mahommedans," etc.

THE LIFE AND TEACHING OF KESHUB CHUNDER SEN.—By P. C. Mazumdar. Second and Cheaper Edition. Rs. 2.

THEOSOPHICAL CHRISTIANITY.—An Address by L. S. Second Edition, Revised and Enlarged. Small 4to. As. 8.

BOMBAY SKETCHES.—By S. Tagore, Bo.C.S. *Printed in Bengali.* Illustrated. Royal 8vo, cloth, gilt. Rs. 8.

KASHGARIA (EASTERN OR CHINESE TURKESTAN).—Historical, Geographical, Military, and Industrial. By Col. Kuropatkin, Russian Army. Translated by Maj. Gowan, H. M.'s Indian Army. 8vo. Rs. 6-8.

THACKER, SPINK AND CO., CALCUTTA.

ANCIENT INDIA AS DESCRIBED BY PTOLEMY.—WITH INTRODUCTION, Commentary, Map of India. By J. W. MCCRINDLE, M.A. 8vo, cloth, lettered. Rs. 4-4.

ANCIENT INDIA AS DESCRIBED BY MEGASTHENES AND ARRIAN. With Introduction, Notes, and a Map of Ancient India. By J. W. MCCRINDLE, M.A. 8vo. Rs. 2-8.

THE COMMERCE AND NAVIGATION OF THE ERYTHRÆAN SEA; Periplus Maris Erythræi; and of Arrian's Account of the Voyage of Nearkhos. With Introduction, Commentary, Notes, and Index. By J. W. MCCRINDLE, M.A. 8vo. Rs. 3.

ANCIENT INDIA AS DESCRIBED BY KTESIAS THE KNIDIAN.—A Translation of the Abridgment of his 'Indika,' by Photios. With Introduction, Notes, Index. By J. W. MCCRINDLE, M.A. 8vo. Rs. 3.

A MEMOIR OF CENTRAL INDIA, INCLUDING MALWA AND ADJOINING PROVINCES, with the History, and copious Illustrations, of the Past and Present condition of that country. By Maj.-Gen. S. J. MALCOLM, G.C.B., &c. *Reprinted from Third Edition.* 2 vols. Crown 8vo, cloth. Rs. 5.

BOOK OF INDIAN ERAS.—WITH TABLES FOR CALCULATING INDIAN DATES. By ALEXANDER CUNNINGHAM, C.S.I., C.I.E., Major-General, Royal Engineers. Royal 8vo, cloth. Rs. 12.

TALES FROM INDIAN HISTORY.—BEING THE ANNALS OF INDIA retold in Narratives. By J. TALBOYS WHEELER. Crown 8vo, cloth, Rs. 3. School Edition, cloth, limp, Re. 1-8.

"The history of our great dependency made extremely attractive reading. Altogether this is a work of rare merit."—*Broad Arrow.*

"Will absorb the attention of all who delight in drilling records of adventure and daring. It is no mere compilation, but an earnest and brightly written book."—*Daily Chronicle.*

A CRITICAL EXPOSITION OF THE POPULAR "JIHAD."—Showing that all the Wars of Mahammad were defensive, and that Aggressive War or Compulsory Conversion is not allowed in the Koran, &c. By Moulavi CHERAGH ALI, author of "Reforms under Moslem Rule," "Hyderabad under Sir Salar Jung." 8vo. Rs. 6.

MAYAM-MA: THE HOME OF THE BURMAN.—BY TSAYA (REV. H. POWELL). Crown 8vo. Rs. 2.

AN INTRODUCTION TO THE STUDY OF HINDUISM.—BY GURU PRISHAD SEN. Crown 8vo. [*In the Press.*

THACKER, SPINK AND CO., CALCUTTA.

CHIN-LUSHAI LAND.—INCLUDING A DESCRIPTION OF THE VARIOUS Expeditions into the Chin-Lushai Hills and the Final Annexation of the Country. By Surgn.-Lieut.-Colonel A. S. REID, M.B., Indian Medical Service. With three Maps and nine Phototint Illustrations.

THE IMAGE OF WAR, OR SERVICE IN THE CHIN HILLS.—A COLLECTION of nearly 150 Photo Reproductions from negatives. By Surgeon-Captain A. G. NEWLAND. With Introductory Notes, by J. D. MACNABB, Esq., B.C.S.

THE RACES OF AFGHANISTAN.—BEING A BRIEF ACCOUNT of the principal Nations inhabiting that country. By Surg.-Maj. H. W. BELLEW, C.S.I., late on Special Political Duty at Kabul. 8vo, cloth. Rs. 3-8.

KURRACHEE: ITS PAST, PRESENT, AND FUTURE.—BY ALEXANDER F. BAILLIE, F.R.G.S., author of "A Paraguayan Treasure," &c. With Maps, Plans, and Photographs, showing the most recent improvements Super-royal 8vo, cloth. Rs. 15.

THE TRIAL OF MAHARAJA NANDA KUMAR.—A NARRATIVE OF A JUDICIAL MURDER. By H. BEVERIDGE, B.C.S. Demy 8vo. Rs. 5.

"Mr. Beveridge has given a great amount of thought, labour, and research to the marshalling of his facts, and he has done his utmost to put the exceedingly complicated and contradicting evidence in a clear and intelligible form."—*Home News.*

THE EMPEROR AKBAR.—A CONTRIBUTION TOWARDS THE HISTORY OF INDIA in the 16th Century. By FREDERICK AUGUSTUS, Count of Noer. Translated from the German by ANNETTE S. BEVERIDGE. 2 vols. 8vo, cloth, gilt. Rs. 5.

ECHOES FROM OLD CALCUTTA.—BEING CHIEFLY REMINISCENCES of the days of Warren Hastings, Francis, and Impey. By H. E. BUSTEED. Second Edition, Enlarged and Illustrated. Post 8vo. Rs. 6.

"The book will be read by all interested in India."—*Army & Navy Magazine.*

"Dr. Busteed's valuable and entertaining 'Echoes from Old Calcutta' has arrived at a second edition, revised, enlarged and illustrated with portraits and other plates rare or quaint. It is a pleasure to reiterate the warm commendation of this instructive and lively volume which its appearance called forth some years since."—*Saturday Review.*

"A series of illustrations which are highly entertaining and instructive of the life and manners of Anglo-Indian society a hundred years ago . . . The book from first to last has not a dull page in it, and it is a work of the kind of which the value will increase with years."—*Englishman.*

HISTORY OF CIVILIZATION IN ANCIENT INDIA.—Based on Sanscrit Literature. By ROMESH CHUNDER DUTT, C S. Cheap Edition. In one vol. Rs. 5.

THACKER, SPINK AND CO., CALCUTTA.

CAPT. HAYES' WORKS ON HORSES.

ON HORSE BREAKING.—By Captain M. H. Hayes. Numerous Illustrations by J. H. Oswald-Brown. Square. Rs. 16.

(1) Theory of Horse Breaking. (2) Principles of Mounting. (3) Horse Control. (4) Rendering Docile. (5) Giving Good Mouths. (6) Teaching to Jump. (7) Mount for the First Time. (8) Breaking for Ladies' Riding. (9) Breaking to Harness. (10) Faults of Mouth. (11) Nervousness and Impatience. (12) Jibbing. (13) Jumping Faults. (14) Faults in Harness. (15) Aggressiveness. (16) Riding and Driving Newly-Broken Horse. (17) Stable Vices.

"One great merit of the book is its simplicity."—*Indian Daily News.*

"A work which is entitled to high praise at being far and away the best reasoned-out one on breaking under a new system we have seen."—*Field.*

"Clearly written."—*Saturday Review.*

"The best and most instructive book of its class that has appeared for many years."—*Times of India.*

RIDING: ON THE FLAT AND ACROSS COUNTRY.—A Guide to Practical Horsemanship. By Captain M. H. Hayes. With 70 Illustrations by Sturgess and J. H. Oswald-Brown. Third Edition, Revised and Enlarged. Rs. 7-8.

The whole text has been so revised or re-written as to make the work the most perfect in existence, essential to all who wish to attain the art of riding correctly.

"One of the most valuable additions to modern literature on the subject."—*Civil and Military Gazette.*

"A very instructive and readable book."—*Sport.*

"This useful and eminently practical book."—*Freeman's Journal.*

THE POINTS OF THE HORSE.—A Familiar Treatise on Equine Conformation. Describing the points in which the perfection of each class of horses consists. By Captain M. H. Hayes. Illustrated by 74 Reproductions of Photographs and 225 Line Drawings. Sm. 4to. Rs. 32.

INDIAN RACING REMINISCENCES.—Being Entertaining Narratives, and Anecdotes of Men, Horses, and Sport. By Captain M. H. Hayes. Illustrated with 42 Portraits and Engravings. Imp. 16mo. Rs. 6.

"Captain Hayes has done wisely in publishing these lively sketches of life in India. The book is full of racy anecdote."—*Bell's Life.*

"All sportsmen who can appreciate a book on racing, written in a chatty style and full of anecdote, will like Captain Hayes' latest work."—*Field.*

"Many a racing anecdote and many a curious character our readers will find in the book, which is very well got up, and embellished with many portraits."—*Bailey's Magazine.*

THACKER, SPINK AND CO., CALCUTTA.

VETERINARY NOTES FOR HORSE-OWNERS.—A POPULAR GUIDE to Horse Medicine and Surgery. By Captain M. H. HAYES. Fourth Edition, Enlarged and Revised to the latest Science of the Day. With many New Illustrations by J. H. OSWALD-BROWN. Crown 8vo, buckram. Rs. 9.

The chief new matter in this Edition is—Articles on Contracted Heels, Donkey's Foot Disease, Forging or Clicking, Rheumatic Joint Disease, Abscess, Dislocation of the Shoulder Joint, Inflammation of the Mouth and Tongue, Flatulent Distention of the Stomach, Twist of the Intestines, Relapsing Fever, Cape Horse Sickness, Horse Syphilis, Rabies, Megrims, Staggers, Epilepsy, Sunstroke, Poisoning, Castration by the Ecraseur, and Mechanism of the Foot (in Chapter or Shoeing).

"Of the many popular veterinary books which have come under our notice, this is certainly one of the most scientific and reliable. . . . The description of symptoms and the directions for the application of remedies are given in perfectly plain terms, which the tyro will find no difficulty in comprehending."—*Field.*

"Simplicity is one of the most commendable features in the book."—*Illustrated Sporting and Dramatic News.*

"Captain Hayes, in the new edition of 'Veterinary Notes,' has added considerably to its value, and rendered the book more useful to those non-professional people who may be inclined or compelled to treat their own horses when sick or injured."—*Veterinary Journal.*

"We do not think that horse-owners in general are likely to find a more reliable and useful book for guidance in an emergency."—*Field.*

TRAINING AND HORSE MANAGEMENT IN INDIA.—BY CAPTAIN M. H. HAYES, author of "Veterinary Notes for Horse-Owners," "Riding," &c. Fifth Edition. Crown 8vo. Rs. 6.

"No better guide could be placed in the hands of either amateur horseman or veterinary surgeon."—*Veterinary Journal.*

"A useful guide in regard to horses anywhere. . . . Concise, practical, and portable."—*Saturday Review.*

SOUNDNESS AND AGE OF HORSES.—A VETERINARY AND LEGAL GUIDE to the Examination of Horses for Soundness. By Captain M. H. HAYES, M.R.C.V.S. With 100 Illustrations. Crown 8vo. Rs. 6.

"Captain Hayes is entitled to much credit for the explicit and sensible manner in which he has discussed the many questions—some of them extremely vexed ones—which pertain to soundness and unsoundness in horses."—*Veterinary Journal.*

"All who have horses to buy, sell, or keep will find plenty to interest them in this manual, which is full of illustrations, and still fuller of hints and wrinkles."—*Referee.*

"Captain Hayes' work is evidently the result of much careful research, and the horseman, as well as the veterinarian, will find in it much that is interesting and instructive."—*Field.*

THACKER, SPINK AND CO., CALCUTTA.

THE HORSE-WOMAN.—A Practical Guide to Side-Saddle Riding. By Mrs. Hayes, and Edited by Captain M. H. Hayes. Illustrated by 48 Drawings by J. Oswald-Brown and 4 Photographs. Uniform with "Riding: on the Flat and Across Country." Imp. 16mo. Rs. 7-8.

"This is the first occasion on which a practical horseman and a practical horsewoman have collaborated in bringing out a book on riding for ladies. The result is in every way satisfactory."—*Field.*

"A large amount of sound practical instruction, very judiciously and pleasantly imparted."—*Times.*

"We have seldom come across a brighter book than 'The Horsewoman.'"—*Athenæum.*

"Eminently sensible and practical."—*Daily Chronicle.*

SPORT AND VETERINARY WORKS.

HIGHLANDS OF CENTRAL INDIA.—Notes on their Forests and Wild Tribes, Natural History, and Sports. By Capt. J Forsyth, B.S.C. New Edition. With Map and Tinted Illustrations. Rs. 7-8.

CALCUTTA TURF CLUB RULES OF RACING, together with the Rules relating to Lotteries, Betting, Defaulters, and the Rules of the Calcutta Turf Club. Revised May 1892. Authorized Edition. Rs. 2.

THE RACING CALENDAR, Vol. V, from May 1892 to April 1893, Races Past. Published by the Calcutta Turf Club. Contents:—Rules of Racing, Lotteries, C. T. C., etc., Registered Colours; Licensed Trainers and Jockeys; Assumed Names; List of Horses Aged, Classed and Measured by C. T. C. and W. I. T. C.; Races Run under C. T. C. Rules; Performances of Horses; Appendix and Index. Rs. 4.

THE RACING CALENDAR from 1st August 1888 to 30th April 1889, Races Past. 12mo. cloth. Vol. I, Rs. 4. Vol. II, to April 1890, Rs. 4. Vol. III, to April 1891, Rs. 4. Vol. IV, to April 1892, Rs. 4. Vol. V, to April 1893, Rs. 4.

CALCUTTA RACING CALENDAR.—Published every Fortnight. Annual Subscription Rs. 12.

THE SPORTSMAN'S MANUAL.—In Quest of Game in Kullu, Lahoul, and Ladak to the Tso Morari Lake, with Notes on Shooting in Spiti, Bara Bagahal, Chamba, and Kashmir, and a detailed description of Sport in more than 100 Nalas. With 9 Maps. By Lt.-Col. R. H. Tyacke, late H. M.'s 98th and 34th Regiments. Fcap 8vo, cloth. Rs. 3-8.

THACKER, SPINK AND CO., CALCUTTA.

SEONEE: OR, CAMP LIFE ON THE SATPURA RANGE.—A Tale of Indian Adventure. By R. A. Sterndale, author of "Mammalia of India," "Denizens of the Jungles." Illustrated by the author. With a Map and an Appendix containing a brief Topographical and Historical Account of the District of Seonee in the Central Provinces of India. Crown 8vo, cloth. Rs. 7.

LARGE GAME SHOOTING IN THIBET, THE HIMALAYAS, Northern and Central India. By Brig.-General Alexander A. Kinloch. Containing Descriptions of the Country and of the various Animals to be found; together with extracts from a journal of several years' standing. With 36 Illustrations from photographs and a Map. Third Edition, Revised and Enlarged. Demy 4to, elegantly bound. Rs. 25.

"This splendidly illustrated record of sport, the photogravures, especially the heads of the various antelopes, are life-like; and the letter-press is very pleasant reading."—*Graphic*.

"The book is capitally got up, the type is better than in former editions, and the excellent photogravures give an exceptional value to the work."—*Asian*.

DENIZENS OF THE JUNGLES.—A Series of Sketches of Wild Animals, illustrating their form and natural attitude. With Letter-press Description of each Plate. By R. A. Sterndale, F.R.G.S., F.Z.S., author of "Natural History of the Mammalia of India," "Seonee," &c. Oblong folio. Rs. 10.

I. "Denizens of the Jungles"—Aborigines—Deer—Monkeys.
II. "On the Watch"—Tiger.
III. "Not so Fast Asleep as he Looks"—Panther—Monkeys.
IV. "Waiting for Father"—Black Bears of the Plains.
V. "Rival Monarchs"—Tiger and Elephant.
VI. "Hors de Combat"—Indian Wild Boar and Tiger.
VII. "A Race for Life"—Blue Bull and Wild Dogs.
VIII. "Meaning Mischief"—The Gaur—Indian Bison.
IX. "More than His Match"—Buffalo and Rhinoceros.
X. "A Critical Moment"—Spotted Deer and Leopard.
XI. "Hard Hit"—The Sambur.
XII. "Mountain Monarchs"—Marco Polo's Sheep.

REMINISCENCES OF TWENTY YEARS' PIG-STICKING IN BENGAL. By Raoul. Illustrated with 6 Portraits. Crown 8vo, cloth gilt. Rs. 6-12.

HORSE BREEDING AND REARING IN INDIA.—With Notes on Training for the Flat and Across Country, and on Purchase, Breaking in, and General Management. By Major John Humfrey, B.S.C., F.Z.S. Crown 8vo, cloth. Rs. 3-8.

THACKER, SPINK AND CO., CALCUTTA.

INDIAN HORSE NOTES.—An Epitome of useful Information arranged for ready reference on Emergencies, and specially adapted for Officers and Mofussil Residents. All Technical Terms explained and Simplest Remedies selected. By Major C———, author of "Indian Notes about Dogs." Second Edition, Revised and considerably Enlarged. Fcap. 8vo, cloth. Rs. 2.

DOGS FOR HOT CLIMATES.—A Guide for Residents in Tropical Countries as to suitable Breeds, their Respective Uses, Management and Doctoring. By Vero Shaw and Captain M. H. Hayes. With Illustrations. [*In the Press.*

RIDING FOR LADIES, WITH HINTS ON THE STABLE.—A Lady's Horse Book. By Mrs. Power O'Donoghue. With 75 Illustrations by A. Chantrey Corbould. Elegantly printed and bound. Imp. 16mo, gilt. Rs. 7-8.

INDIAN NOTES ABOUT DOGS.—Their Diseases and Treatment. By Major C———. Fourth Edition. Fcap. 8vo, cloth. Re. 1-8.

ANGLING ON THE KUMAUN LAKES.—With a Map of the Kumaon Lake Country and Plan of each Lake. By Depy. Surgeon-General W. Walker. Crown 8vo, cloth. Rs. 4.

"Written with all the tenderness and attention to detail which characterise the followers of the gentle art."—*Hayes' Sporting News.*

USEFUL HINTS TO YOUNG SHIKARIS ON THE GUN AND RIFLE.—By "The Little Old Bear." Reprinted from *Asian*. Crown 8vo. Rs. 2-8.

THE ARMS ACT (XI OF 1878).—With all the Notices of the Government of India, the Bengal, North-Western Provinces and Punjab Governments, and High Court Decisions and Rulings. By W. Hawkins. Second Edition. [*In the Press.*

POLO RULES.—Rules of the Calcutta Polo Club and of the Indian Polo Association, with the Article on Polo by "An Old Hand." Reprinted from *Hayes' Sporting News*. Fcap. 8vo. Re. 1.

THE POLO CALENDAR, 1892-93.—Compiled by the Indian Polo Association. Vol. I. Contents: Committee of Stewards, Rules for the Regulation of Tournaments, &c.—Rules of the Game—Station Polo—List of Members—List of Existing Polo Ponies, names and description, with Alphabetical List—Records of Tournaments, 1892-93—Previous Winners. Fcap. 8vo, cloth. Re. 1 8.

Rules of Polo.—From the Polo Calendar. As. 8.

LAWS OF FOOTBALL (ASSOCIATION).—Containing the Law of the Game—Definition of Terms—Hints to Referees. For Pocket. As. 4.

THACKER, SPINK AND CO., CALCUTTA.

MEDICINE, HYGIENE, ETC.

AIDS TO PRACTICAL HYGIENE.—By J. C. Battersby, B.A., M.B. B.CH. Univ. Dublin. Fcap. 8vo, cloth. Rs. 2.

"A valuable handbook to the layman interested in sanitation."—*Morning Post.*
"To the busy practitioner or the medical student it will serve the purposes of a correct and intelligent guide."—*Medical Record.*

HINTS FOR THE MANAGEMENT AND MEDICAL TREATMENT OF Children in India. By Edward A. Birch, M.D., Surgeon-Major Bengal Establishment. Second Edition, Revised. Being the Eighth Edition of "Goodeve's Hints for the Management of Children in India." Crown 8vo. Rs. 7.

The Medical Times and Gazette, in an article upon this work and Moore's "Family Medicine for India," says:—"The two works before us are in themselves probably about the best examples of medical works written for non-professional readers. The style of each is simple, and as free as possible from technical expressions. The modes of treatment recommended are generally those most likely to yield good results in the hands of laymen; and throughout each volume the important fact is kept constantly before the mind of the reader, that the volume he is using is but a poor substitute for personal professional advice, for which it must be discarded whenever there is the opportunity."

QUERIES AT A MESS TABLE.—What shall we Eat? What shall we Drink? By Surg.-Maj. Joshua Duke. Fcap. 8vo, cloth, gilt. Rs. 2-4.

BANTING IN INDIA.—With some Remarks on Diet and Things in General. By Surg.-Maj. Joshua Duke. Third Edition. Cloth. Re. 1-8.

OUTLINES OF MEDICAL JURISPRUDENCE FOR INDIA.—By J. D. B. Gribble, M.C.S. (Retired), and Patrick Hehir, M.D., F.R.C.S.E. Third Edition, Revised, Enlarged, and Annotated. Demy 8vo. Rs. 5-8.

RUDIMENTS OF SANITATION.—For Indian Schools. By Patrick Hehir, M.D. Second Edition. 12mo, cloth. Re. 1-4.

THE TEETH.—Their Structure, Disease, and Preservation. With some Notes on Conservative and Prosthetic Dentistry. Nine Plates. By Jos. Miller, L.D.S., R.C.S.E. Second Edition. 8vo, cloth. Rs. 2-8.

THE BABY.—Notes on the Feeding, Rearing and Diseases of Infants. By S. O. Moses, Licentiate of the Royal College of Physicians, Edinburgh, &c. Fcap. 8vo, cloth. Rs. 2.

THACKER, SPINK AND CO., CALCUTTA.

MY LEPER FRIENDS.—An Account of Personal Work among Lepers, and their daily life in India. By Mrs. HAYES. With Illustrations from Photographs, and a Chapter on Leprosy by Dr. G. G. MACLAREN. Imp. square 32mo. Rs. 2-8.

"The author pictures a very sad phase of human misery by relating the story of the inner life of sufferers whom she has known."—*Cork Constitution.*

"It is impossible to read Mrs. Hayes' book without feeling the keenest sympathy with her in her brave and onerous work, and it cannot fail to result in a considerable return for the advantage of the lepers. Mrs. Hayes writes well and vividly, and there is a note of thorough sincerity in all she says that lends an additional charm to the work. . . . There are several illustrations in the book, reproduced from photographs of lepers."—*Home News.*

"On the whole, Mrs. Hayes has written her book in a very sympathising spirit."—*Indian Daily News.*

HYGIENE OF WATER AND WATER SUPPLIES.—By PATRICK HEHIR, M.D., Lecturer on Hygiene, Hyderabad Med. School. 8vo, cloth, flush. Rs. 2.

CHOLERA EPIDEMIC IN KASHMIR, 1892.—By A. MITRA, L.R.C.P., L.R.C.S., Principal Medical Officer in Kashmir. With Map and Tables. 4to, sewed. Re. 1.

A RECORD OF THREE YEARS' WORK OF THE NATIONAL ASSOCIATION for Supplying Female Medical Aid to the Women of India. August 1885 to August 1888. By H. E. THE COUNTESS OF DUFFERIN. Crown 8vo. Re. 1.

THE NATIONAL ASSOCIATION FOR SUPPLYING FEMALE MEDICAL AID to the Women of India. By H. E. THE COUNTESS OF DUFFERIN. Reprinted from the *Asiatic Quarterly Review,* by permission. As. 8.

THE INDIAN MEDICAL SERVICE.—A Guide for intended Candidates for Commissions and for the Junior Officers of the Service. By WILLIAM WEBB, M.B., Surgeon, Bengal Army, late Agency Surgeon at the Court of Bikanir, Superintendent of Dispensaries, Jails, and Vaccination in the Bikanir State, and for some time Guardian to H. H. the Maharajah. Crown 8vo. Rs. 4.

"We recommend the book to all who think of competing for admission into the Indian Medical Service."—*Lancet.*

THE CARLSBAD TREATMENT FOR TROPICAL AILMENTS, AND HOW TO CARRY IT OUT IN INDIA. By Surgn.-Captain L. TARLETON YOUNG. Ex. fcap. 8vo. [*In the Press.*

THACKER, SPINK AND CO., CALCUTTA.

AGUE; OR, INTERMITTENT FEVER.—By M. D. O'CONNEL, M.D. 8vo, sewed. Rs. 2.

THE LANDMARKS OF SNAKE-POISON LITERATURE.—Being a Review of the more important Researches into the Nature of Snake-Poisons. By VINCENT RICHARDS, F.R.C.S. ED., &c., Civil Medical Officer of Goalundo, Bengal. Rs. 2-8.

MALARIA; ITS CAUSE AND EFFECTS; MALARIA AND THE SPLEEN; Injuries of the Spleen: An Analysis of 39 cases. By E. G. RUSSELL, M.B., B.S.C. 8vo, cloth. Rs. 8.

PERSONAL AND DOMESTIC HYGIENE FOR THE SCHOOL AND HOME; being a Text-book on Elementary Physiology, Hygiene, Home Nursing, and First Aid to the Injured; for Senior Schools and Family Reference By Mrs. HAROLD HENDLEY. Illustrated. Ex. fcap. 8vo. Rs. 2-8.

MEDICAL JURISPRUDENCE FOR INDIA.—By J. B. LYON, F.C.S., F.C.- Brigade Surgeon, Professor of Medical Jurisprudence, Grant Medical College, Bombay. The Legal Matter revised by J. D. INVERARITY, Bar.-at-law. Second Edition. Illustrated. 8vo. Rs. 16.

INDIAN MEDICAL GAZETTE.—Published monthly. Subscription Rs. 18 yearly.

DOMESTIC BOOKS.

THE INDIAN COOKERY BOOK.—A PRACTICAL HANDBOOK TO THE KITCHEN IN INDIA, adapted to the Three Presidencies. Containing Original and Approved Recipes in every department of Indian Cookery; Recipes for Summer Beverages and Home-made Liqueurs; Medicinal and other Recipes; together with a variety of things worth knowing. By a Thirty-five Years' Resident. Rs. 3.

FIRMINGER'S MANUAL OF GARDENING FOR INDIA.—A New Edition (the fourth) thoroughly Revised and Re-written. With many Illustrations. By H. ST. J. JACKSON. Imp. 16mo, cloth, gilt. Rs. 10.

POULTRY KEEPING IN INDIA.—A SIMPLE AND PRACTICAL BOOK on their care and treatment, their various breeds, and the means of rendering them profitable. By ISA TWEED, author of "Cow-Keeping in India." With Illustrations. [*In the Press.*

THACKER, SPINK AND CO., CALCUTTA.

COW-KEEPING IN INDIA.—A SIMPLE AND PRACTICAL BOOK on their care and treatment, their various breeds, and the means of rendering them profitable. By ISA TWEED. With 37 Illustrations of the various Breeds, &c. Crown 8vo, cloth, gilt. Rs. 4-8.

"A most useful contribution to a very important subject, and we can strongly recommend it."—*Madras Mail.*

"A valuable contribution to Agricultural Literature in the East."—*Ceylon Observer.*

ENGLISH ETIQUETTE FOR INDIAN GENTLEMEN.—By W. TREGO WEBB, Bengal Educational Department. Second Edition. Fcap. 8vo, cloth, Re. 1-4. Paper, Re. 1.

The book comprises chapters on General Conduct, Calls, Dining-out, Levées, Balls, Garden-parties, Railway-travelling, &c. It also contains a chapter on Letter-writing, proper Modes of Address, &c., together with hints on how to draw up Applications for Appointments, with Examples.

PERSONAL AND DOMESTIC HYGIENE FOR THE SCHOOL AND HOME; being a Text-book on Elementary Physiology, Hygiene, Home Nursing, and First Aid to the Injured; for Senior Schools and Family Reference. By Mrs. HAROLD HENDLEY. Ex. fcap. 8vo.

THE AMATEUR GARDENER IN THE HILLS.—With a few Hints on Fowls, Pigeons, and Rabbits. By an Amateur. Second Edition, Revised and Enlarged. [*In the Press.*

HINTS FOR THE MANAGEMENT AND MEDICAL TREATMENT OF CHILDREN IN INDIA. By EDWARD A. BIRCH, M.D., Surgeon-Major, Bengal Establishment. Second Edition, Revised. Being the Eighth Edition of "Goodeve's Hints for the Management of Children in India." Crown 8vo. Rs. 7.

Dr. Goodeve.—"I have no hesitation in saying that the present edition is for many reasons superior to its predecessors. It is written very carefully, and with much knowledge and experience on the author's part, whilst it possesses the great advantage of bringing up the subject to the present level of Medical Service."

QUERIES AT A MESS TABLE.—WHAT SHALL WE EAT? WHAT SHALL WE DRINK? By Surg.-Maj. JOSHUA DUKE. Fcap. 8vo, cloth, gilt, Rs. 2-4.

THE MEM-SAHIB'S BOOK OF CAKES, BISCUITS, ETC.—With Remarks on Ovens, & Hindustani Vocabulary, Weights & Measures. [*In the Press.*

THACKER, SPINK AND CO., CALCUTTA.

GUIDE BOOKS.

INCE'S KASHMIR HANDBOOK.—A Guide for Visitors. Re-Written and much Enlarged by Joshua Duke, Surg.-Lt.-Col., Bengal Medical Service, formerly Civil Surgeon, Gilgit and Srinagar. Fcap. 8vo, cloth, Maps in cloth case. With Appendix containing the Jhelum Valley Road. Rs. 6-8.

The Chief Contents are:—An Account of the Province of Kashmir, its Rivers, Lakes, Mountains, Vales, Passes, Inhabitants—Srinagar—Arts and Manufactures, Antiquities, etc.—Requisites for the Journey—Cost—Official Notification to Travellers—Useful Hints—Routes, Gujrat and Pir Panjal—Jhelum, Tangrot and Kotli Poonch—Rawal Pindi and Murree—The New Road—Husan Abbal, Abbottabad, the Jhelum—The Kishengunga Valley—Eastern Portion of Kashmir—Leh—Western Portion of Kashmir—Woolar Lake—Gulmarg—Lolab Valley, Ladak—Pangkong Lake—Gilgit—Astor—Skardu—The Tilaib Valley, &c., and the following—

Maps:—(1) Jammu and Kashmir with adjoining countries. (2) Map showing Routes to Skardu, etc. (3) Map showing Leh to Himis Monastery, Salt Lake Valley, Pangkong Lake, Kamri Pass, Burail Pass. (4) Astor and Gilgit with surrounding country. *The Maps are finely executed by the Survey of India Dept.*

RAWAL PINDI TO SRINAGAR.—A Detailed Account of the New Jhelum Valley Road; together with a Brief Note of five other Routes leading into the Valley. Being an Appendix to Ince's Handbook to Kashmir. Re. 1-8.

FROM SIMLA TO SHIPKI IN CHINESE THIBET.—An Itinerary of the Roads and various minor Routes, with a few Hints to Travellers, and Sketch Map. By Major W. F. Gordon-Forbes, Rifle Brigade. Fcap. 8vo, cloth. Rs. 2.

Itineraries—Simla to Shipki, 'Charling' Pass, 'Sarahan to Narkunda' Forest Road, Simla to the 'Chor,' Pooi to Dankar, Chini to Landour, and the 'Shalle.'

HANDBOOK FOR VISITORS TO AGRA AND ITS NEIGHBOURHOOD. By H. G. Keene, c.s. Fifth Edition, Revised. Maps, Plans, &c. Fcap. 8vo, cloth. Rs. 2-8.

A HANDBOOK FOR VISITORS TO DELHI AND ITS NEIGHBOURHOOD. By H. G. Keene, c.s. Third Edition. Maps. Fcap. 8vo, cloth. Rs. 2-8.

HILLS BEYOND SIMLA.—Three Months' Tour from Simla, through Bussahir, Kunowar, and Spiti to Lahoul. ("In the Footsteps of the Few.") By Mrs. J. C. Murray-Aynsley. Crown 8vo, cloth. Rs. 3.

THACKER, SPINK AND CO., CALCUTTA.

THACKER'S GUIDE TO DARJEELING.—With two Maps. Fcap. 8vo, sewed. Rs. 2.

THE 4-ANNA RAILWAY GUIDE.—With Maps. Published monthly. 4 annas.

THACKER'S GUIDE TO CALCUTTA.—WITH CHAPTERS ON ITS BY-PATHS, etc., and a chapter on the Government of India, and Maps of the European Residence Portion and Official and Business Portion of the City. Fcap. 8vo, cloth. Rs. 3.

CALCUTTA TO LIVERPOOL, BY CHINA, JAPAN, AND AMERICA, IN 1877. By Lieut.-General Sir HENRY-NORMAN. Second Edition. Fcap. 8vo, cloth. Rs. 2-8.

GUIDE TO MASURI, LANDAUR, DEHRA DUN, AND THE HILLS NORTH OF DEHRA; including Routes to the Snows and other places of note; with Chapter on Garhwa (Tehri), Hardwar, Rurki, and Chakrata. By JOHN NORTHAM. Rs. 2-8.

THE SPORTSMAN'S MANUAL.—IN QUEST OF GAME IN KULLU, Lahoul, and Ladak to the Tso Morari Lake, with Notes on Shooting in Spiti, Bara Bagahal, Chamba, and Kashmir, and a detailed description of Sport in more than 100 Nalas. With nine Maps. By Lt.-Col. R. H. TYACKE, late H. M.'s 98th & 34th Regts. Fcap. 8vo, cloth. Rs. 3-8.

FROM THE CITY OF PALACES TO ULTIMA THULE.—With a Map of Iceland, Icelandic Vocabulary, Money Tables, &c. By H. K. GORDON. Crown 8vo, sewed. Re. 1.

THACKER'S INDIAN DIRECTORIES AND MAPS.

MAP OF THE CIVIL DIVISIONS OF INDIA.—Including Governments, Divisions and Districts, Political Agencies, and Native States; also the Cities and Towns with 10,000 Inhabitants and upwards. Coloured. 20 in. × 36 in. Folded, Re. 1. On linen, Rs. 2.

CALCUTTA.—PLANS OF THE OFFICIAL AND BUSINESS PORTION, with houses numbered, and Index of Government Offices and Houses of Business on the Map. Plan of the Residence portion of Calcutta with houses numbered so that their position may easily be found. Two maps in pocket case. The maps are on a large scale. As. 12.

THACKER, SPINK AND CO., CALCUTTA.

1893.—THACKER'S INDIAN DIRECTORY.—Official, Legal, Educational, Professional, and Commercial Directories of the whole of India. General Information; Holidays, &c.; Stamp Duties, Customs Tariff, Tonnage Schedules; Post Offices in India, forming a Gazetteer; List of Governors-General and Administrators of India from beginning of British Rule; Orders of the Star of India, Indian Empire, &c.; Warrant of Precedence, Table of Salutes, &c.; The Civil Service of India; An Army List of the Three Presidencies; A Railway Directory; A Newspaper and Periodical Directory; A Conveyance Directory; Tea, Indigo, Silk, and Coffee Concerns; List of Clubs in India; Alphabetical List of Residents. In thick Royal Octavo. With a Railway Map of India. A Map of the Official and Business portion of Calcutta and a Map of the European Residence Portion of Calcutta. Rs. 20.

A COMPLETE LIST OF INDIAN AND CEYLON TEA GARDENS, Indigo Concerns, Silk Filatures, Sugar Factories, Cinchona Concerns, and Coffee Estates. With their Capital, Directors, Proprietors, Agents, Managers, Assistants, &c., and their Factory Marks by which the Chests may be identified in the Market. [1893] Rs. 2-8.

THACKER'S MAP OF INDIA, WITH INSET PHYSICAL MAPS, SKETCH PLANS of Calcutta, Bombay, and Madras. Edited by J. G. BARTHOLOMEW. Corrected to present date. With Railways, Political Changes, and an Index of 10,000 Names, being every place mentioned in "Hunter's Imperial Gazetteer." In book form, Rs. 5; mounted on rollers, varnished, with Index, Rs. 8.

"An excellent map."—*Glasgow Herald.*

"This is a really splendid map of India, produced with the greatest skill and care."—*Army and Navy Gazette.*

"For compactness and completeness of information few works surpassing or approaching it have been seen in cartography."—*Scotsman.*

NATURAL HISTORY, BOTANY, ETC.

THE FUTURE OF THE DATE PALM IN INDIA (PHŒNIX DACTYLIPTERA). By E. BONAVIA, M.D., Brigade-Surgeon, Indian Medical Department. Crown 8vo, cloth. Rs. 2-8.

GAME, SHORE, AND WATER BIRDS OF INDIA.—BY COL. A. LE MESSURIER, R.E. A *vade mecum* for Sportsmen. With 121 Illustrations. 8vo. Rs. 10.

THACKER, SPINK AND CO., CALCUTTA.

HANDBOOK TO THE FERNS OF INDIA, CEYLON, AND THE MALAY
PENINSULA. By Colonel R. H. BEDDOME, author of the "Ferns of British India." With 300 Illustrations by the author. Imp. 16mo. Rs. 10.

"A most valuable work of reference."—*Garden.*

"It is the first special book of portable size and moderate price which has been devoted to Indian Ferns, and is in every way deserving."—*Nature.*

SUPPLEMENT TO THE FERNS OF BRITISH INDIA, CEYLON AND THE
MALAY PENINSULA, containing Ferns which have been discovered since the publication of the "Handbook to the Ferns of British India," &c. By Col. R. H. BEDDOME, F.L.S. Crown 8vo, sewed. Rs. 2-12.

GOLD, COPPER, AND LEAD IN CHOTA-NAGPORE.—COMPILED BY W. KING, D. SC., Director of the Geological Survey of India, and T. A. POPE, Deputy Superintendent, Survey of India. With Map showing the Geological Formation and the Areas taken up by the Various Prospecting and Mining Companies. Crown 8vo, cloth. Rs. 5.

ON INDIGO MANUFACTURE.—A PRACTICAL AND THEORETICAL GUIDE to the Production of the Dye. With numerous Illustrative Experiments. By J. BRIDGES LEE, M.A., F.G.S. Crown 8vo, cloth. Rs. 4.

"The book is thoroughly practical, and is as free from technicalities as such a work can well be, and it gives as much information as could well be imparted in so small a compass."—*Indian Daily News.*

"Instructive and useful alike to planter and proprietor . . . A very clear and undoubtedly valuable treatise for the use of practical planters, and one which every planter would do well to have always at hand during his manufacturing season. For the rest, a planter has only to open the book for it to commend itself to him."—*Pioneer.*

MANUAL OF AGRICULTURE FOR INDIA.—BY LIEUT. FREDERICK POGSON. Illustrated. Crown 8vo, cloth, gilt. Rs. 5.

THE CULTURE AND MANUFACTURE OF INDIGO.—With a Description of a Planter's Life and Resources. By WALTER MACLAGAN REID. Crown 8vo. With 19 full-page Illustrations. Rs. 5.

"It is proposed in the following Sketches of Indigo Life in Tirhoot and Lower Bengal to give those who have never witnessed the manufacture of Indigo, or seen an Indigo Factory in this country, an idea of how the finished marketable article is produced: together with other phases and incidents of an Indigo Planter's life, such as may be interesting and amusing to friends at home."—*Introduction.*

ROXBURGH'S FLORA INDICA; OR, DESCRIPTION OF INDIAN PLANTS.
Reprinted *litteratim* from Cary's Edition. 8vo, cloth. Rs. 5.

THACKER, SPINK AND CO., CALCUTTA.

A NATURAL HISTORY OF THE MAMMALIA OF INDIA, BURMAH AND CEYLON. By R. A. STERNDALE, F.R.G.S., F.Z.S., &c., author of "Seonee," "The Denizens of the Jungle." With 170 Illustrations by the author and others. Imp. 16mo. Rs. 10.

"The very model of what a popular natural history should be."—*Knowledge*.

"The book will, no doubt, be specially useful to the sportsman, and, indeed, has been extended so as to include all territories likely to be reached by the sportsman from India."—*The Times*.

A TEA PLANTER'S LIFE IN ASSAM.—By GEORGE M. BARKER. With 75 Illustrations by the author. Crown 8vo. Rs. 6-8.

"Mr. Barker has supplied us with a very good and readable description accompanied by numerous illustrations drawn by himself. What may be called the business parts of the book are of most value"—*Contemporary Review*.

"Cheery, well-written little book."—*Graphic*.

"A very interesting and amusing book, artistically illustrated from sketches drawn by the author."—*Mark Lane Express*.

A TEXT-BOOK OF INDIAN BOTANY: MORPHOLOGICAL, PHYSIOLOGICAL, and SYSTEMATIC. By W. H. GREGG, B.M.S., Lecturer on Botany at the Hugli Government College. Profusely Illustrated. Crown 8vo. Rs. 5.

THE INLAND EMIGRATION ACT, AS AMENDED BY ACT VII OF 1893, The Health Act; Sanitation of Emigrants; The Artificer's Act; Land Rules of Assam, etc. Crown 8vo, cloth. Rs. 2.

ENGINEERING, SURVEYING, ETC.

STATISTICS OF HYDRAULIC WORKS, AND HYDROLOGY OF ENGLAND, CANADA, EGYPT, AND INDIA. Collected and reduced by LOWIS D'A. JACKSON, C.E. Royal 8vo. Rs. 10.

PERMANENT WAY POCKET-BOOK.—CONTAINING COMPLETE FORMULÆ for Laying Points, Crossings, Cross-Over Roads, Through Roads, Diversions, Curves, etc., suitable for any Gauge. With Illustrations. By T. W. JONES. Pocket-Book Form, cloth. Rs. 3.

THE INDIAN ENGINEER.—Published weekly. Subscription Rs 20 yearly.

A HAND-BOOK OF PRACTICAL SURVEYING FOR INDIA.—Illustrated with Plans, Diagrams, etc. Fourth Edition, Revised. By F. W. KELLY, late of the Indian Survey. With 24 Plates. 8vo. Rs. 8.

THACKER, SPINK AND CO., CALCUTTA.

IRRIGATED INDIA.—AN AUSTRALIAN VIEW OF INDIA AND CEYLON, their Irrigation and Agriculture. By the Hon. ALFRED DEAKIN, M.L.A., formerly Chief Secretary and Minister of Water-Supply of Victoria, Australia. With a Map. 8vo, cloth. Rs. 7-8.

CONTENTS:—Introduction—India and Australia—The British in India—The Native Population—Physical and Political Divisions—Ceylon—Madras—Lower Bengal—Bombay—The Independent States—The North-West Provinces and the Punjab—The Agriculture of India—Indian Wheat and Australian Trade—Irrigation Generally—The Kaveri Scheme—Ekruk and Khadabvasla—Powai, Vehar and Tansa—The Ganges Canal System—The Bari Doab Canal—The Sirhind Canal—Indian Irrigation.

APPENDICES:—Irrigation in Ceylon—Irrigation in Madras—Madras Company's Canal—Irrigation in Bombay—Irrigation in Lower Bengal—Irrigation in the North-West Provinces—Irrigation in the Punjab.

"I think that I may again with profit refer to Mr. Deakin's Book on Irrigated India, the perusal of which I am glad to have this opportunity of recommending to the attention of those who are interested in the welfare of this country."—*C. W. Odling*, M.R., *in a Lecture on Irrigation Canals, delivered at Sibpur.*

"He approaches Indian problems with an Australian freshness of view and frankness of comment that are often singularly suggestive."—*Times.*

"Contains a masterly account of the great gift of the English to India—the irrigation works."—*Manchester Guardian.*

"It is the work of an observer of no ordinary capacity and fitness for the work of observing and describing."—*Scotsman.*

AN EXPLANATION OF QUADRUPLEX TELEGRAPHY.—With 12 Diagrams. By BEN. J. STOW, Telegraph Master. Fcap. 4to. Rs. 2.

AN EXPLANATION ON DUPLEX, QUADRUPLEX, OPEN AND TRANSLATION WORKING AND OTHER CIRCUITS.—Testing of Currents, Batteries, Instruments, Earths, and Line, with the Tangent Galvanometer. With 12 Plates. By E. H. NELTHROPP, Telegraph Master. Crown 8vo, sewed. Rs. 2.

MANUAL OF SURVEYING FOR INDIA.—DETAILING THE MODE OF operations on the Trigonometrical, Topographical, and Revenue Surveys of India. By Col. H. L. THUILLIER and Lieut.-Col. H. SMYTH. Third Edition, Revised and Enlarged. Royal 8vo, cloth. Rs. 12.

COLEBROOKE'S TRANSLATION OF THE LILAVATI.—With Notes. By HARAN CHANDRA BANERJI, M.A., B.L. 8vo, cloth. Rs. 4.

This edition includes the Text in Sanskrit. The Lilavati is a standard work on Hindu mathematics written by Bháskaráchárya, a celebrated mathematician of the twelfth century.

THACKER, SPINK AND CO., CALCUTTA.

A HAND-BOOK OF PHOTOGRAPHY.—WRITTEN ESPECIALLY FOR INDIA. By GEORGE EWING, Honorary Treasurer of the Photographic Society of India. [*In the Press.*

THE PHOTOGRAPHER'S POCKET-BOOK.—A Compilation of all Information regarding Photography in a small handy form. [*In the Press.*

THE JOURNAL OF THE PHOTOGRAPHIC SOCIETY.—Published monthly. With Illustrations. Subscription Rs. 5 yearly.

MILITARY WORKS.

THE RECONNOITRER'S GUIDE AND FIELD BOOK.—ADAPTED FOR INDIA. By Major M. J. KING-HARMAN, B.S.C. Second Edition, Revised and Enlarged. In roan. Rs. 4.

It contains all that is required for the guidance of the Military Reconnoitrer in India: it can be used as an ordinary Pocket Note Book, or as a Field Message Book; the pages are ruled as a Field Book, and in sections, for written description or sketch.

The book has been highly approved by Lord Roberts, who regards it as a most valuable and practical composition.

"To Officers serving in India the Guide will be invaluable."—*Broad Arrow.*

"It appears to contain all that is absolutely required by the Military Reconnoitrer in India, and will thus dispense with many bulky works. In fact it contains just what is wanted and nothing not likely to be wanted."—*Naval and Military Gazette.*

"It has been found invaluable to many a Staff Officer and Commandant of a Regiment, as well as of the greatest possible assistance to officers studying for the Garrison Course Examination. The book will go into the breast pocket of a regulation khaki jacket, and can therefore always fulfil the office of a *vademecum*."—*Madras Mail.*

INDIAN MOUNTED VOLUNTEERS' GUIDE TO EQUITATION AND THE TRAINING OF HORSES. Compiled from Regulations. By Troop Sergeant Major J. P. BURKE. Re. 1.

THE QUARTERMASTER'S ALMANAC.—A DIARY OF THE DUTIES, with other information. By Lieut. HARRINGTON BUSH. 8vo. Re. 1-8.

MUSKETRY INSTRUCTION IN THE FORM OF QUESTIONS & ANSWERS. By Capt. L. E. DU MOULIN. Fcap. 8vo. Rs. 2.

REGIMENTAL RECORDS OF THE BENGAL ARMY (uniform with above). Edited by Lt. F. G. CARDEW, 10th Beng. Lancers. [*In prepn.*

BENGAL CAVALRY. One Volume. | BENGAL INFANTRY. Two Volumes.
THE PUNJAB FRONTIER FORCE. One Volume.

THACKER, SPINK AND CO., CALCUTTA.

A SKETCH OF THE SERVICES OF THE BENGAL NATIVE ARMY.
Compiled in the Office of the Adjutant-General by Lieut. F. G. CARDEW, 10th Bengal Lancers, and published under the Instructions of the Govt. of India. With 8 Coloured Illustrations. Royal 8vo. Rs. 2-8. [*Nearly ready.*

LETTERS ON TACTICS AND ORGANIZATION.—BY CAPT. F. N. MAUDE, R.E. (Papers reprinted from the *Pioneer* and *Civil and Military Gazette.*) Crown 8vo, cloth. Rs. 5.

"The author displays considerable knowledge of the subjects with which he deals, and has evidently thought much on them. His views are broad and advanced."—"Every soldier should read this book."—*Athenæum.*

"On the whole, Captain Maude may be most warmly congratulated upon the production of a book, of which, disagreeing as we do with some of his conclusions, we are glad to speak, as it deserves, in terms of the most unstinted and ungrudging praise."—*Whitehall Review.*

THE TRAINING AND MANAGEMENT OF CHARGERS.—BY G. W. KING, Lieut., Ghazipur Light Horse. Cloth. Re. 1-8.

THE INVASION AND DEFENCE OF ENGLAND.—BY CAPT. F. N. MAUDE, R.E. Crown 8vo, cloth. Re. 1-8.

"This little book only deals with the case of possible invasion by France, but it is one of the best we have read on the subject, and will well repay perusal."—*Allen's Indian Mail.*

"His little book is a useful and interesting contribution to the invasion of England question; it contains a good deal of information, and, without being written in an alarmist style, exposes very clearly the danger in which England stands."—*Englishman.*

"The lay reader will welcome as an able, thoughtful, and original contribution to a topic of unsurpassable importance."—*Home News.*

"The book is ably written, and is full of suggestive matter of the highest importance to the security of the country."—*Glasgow Herald.*

NOTES FOR OFFICERS QUALIFYING FOR THE TRANSPORT DEPARTMENT in India. By Lieut. P. R. MOCKLER. 32mo, cloth. Re. 1.

THE SEPOY OFFICER'S MANUAL.—Second Edition, Revised. By Capt. E. G. BARROW. Rs. 2-8.

"It seems to contain almost everything required in one of the modern type of Civilian Soldiers . . . . In the most interesting part of the book is an account of the composition of the Bengal Army with descriptive note on the Brahmans, Rajputs, Sikhs, Goorkhas, Pathans and other races."—*Englishman.*

"A vast amount of technical and historical data of which no Anglo-Indian Officer should be ignorant."—*Broad Arrow.*

"The notes are brief and well digested, and contain all that it is necessary for a candidate to know."—*Army and Navy Gazette.*

THACKER, SPINK AND CO., CALCUTTA.

MUSKETRY MADE EASY FOR NATIVE OFFICERS AND NON-COMMISSIONED OFFICERS, Native Army. By Lieut. R. E. S. TAYLOR, Adjutant, 28th Bengal Infantry. Arranged in Questions and Answers. English and Urdu. As. 8.

THE INDIAN ARTICLES OF WAR.—ANNOTATED. BY CAPT. H. S. HUDSON, late 27th Madras Infantry. Second Edition. Revised by an Officer of the Indian Staff Corps. Crown 8vo, cloth. Rs. 4.

"Likely to be useful to Examiners."—*Army and Navy Gazette.*
"Complete, intelligible, and attractive."—*Englishman.*
"Extremely useful to those who have to deal with cases rising under the Indian Articles of War."—*Broad Arrow.*

THE INDIAN MESSAGE BOOK.—INTERLEAVED FOR KEEPING COPIES. With 12 Authorised Pattern Envelopes. Each Re. 1-4.

NOTES ON THE COURSE OF GARRISON INSTRUCTION, TACTICS, Topography, Fortifications, condensed from the Text-Books, with explanations and additional matter. With Diagrams. By Major E. LLOYD, Garrison Instructor. Crown 8vo, cloth. Rs. 2-8.

LECTURES DELIVERED TO TRANSPORT CLASSES.—A complete Epitome of Transport Duties and Veterinary for use in Classes and for Ready Reference in the Field. By a Deputy Assistant Commissary-General. *[In the Press.*

LEE-METFORD MUSKETRY REGULATIONS.—ALTERATIONS AND ADDITIONS to the 1892 Regulations, in accordance with Army Order 238, December 1892. Printed only on one side of the paper. As. 6.

THE IMAGE OF WAR; OR, SERVICE ON THE CHIN HILLS.—With Introductory Notes. By J. D. MAXWELL, B.SC. Illustrated by about 140 full-plate Phototints and Illustrations in the Text. *[In the Press.*

HINDUSTANI, PERSIAN, ETC.

GLOSSARY OF MEDICAL AND MEDICO-LEGAL TERMS, including those most frequently met with in the Law Courts. By R. F. HUTCHISON, M.D., Surgeon-Major. Second Edition. Fcap. 8vo, cloth. Rs. 2.

HIDAYAT AL HUKUMA.—A GUIDE TO MEDICAL OFFICERS AND SUBORDINATES of the Indian Service. English and Hindustani. By GEO. S. RANKING, M.D., Surgeon-Major. 18mo, sewed. Re. 1-4.

THACKER, SPINK AND CO., CALCUTTA.

THE DIVAN-I-HAFIZ.—The Divan written in the fourteenth century by Khwaja-Shame-ud-din Mohammad-i-Hafiz-i-Shirazi, translated for the first time out of the Persian into English Prose, with Critical and Explanatory remarks, with an Introductory Preface, a Note on Sufi'ism, and Life of the author. By Lieut.-Col. H. Wilberforce Clarke, author of "The Persian Manual," translator of "The Bustan-i-Sa'di," "The Sekandar Namah-i-Nizami," etc. 2 vols. 4to. Rs. 25.

THE 'AWARIFU-L-MA'ARIF.—Written in the Thirteenth Century by Shaikh Shahab-ud-din—'Umar bin Muhammad-i-Sahrwardi; translated (out of the Arabic into Persian) by Mamud bin 'Ali al Kashani, Companion in Sufi'ism to the Divan-i-Khwaja Hafiz; translated for the first time (out of the Persian into English) by Lieut.-Col. H. Wilberforce Clarke. 4to. Rs. 13.

HISTORY OF THE SIKHS: or, Translation of the Sikkhan de Raj di Vikhia, as laid down for the Examination in Panjabi, &c., together with a short Gurmukhi Grammar. By Lt.-Col. Major Henry Court. Royal 8vo, cloth. Rs. 8.

THE RUSSIAN CONVERSATION GRAMMAR.—By Alex. Kinloch, late Interpreter to H. B. M. Consulate and British Consul in the Russian Law Courts; Instructor for Official Examinations. Crown 8vo, cloth. Rs. 6-8.

This work is constructed on the excellent system of Otto in his "German Conversation Grammar," with illustrations accompanying every rule, in the form of usual phrases and idioms, thus leading the student by easy but rapid gradations to a colloquial attainment of the language.

VOCABULAIRE FRANCAIS HINDOUSTANI.—Par Dr. C. Rougier, Médecin de la Cie, Messageries Maritimes, et le Dr. Garnon, Medecin de 1-ere Classe de la Marine. [*In the Press.*

TRANSLATIONS INTO PERSIAN.—Selections from *Murray's History of India, Foliorum Centuria—Gibbon's Roman Empire—Our Faithful Ally the Nizam.* By Major A. C. Talbot. Part I, English. Part II, Persian. 2 vols. 8vo. Rs. 10.

UTTARA RAMA CHARITA.—A Sanskrit Drama. By Bhavabhuti. Translated into English Prose by C. H. Tawney, M.A. Second Edition. Adapted to Pundit I. C. Vidyasagara's edition of the Text. 8vo, sewed. Re. 1-8.

THACKER, SPINK AND CO., CALCUTTA.

A GUIDE TO HINDUSTANI (Talim-i-Zaban-i-Urdu). Specially designed for the use of students and men serving in India. By Surgeon-Major Geo. S. Ranking, Offg. Secretary to the Board of Examiners, Fort William. Second Edition. 8vo, cloth. Rs. 6.

Printed throughout in Persian character. With *fac-simile* MS. Exercises, Petitions, &c.

"The work on the whole, we believe, will meet a want. . . . . . It contains an excellent list of technical military terms and idioms, and will prove especially serviceable to any one who has to act as an interpreter at courts-martial and cognate enquiries."—*Civil and Military Gazette.*

"There can be no question as to the practical utility of the book."—*Pioneer.*

"Surgeon-Major Ranking has undoubtedly rendered good service to the many military men for whom knowledge of Hindustani is essential."—*Athenæum.*

"Has the merit of conciseness and portability, and the selections at the end, of the historical and colloquial style, are well chosen."—*Saturday Review.*

"A well-conceived book, and has much useful matter in it. The sentences are very good, practical and idiomatic."—*Homeward Mail.*

"Supplies a want long felt, by none more than by young Medical Officers of the Army of India. We think the work admirably adapted for its purpose."—*British Medical Journal.*

MALAVIKAGNIMITRA.—A Sanskrit Play by Kalidasa. Literally translated into English Prose by C. H. Tawney, m.a., Principal, Presidency College, Calcutta. Second Edition. Crown 8vo. Re. 1-8.

TWO CENTURIES OF BHARTRIHARI.—Translated into English Verse by C. H. Tawney, m.a. Fcap. 8vo, cloth. Rs. 2.

HINDUSTANI AS IT OUGHT TO BE SPOKEN.—By J. Tweedie, Bengal Civil Service. Second Edition. Crown 8vo, pp. xvi, 350, cloth. Rs. 4-8.

Supplement containing Key to the Exercises and Translation of the Reader with Notes. Rs. 2.

The work has been thoroughly Revised and partly Re-Written, and much additional matter added. The Vocabularies have been improved, and all words used in the book have been embodied in the Glossaries, English-Hindustani—Hindustani-English. A Reader is also given, and a General Index to the whole book.

"The Young Civilian or Officer, reading for his Examination, could not do better than master this Revised Edition from cover to cover."—*I. Daily News.*

"The book is divided into twelve easy lessons, and there is nothing to prevent the most khansamah-worried *mem-saheb* from mastering one of these a day. At the end of a fortnight she will have acquired a small useful vocabulary, and should be quite certain how to use the words she knows."—*Englishman.*

THACKER, SPINK AND CO., CALCUTTA.

BOOK-KEEPING AND OFFICE MANUALS.

A GUIDE TO BOOK-KEEPING.—By Single, Mixed and Double Entries. Commercial Accounts of the most intricate nature fully illustrated by Examples and Annotations; Answers to Examination Questions on Book-Keeping, for Promotion to Assistant Examiner (1st grade) and to Accountant (2nd grade), from 1880 to 1891. By S. George, late Chief Accountant, P. W. D., Bengal. Demy 8vo, cloth. Rs. 2-8.

PHONOGRAPHY IN BENGALI.—By Dwijendra Nath Shinghaw, Professor of Phonography in Calcutta. Being a Handbook for the study of Shorthand on the principle of Pitman's System. 12mo. As. 8. With a Key. 12mo. As. 4 extra.

THE INDIAN SERVICE MANUAL; or, Guide to the Several Departments of the Government of India, containing the Rules for Admission, Notes on the working of each Department, &c. By C. R. Hardless, author of "The Clerk's Manual."

SPENS' THE INDIAN READY RECKONER.—Containing Tables for ascertaining the value of any number of articles, &c., from three pies to five rupees; also Tables of Wages from four annas to twenty-five rupees. By Captain A. T. Spens. Re. 1-8.

THE INDIAN LETTER-WRITER.—Containing an Introduction on Letter Writing, with numerous Examples in the various styles of Correspondence. By H. Anderson. Crown 8vo, cloth. Re. 1.

THE CLERK'S MANUAL.—A Complete Guide to General Office Routine (Government and Business). By Charles R. Hardless. Second Edition, Revised. 12mo, boards. Rs. 2.

RICARDO'S EXCHANGE REMEDY.—A Prosposal to Regulate the Rupee Currency by making it expand and contract automatically at fixed sterling rates, with the aid of the silver clause of the English Bank Act. By A. M. L., Fellow of the Bankers' Institute. 8vo, sewed. As. 8.

INDIAN WAGES TABLES.—Calculated for months of 28 to 31 working days at rates from 2 to 18 rupees per month, giving the calculation at Sight for 1 to 1,000 days from 2 to 8½ rupees per month and to 20,000 days by one addition: and for 1 to 300 days from 9 to 18 rupees per month. Also 3 Tables of Sirdaree for those who require them. By G. G. Playfair, Secretary of the Lebong Tea Co., Limited, and formerly one of the Brahmaputra Tea Co., Ld. [*In the Press.*

THACKER, SPINK AND CO., CALCUTTA.

EDUCATIONAL BOOKS.

HINTS ON THE STUDY OF ENGLISH.—By F. J. Rowe, M.A., and W. T. Webb, M.A., Professors of English Literature, Presidency College, Calcutta. New Edition. With an additional chapter on the Structure and Analysis of Sentences, and Exercises on the correction of mistakes commonly made by Students. Crown 8vo, cloth. Rs. 2-8.

AN EASY ENGLISH GRAMMAR FOR SCHOOLS IN INDIA.—Containing numerous Exercises in Idiom. By F. J. Rowe, M.A., and W. T. Webb, M.A., authors of "Hints on the Study of English." [*In the Press.*

A COMPANION READER TO "HINTS ON THE STUDY OF ENGLISH." (Eighteenth Thousand.) Demy 8vo. Re. 1-4.

A KEY TO THE COMPANION READER TO "HINTS ON THE STUDY OF ENGLISH." With an Appendix, containing Test Examination Questions By F. J. Rowe, M.A. Fcap. 8vo. Rs. 2.

ENTRANCE TEST EXAMINATION QUESTIONS AND ANSWERS in English, being the Questions appended to "Hints on the Study of English," with their Answers, together with Fifty Supplementary Questions and Answers. By W. T. Webb, M.A. 12mo, sewed. Re. 1.

PRINCIPAL EVENTS IN INDIAN AND BRITISH HISTORY.—With their Dates in Suggestive Sentences. In Two Parts. By Miss Adams, La Martinière College for Girls, Calcutta. Second Edition. Demy 8vo boards. Re. 1.

HISTORY OF INDIA FOR BEGINNERS.—By Moulvie Abdul Karim, B.A., Assistant Inspector of Schools. Fcap. 8vo, sewed. As. 12.

ELEMENTARY STATICS AND DYNAMICS.—By W. N. Boutflower, B.A., late Scholar of St. John's College, Cambridge, and Professor of Mathematics, Muir Central College, Allahabad. Second Edition. Crown 8vo. Rs. 3-8.

THE STUDENT'S HANDBOOK TO HAMILTON AND MILL.—By W. Bell, M.A., Professor of Philosophy and Logic, Government College Lahore. 8vo, boards. Rs. 2.

ELEMENTARY HYDROSTATICS.—With numerous Examples and University Papers. By S. B. Mukerjee, M.A., B.L., Assistant Professor, Government College, Lahore. 12mo, cloth. Re. 1-8.

THACKER, SPINK AND CO., CALCUTTA.

ENGLISH SELECTIONS APPOINTED BY THE SYNDICATE OF THE CAL-
CUTTA UNIVERSITY for the Entrance Examination. Crown 8vo, cloth.
Re. 1-8.

WEBB'S KEY TO THE ENTRANCE COURSE.—1894 and 1895. *Each* Rs. 2.

THE LAWS OF WEALTH.—A PRIMER ON POLITICAL ECONOMY FOR
THE MIDDLE CLASSES IN INDIA. By HORACE BELL, C.E. Seventh
Thousand. Fcap. 8vo. As. 8.

THE INDIAN LETTER-WRITER.—CONTAINING AN INTRODUCTION ON
LETTER WRITING, with numerous Examples in the various styles of Correspondence. By H. ANDERSON. Crown 8vo, cloth. Re. 1.

A CATECHISM ON THE RUDIMENTS OF MUSIC.—SIMPLIFIED FOR
BEGINNERS. By I. LITTLEPAGE. 12mo, sewed. Re. 1.

CALCUTTA UNIVERSITY CALENDAR FOR THE YEAR 1893.—Containing Acts, Bye-Laws, Regulations, The University Rules for Examination, Text-Book Endowments, Affiliated Institutions, List of Graduates
and Under-Graduates, Examination Papers, 1892. Cloth. Rs. 5.
CALENDAR for previous years. *Each* Rs. 5.

CALCUTTA UNIVERSITY CALENDAR.—THE EXAMINATION PAPERS,
1890 and 1891. Cloth. *Each* Re. 1-8.

FIFTY GRADUATED PAPERS IN ARITHMETIC, ALGEBRA, AND GEO-
METRY for the use of Students preparing for the Entrance Examinations
of the Indian Universities. With Hints on Methods of Shortening Work
and on the Writing of Examination Papers. By W. H. WOOD, B.A.,
F.C.S., Principal, La Martinière College. Re. 1-8.

THE PRINCIPLES OF HEAT.—FOR THE F. A. EXAMINATION of the
Calcutta University. By LEONARD HALL, M.A. Crown 8vo. As. 8.

ANALYSIS OF REID'S ENQUIRY INTO THE HUMAN MIND.—With
Copious Notes. By W. C. FINK. Second Edition. Re. 1-12.

THE ENGLISH PEOPLE AND THEIR LANGUAGE.—Translated from
the German of Loth by C. H. TAWNEY, M.A., Professor in the Presidency College, Calcutta. Stitched. As. 8.

TALES FROM INDIAN HISTORY.—BEING THE ANNALS OF INDIA
retold in Narratives. By J. TALBOYS WHEELER. Crown 8vo, cloth.
School Edition. Re. 1-8.

A NOTE ON THE DEVANAGARI ALPHABET FOR BENGALI STUDENTS.
By GURU DAS BANERJEE, M.A., D.L. Crown 8vo. As. 4.

THACKER, SPINK AND CO., CALCUTTA.

THE GOVERNMENT OF INDIA.—A PRIMER FOR INDIAN SCHOOLS.
By HORACE BELL, C.E. Third Edition. Fcap. 8vo, sewed, As. 8; in cloth, Re. 1.

Translated into Bengali. By J. N. BHATTACHARJEE. 8vo. As. 12.

AN INQUIRY INTO THE HUMAN MIND ON THE PRINCIPLES OF COMMON SENSE. By THOMAS REID, D.D. 8vo, cloth. Re. 1-4.

A TEXT-BOOK OF INDIAN BOTANY: MORPHOLOGICAL, PHYSIOLOGICAL, and SYSTEMATIC. By W. H. GREGG, B.M.S., Lecturer on Botany at Hugli Government College. Profusely Illustrated. Crown 8vo. Rs. 5.

A MORAL READING BOOK FROM ENGLISH AND ORIENTAL SOURCES. By ROPER LETHBRIDGE, C.I.E., M.A. Crown 8vo, cloth. As. 14.

A PRIMER CATECHISM OF SANITATION FOR INDIAN SCHOOLS.— Founded on Dr. Cunningham's Sanitary Primer. By L. A. STAPLEY. Second Edition. As. 4.

NOTES ON MILL'S EXAMINATION OF HAMILTON'S PHILOSOPHY. By THOMAS EDWARDS, F.E.I.S. Fcap., sewed. Re. 1.

A SHORT HISTORY OF THE ENGLISH LANGUAGE.—By THOMAS EDWARDS, F.E.I.S. 18mo. Re. 1-4.

LAMB'S TALES FROM SHAKESPEARE.—AN EDITION IN GOOD TYPE. Cloth. As. 1

LAND TENURES AND LAND REVENUE.

AZIZUDDIN AHMED.—THE N.-W. PROVINCES LAND REVENUE ACT. Being Act XIX of 1873 as amended by Acts I and VIII of 1879, XII of 1881, XIII and XIV of 1882, XX of 1890, and XII of 1891. With Notes, Government Orders, Board Circulars and Decisions, and Rulings of the Allahabad High Court. By AZIZUDDIN AHMED, Deputy Collector and Magistrate. Demy 8vo, cloth. Rs. 8.

FINUCANE AND RAMPINI.—THE BENGAL TENANCY ACT.—Being Act VIII of 1885. With Notes and Annotations, Judicial Rulings and the Rules framed by the Local Government and the High Court under the Act, for the guidance of Revenue Officers and the Civil Courts. By R. F. RAMPINI, M.A., C.S., Barrister-at-Law, and M. FINUCANE, M.A., C.S. Second Edition. Rs. 7.

THACKER SPINK AND CO., CALCUTTA.

BEVERLEY.—THE LAND ACQUISITION ACTS (Acts X of 1870 and XVIII of 1885). With Introduction and Notes. The whole forming a complete Manual of Law and Practice on the subject of Compensation for Lands taken for Public Purposes. Applicable to all India. By H. BEVERLEY, M.A., B.C.S. Second Edition. 8vo, cloth. Rs. 6.

FORSYTH.—REVENUE SALE-LAW OF LOWER BENGAL, comprising Act XI of 1859; Bengal Act VII of 1868; Bengal Act VII of 1880 (Public Demands Recovery Act), and the unrepealed Regulations and the Rules of the Board of Revenue on the subject. With Notes. Edited by WM. E. H. FORSYTH. Demy 8vo, cloth. Rs. 5.

PHILLIPS.—MANUAL OF REVENUE AND COLLECTORATE LAW. With Important Rulings and Annotations. By H. A. D. PHILLIPS, Bengal Civil Service. Crown 8vo, cloth. [1884] Rs. 10.

CONTENTS:—Alluvion and Diluvion, Certificate, Cesses, Road and Public Works, Collectors, Assistant Collectors, Drainage, Embankment, Evidence, Excise, Lakhiraj Grants and Service Tenures, and Land Acquisition, Land Registration, Legal Practitioners, License Tax, Limitation, Opium, Partition, Public Demands Recovery, Purni Sales, Registration, Revenue Sales, Salt, Settlement, Stamps, Survey and Wards.

REYNOLDS.—THE NORTH-WESTERN PROVINCES RENT ACT.— With Notes, &c. By H. W. REYNOLDS, C.S. Demy 8vo. [1886] Rs. 7.

FIELD.—LANDHOLDING, AND THE RELATION OF LANDLORD AND TENANT in various countries of the world. By C. D. FIELD, M.A., LL.D. Second Edition. 8vo, cloth. Rs. 16.

N.B.—This edition contains "The Bengal Tenancy Act, 1885," with Notes and Observations: and an Index to the whole of the Law of Landlord and Tenant in Bengal.

"We may take it that, as regards Indian laws and customs, Mr. Field shows himself to be at once an able and skilled authority. In order, however, to render his work more complete, he has compiled, chiefly from Blue-books and similar public sources, a mass of information having reference to the land-laws of most European countries, of the United States of America, and our Australasian colonies."—*Field.*

GRIMLEY.—MANUAL OF THE REVENUE SALE LAW AND CERTIFICATE PROCEDURE of Lower Bengal, including the Acts on the Subject and Selections from the Rules and Circular Orders of the Board of Revenue. With Notes. By W. H. GRIMLEY, B.A., C.S. 8vo. Rs. 5-8; interleaved, Rs. 6.

THACKER, SPINK AND CO., CALCUTTA.

PHILLIPS.—THE LAW RELATING TO THE LAND TENURES OF
LOWER BENGAL. (Tagore Law Lectures, 1875.) By ARTHUR PHILLIPS.
Royal 8vo, cloth. Rs. 10.

REGULATIONS OF THE BENGAL CODE.—A SELECTION intended
chiefly for the use of Candidates for appointments in the Judicial and
Revenue Departments. Royal 8vo, stitched. Rs. 4.

PHILLIPS —OUR ADMINISTRATION OF INDIA.—BEING A COMPLETE
Account of the Revenue and Collectorate Administration in all departments, with special reference to the work and duties of a District Officer in Bengal. By H. A. D. PHILLIPS. Rs. 5.

"In eleven chapters Mr. Phillips gives a complete epitome of the civil, in distinction from the criminal, duties of an Indian Collector."—*London Quarterly Review.*

WHISH.—A DISTRICT OFFICE IN NORTHERN INDIA.—With some
suggestions on Administration. By C. W. WHISH, B.C.S. Demy 8vo, cloth. Rs. 4.

"Mr. Whish has produced an extremely useful and thoughtful book, which will pave the way for the junior members of his service. It is above all things practical, and sets forth the whole scheme of district duties in a clear and systematic manner."—*Englishman.*

FIELD.—INTRODUCTION TO THE REGULATIONS OF THE BENGAL
CODE. By C. D. FIELD, M.A., LL.D. Crown 8vo. Rs. 3.

CONTENTS: (I) The Acquisition of Territorial Sovereignty by the English in the Presidency of Bengal. (II) The Tenure of Land in the Bengal Presidency. (III) The Administration of the Land Revenue. (IV) The Administration of Justice.

MARKBY.—LECTURES ON INDIAN LAW.—BY WILLIAM MARKBY
M.A. Crown 8vo, cloth. Rs. 3.

CONTENTS: (I) Resumption of Lands held Rent-free. (II) The Revenue Sale Land of the Permanently Settled Districts. (III) Shekust Pywust, or Alluvion and Diluvion. (IV-V) The charge of the Person and Property of Minors. (VI) Of the protection afforded to Purchasers and Mortgagees when their title is impeached. Appendix—The Permanent Settlement—Glossary.

HOUSE.—THE N.-W. PROVINCES RENT ACT.—BEING ACT XII OF
1881, as amended by subsequent Acts. Edited with Introduction, Commentary and Appendices. By H. F. HOUSE, C.S. 8vo, cloth. Rs. 10.

THACKER, SPINK AND CO., CALCUTTA.

CIVIL LAW.

ALEXANDER.—INDIAN CASE-LAW ON TORTS. By the late R. D. Alexander, c.s. An entirely new Edition, Re-written and Enlarged by R. F. Rampini, c.s. 8vo, cloth. Rs. 8.

CHALMERS.—THE NEGOTIABLE INSTRUMENTS ACT, 1881.—Being an Act to define and amend the Law relating to Promissory Notes, Bills of Exchange, and Cheques. Edited by M. D. Chalmers, m.a., Barrister-at-law, author of "A Digest of the Law of Bills of Exchange," &c.; and editor of Wilson's "Judicature Acts." 8vo, cloth.

COLLETT.—THE LAW OF SPECIFIC RELIEF IN INDIA.—Being a Commentary on Act I of 1877. By Charles Collett, late of the Madras Civil Service, of Lincoln's Inn, Barrister-at-Law, and formerly a Judge of the High Court at Madras. Second Edition. [*In the Press.*

KELLEHER.—PRINCIPLES OF SPECIFIC PERFORMANCE AND MISTAKE. By J. Kelleher, c.s. 8vo, cloth. Rs. 8.

"The work is well written, and the rules deduced from the authorities are generally accurately and always clearly expressed. We can therefore recommend the book to all students of English law, not doubting but that they will find it very useful for their purposes."—*Civil and Military Gazette.*

KELLEHER.—MORTGAGE IN THE CIVIL LAW.—Being an outline of the Principles of the Law of Security, followed by the text of the Digest of Justinian, with Translation and Notes; and a translation of the corresponding titles of the Indian Code. By J. Kelleher, b.c.s., author of "Possession in the Civil Law." Royal 8vo. Rs. 10.

KELLEHER.—POSSESSION IN THE CIVIL LAW.—Abridged from the Treatise of Von Savigny, to which is added the Text of the Title on Possession from the Digest. By J. Kelleher, c.s. 8vo, cloth. Rs. 8.

SUTHERLAND.—THE INDIAN CONTRACT ACT (IX of 1872) AND THE SPECIFIC RELIEFS ACT (I of 1877). With a Full Commentary. By D. Sutherland. Second Edition. Royal 8vo, cloth. Rs. 5.

CASPERSZ.—THE LAW OF ESTOPPEL IN INDIA.—Part I, Estoppel by Representation. Part II, Estoppel by Judgment. Being Tagore Law Lectures, 1893. By A. Caspersz, Bar.-at-Law. Royal 8vo, cloth. Rs. 12.

THE INDIAN INSOLVENCY ACT.—Being a Reprint of the Law as to Insolvent Debtors in India, 11 and 12 Vict. Cap. 21 (June 1848). Royal 8vo, sewed. (Uniform with Acts of the Legislative Council.) Re. 1-8.

THACKER, SPINK AND CO., CALCUTTA.

GHOSE.—THE LAW OF MORTGAGE IN INDIA, WITH THE TRANSFER OF PROPERTY ACT AND NOTES. By RASHBEHARI GHOSE, M.A., D.L., Tagore Law Professor, 1876. Second Edition, Revised and Enlarged. New Edition. [In preparation.

RIVAZ.—THE INDIAN LIMITATION ACT.—WITH NOTES. By the Hon'ble H. T. RIVAZ, Barrister-at-Law, Judge of the High Court of the Punjab. Fourth Edition. [In the Press.

SUCCESSION, ADMINISTRATION, ETC.

FORSYTH.—THE PROBATE AND ADMINISTRATION ACT.—Being Act V of 1881. With Notes. By W. E. H. FORSYTH. Edited, with Index, by F. J. COLLINSON. Demy 8vo, cloth. Rs. 5.

HENDERSON.—THE LAW OF INTESTATE AND TESTAMENTARY SUCCESSION IN INDIA; including the Indian Succession Act (X of 1865), with a Commentary; and the Parsee Succession Act (XXI of 1865), the Hindu Wills Act (XXI of 1870), the Probate and Administration Act, &c. With Notes and Cross References. By GILBERT S. HENDERSON, M.A., Barrister-at-Law, and Advocate of the High Court at Calcutta.

HENDERSON.—THE LAW OF TESTAMENTARY DEVISE.—As administered in India, or the Law relating to Wills in India. With an Appendix, containing:—The Indian Succession Act (X of 1865), the Hindu Wills Act (XXI of 1870), the Probate and Administration Act (V of 1881) with all amendments, the Probate Administration Act (VI of 1889), and the Certificate of Succession Act (VII of 1889). By G. S. HENDERSON, M.A., Barrister-at-Law. (Tagore Law Lectures, 1887.) Royal 8vo, cloth. Rs. 16.

CIVIL PROCEDURE, SMALL CAUSE COURT, ETC.

BROUGHTON.—THE CODE OF CIVIL PROCEDURE.—BEING ACT X OF 1877. With Notes and Appendix. By the Hon'ble L. P. DELVES BROUGHTON, assisted by W. F. AGNEW and G. S. HENDERSON. Royal 8vo, cloth. Reduced to Rs. 7.

O'KINEALY.—THE CODE OF CIVIL PROCEDURE (ACT XIV OF 1882). With Notes, Appendices, &c. By the Hon'ble J. O'KINEALY. Fourth Edition. Royal 8vo. Rs. 16.

THACKER, SPINK AND CO., CALCUTTA.

MACEWEN.—THE PRACTICE OF THE PRESIDENCY COURT OF SMALL CAUSES OF CALCUTTA, under the Presidency Small Cause Courts Act (XV of 1882). With Notes and an Appendix. By R. S. T. MAC-EWEN, of Lincoln's Inn, Barrister-at-Law, one of the Judges of the Presidency Court of Small Causes of Calcutta. Thick 8vo. Rs. 10.

RYVES.—PROVINCIAL SMALL CAUSE COURT MANUAL.—BY A. E. RYVES, B.A., Advocate of the High Court, N.-W. P. [*In preparation.*

POCKET CODE OF CIVIL LAW.—CONTAINING THE CIVIL PROCEDURE CODE (Act XIV of 1882), The Court Fees Act (VII of 1870), The Evidence Act (I of 1872), The Specific Reliefs Act (I of 1877), The Registration Act (III of 1877), The Limitation Act (XV of 1877), The Stamp Act (I of 1879). With Supplement containing the Amending Act of 1888, and a General Index. Revised 1891. Fcap. 8vo, cloth. Rs. 4.

LOCAL SELF-GOVERNMENT.

STERNDALE.—MUNICIPAL WORK IN INDIA.—OR, HINTS ON SANITATION, General Conservancy and Improvement in Municipalities, Towns, and Villages. By R. C. STERNDALE. Crown 8vo, cloth. Rs. 3.

COLLIER.—THE BENGAL LOCAL SELF-GOVERNMENT MANUAL.—Being ACT III OF 1885, B. C., and the General Rules framed thereunder. With Notes, Hints regarding Procedure, and References to Leading Cases; an Appendix, containing the principal Acts referred to, &c. &c. By F. R. STANLEY COLLIER, B.C.S. Third Edition, thoroughly revised and brought up to date. Crown 8vo. Rs. 5.

COLLIER.—THE BENGAL MUNICIPAL MANUAL.—BEING B. C. ACT III OF 1884. With Notes and an Appendix containing all the Acts and Rules relating to Municipalities. By F. R. STANLEY COLLIER, C.S. Third Edition. [*In preparation.*

CRIMINAL LAW.

COLLETT.—COMMENTARIES ON THE INDIAN PENAL CODE.—BY CHARLES COLLETT, Barrister-at-Law. 8vo. Rs. 5.

POCKET PENAL, CRIMINAL PROCEDURE, AND POLICE CODES.—Also the Whipping Act and the Railway Servants' Act, being Acts XLV of 1860 (with Amendments), X of 1882, V of 1861, VI of 1864, and XXXI of 1867. With a General Index. Revised 1892. Fcap. 8vo, cloth. Rs. 4.

THACKER, SPINK AND CO., CALCUTTA.

Criminal Law.

AGNEW AND HENDERSON.—THE CODE OF CRIMINAL PROCEDURE (ACT X OF 1882), together with Rulings, Circular Orders, Notifications, &c., of all the High Courts in India, and Notifications and Orders of the Government of India and the Local Governments. Edited, with Copious Notes and Full Index, by W. F. AGNEW, Bar.-at-Law, author of "A Treatise on the Law of Trusts in India"; and GILBERT S. HENDERSON, M.A., Bar.-at-Law, author of "A Treatise on the Law of Testamentary and Intestate Succession in India." Third Edition. Rs. 14.

O'KINEALY.—THE INDIAN PENAL CODE.—BEING ACT XLV OF 1860, and other Laws and Acts of Parliament relating to the Criminal Courts of India; containing Rulings on Points of Procedure and Decisions of the High Court of Calcutta. Third Edition. By the Hon'ble J. O'KINEALY. Royal 8vo. [1886] Rs. 12.

PHILLIPS.—MANUAL OF INDIAN CRIMINAL LAW.—Being the Penal Code, Criminal Procedure Code, Evidence, Whipping, General Clauses, Police, Cattle-Trespass, Extradition Acts, with Penal Clauses of Legal Practitioners' Act, Registration, Arms, Stamp, &c., Acts. Fully Annotated, and containing all Applicable Rulings of all High Courts arranged under the Appropriate Sections up to date; also Circular Orders and Notifications. By H. A. D. PHILLIPS, C.S. Second Edition. Thick crown 8vo. Rs. 10.

PHILLIPS.—COMPARATIVE CRIMINAL JURISPRUDENCE.—Showing the Law, Procedure, and Case-Law of other Countries, arranged under the corresponding sections of the Indian Codes. By H. A. D. PHILLIPS, B.C.S. Vol. I, Crimes and Punishments. Vol. II, Procedure and Police. Demy 8vo, cloth. Rs. 12.

PRINSEP.—CODE OF CRIMINAL PROCEDURE (ACT X OF 1882), and other Laws and Rules of Practice relating to Procedure in the Criminal Courts of British India. With Notes. By the Hon'ble H. T. PRINSEP, Judge, High Court, Calcutta. Tenth Edition, brought up to June 1892. Royal 8vo. Rs. 12.

TOYNBEE.—THE VILLAGE CHAUKIDARI MANUAL.—BEING ACT VI (B. C.) OF 1870, as amended by Acts I (B. C.) of 1871 and 1886. With Notes, Appendices, &c. By G. TOYNBEE, C.S., Magistrate of Hooghly. Second Edition, Revised. Crown 8vo, cloth. Re. 1.

THACKER, SPINK AND CO., CALCUTTA.

SWINHOE.—THE CASE NOTED PENAL CODE, AND OTHER ACTS. Act XLV of 1860 as amended with references to all Reported Cases decided under each section. *[In the Press.*

EVIDENCE.

FIELD.—THE LAW OF EVIDENCE IN BRITISH INDIA.—Being a Treatise on the Indian Evidence Act as amended by Act XVIII of 1872. By the Hon'ble C. D. FIELD, M.A., LL.D. Fifth Edition. *[In the Press.*

STEPHEN.—THE PRINCIPLES OF JUDICIAL EVIDENCE.—An Introduction to the Indian Evidence Act, 1872. By SIR JAMES FITZ-JAMES STEPHEN, formerly Legislative Member of the Supreme Council of India. A New Edition. Crown 8vo, cloth. Rs. 3.

MEDICAL JURISPRUDENCE.

LYON.—MEDICAL JURISPRUDENCE FOR INDIA.—By J. B. LYON, F.C.S., F.C., Brigade-Surgeon, Professor of Medical Jurisprudence, Grant Medical College, Bombay. The Legal Matter revised by J. D. INVERARITY, Barrister-at-Law. Second Edition. Illustrated. 8vo. Rs. 16.

GRIBBLE.—OUTLINES OF MEDICAL JURISPRUDENCE FOR INDIA. By J. D. B. GRIBBLE, M.C.S. (Retired), PATRICK HEHIR, M.D., F.R.C.S.E., Third Edition, Revised, Enlarged, and Annotated. Demy 8vo. Rs. 5-8.

DIGESTS.

SUTHERLAND.—THE DIGEST OF INDIAN LAW REPORTS.—A Compendium of the Rulings of the High Court of Calcutta from 1862, and of the Privy Council from 1831 to 1876. By D. SUTHERLAND, Barrister-at-Law. Imp. 8vo, Rs. 8. Vol. II, 1876 to 1890, thick cloth, imp. 8vo. Rs. 12.

WOODMAN.—A DIGEST OF THE INDIAN LAW REPORTS and of the Reports of the cases heard in appeal by the Privy Council, 1887 to 1889. Edited by J. V. WOODMAN. Super-royal 8vo.

THACKER, SPINK AND CO., CALCUTTA.

HINDU AND MAHOMMEDAN LAW.

AMEER ALI.—THE STUDENT'S HAND-BOOK OF MAHOMMEDAN LAW. By the Hon'ble SYED AMEER ALI, C.I.E., author of "The Law relating to Gifts, Trusts, &c., among the Mahommedans;" "Personal Law of the Mahommedans," &c., &c. Crown 8vo. Rs. 3.

AMEER ALI.—MAHOMMEDAN LAW, VOL. I.—BY THE HON'BLE SYED AMEER ALI, C.I.E., Barrister-at-Law. Containing the Law relating to Gifts, Wakfs, Wills, Pre-emption, and Bailment. With an Introduction on Mahommedan Jurisprudence and Works on Law. (Being the Second Edition of Tagore Law Lectures, 1884. Royal 8vo, cloth. Rs. 16.

AMEER ALI.—MAHOMMEDAN LAW, VOL. II.—THE PERSONAL LAW OF THE MAHOMMEDANS. By the Hon'ble SYED AMEER ALI, M.A., C.I.E., Barrister-at-Law. Second Edition. Revised. [*In the Press.*

COWELL.—HINDU LAW.—BEING A TREATISE ON THE LAW ADMINISTERED EXCLUSIVELY TO HINDUS by the British Courts in India. (Tagore Law Lectures, 1870 and 1871.) By HERBERT COWELL, Barrister-at-Law. Royal 8vo, cloth. Lectures, 1870, Rs. 12; Lectures, 1871, Rs. 8.

JOLLY.—THE HINDU LAW OF INHERITANCE, PARTITION, AND ADOPTION according to the Smritis. By Prof. JULIUS JOLLY, of Wurtzburg. (Tagore Law Lectures, 1883.) Royal 8vo. Rs. 10.

RUMSEY.—AL SIRAJIYYAH.—OR, THE MAHOMMEDAN LAW OF INHERITANCE, with Notes and Appendix. By ALMARIC RUMSEY. Second Edition. Revised, with Additions. Crown 8vo. Rs. 4-8.

SIROMANI.—A COMMENTARY ON HINDU LAW OF INHERITANCE, Succession, Partition, Adoption, Marriage, Stridhan, and Testamentary Disposition. By Pundit JOGENDRO NATH BHATTACHARJEE, M.A., B.L. Second Edition. 8vo. Rs. 16.

WILSON.—INTRODUCTION TO THE STUDY OF ANGLO-MAHOMMEDAN LAW. By Sir ROLAND KNIGHT WILSON, Bart., M.A., L.M.M., late Reader in Indian Law to the University of Cambridge, author of "Modern English Law." [*In the Press.*

WILSON—A DIGEST OF ANGLO-MUHAMMADAN LAW.—Being an attempt to set forth, in the form of a Code, the rules now actually administered to Muhammadans only by the Civil Courts of British India, with explanatory Notes and full reference to Modern Case-Law, as well as to the ancient authorities. [*In the Press.*

THACKER, SPINK AND CO., CALCUTTA.

LAW MANUALS, ETC.

COWELL.—THE HISTORY AND CONSTITUTION OF THE COURTS AND LEGISLATIVE AUTHORITIES IN INDIA. Second Edition, Revised. By HERBERT COWELL. 8vo, cloth. [1884] Rs. 6.

HAND-BOOK OF INDIAN LAW.—A POPULAR AND CONCISE STATEMENT OF THE LAW generally in force in British India, designed for non-legal people, on subjects relating to Person and Property. By a Barrister-at-Law and Advocate of the High Court at Calcutta. [*In the Press.*

CARNEGY.—KACHAHRI TECHNICALITIES.—A GLOSSARY OF TERMS, Rural, Official and General, in daily use in the Courts of Law, and in illustration of the Tenures, Customs, Arts, and Manufactures of Hindustan. By P. CARNEGY. Second Edition. 8vo. cloth. Rs. 9.

CURRIE.—THE INDIAN LAW EXAMINATION MANUAL.—BY FENDALL CURRIE, of Lincoln's Inn, Barrister-at-Law. Fourth Edition, Revised. Demy 8vo. [1892] Rs. 5.

CONTENTS:—Introduction—Hindoo Law—Mahommedan Law—Indian Penal Code—Code of Civil Procedure—Evidence Act—Limitation Act—Succession Act—Contract Act—Registration Act—Stamp and Court-Fees Acts—Mortgage—Code of Criminal Procedure—The Easements Act—The Trust Act—The Transfer of Property Act—The Negotiable Instruments Act.

LEGISLATIVE ACTS OF THE GOVERNOR-GENERAL OF INDIA IN COUNCIL OF 1891. With Table of Contents and Index. Royal 8vo, cloth. Rs. 6.

DONOGH.—THE STAMP LAW OF BRITISH INDIA.—As constituted by the Indian Stamp Act (I of 1879), Rulings and Circular Orders, Notifications, Resolutions, Rules, and Orders, together with Schedules of all the Stamp Duties chargeable on Instruments in India from the earliest times. Edited, with Notes and complete Index, by WALTER R. DONOGH, M.A., of the Inner Temple, Barrister-at-Law. Demy 8vo, cloth, gilt. [1886] With Supplement. Rs. 8.

SUPPLEMENT CONTAINING AMENDMENTS, annotated to June 1890. As. 8.

GRIMLEY.—AN INCOME TAX MANUAL.—Being Act II of 1886. With Notes. By W. H. GRIMLEY, B.A., C.S., Commissioner of Income-Tax, Bengal. Royal 8vo. Rs. 3-8. Interleaved, Rs. 4.

THACKER, SPINK AND CO., CALCUTTA.

INDIAN MEDICAL GAZETTE.

A Record of Medicine, Surgery and Public Health, and of General Medical Intelligence, Indian and European.

Edited by W. J. SIMPSON, M.D.

Published monthly. Subscription Rs. 18 per annum. Single copy Rs. 2.

The *Indian Medical Gazette* was established nineteen years ago, and has earned for itself a world-wide reputation by its solid contributions to Tropical Medicine and Surgery. It is the **Sole** representative medium for recording the work and experience of the Medical Profession in India; and its very numerous **Exchanges** with all the leading Medical Journals in Great Britain and America enable it not only to diffuse this information broadcast throughout the world, but also to cull for its Indian readers, from an unusual variety of sources, all information which has any practical bearing on medical works in India.

The *Indian Medical Gazette* is indispensable to every member of the Medical Profession in India who wishes to keep himself abreast of medical progress, for it brings together and fixes the very special knowledge which is only to be obtained by long experience and close observation in India. In this way it constitutes itself a record of permanent value for reference, and a journal which ought to be in the library of every medical man in India or connected with that country. The Transactions of the Calcutta Medical Society, which meets monthly, is printed *in extenso*, and is a very valuable feature in the Gazette.

The Gazette covers altogether different ground from *The Lancet* and *British Medical Journal*, and in no way competes with these for general information, although it chronicles the most important item of European Medical Intelligence. The whole aim of the Gazette is to make itself of special use and value to Medical Officers in India and to assist and support them in the performance of their difficult duties.

It is specially devoted to the best interests of **The Medical Services**, and its long-established reputation and authority enable it to command serious attention in the advocacy of any desirable reform or substantial grievance.

The Contributors to the *Indian Medical Gazette* comprise the most eminent and representative men in the profession.

THACKER, SPINK AND CO., CALCUTTA.

THE INDIAN ENGINEER.
AN ILLUSTRATED WEEKLY JOURNAL
FOR
Engineers, Merchants, Buyers of Machinery & Hardware, and others interested in the Engineering and allied professions.

The Oldest Engineering Journal in India.

"THE INDIAN ENGINEER" contains the latest and most authentic information on all subjects connected with engineering enterprise; it includes illustrations aud descriptions of important works in progress or completed. Provincial and Foreign Industries and News-Letters; Railway news, enterprise and statistics; Leading Articles on subjects of the day. Miscellaneous matters, scientific and useful.

Subscribed to by Engineers both Civil and Military, Municipalities, Railways, Merchants, Architects, Contractors, &c., &c.

RATES OF SUBSCRIPTION
Including a copy of the Indian Engineer's Diary and Reference Book.

Thick Paper Edition, yearly	...	... Rs. 20
Thin Paper Edition, yearly	...	... „ 10

THACKER, SPINK AND CO., CALCUTTA.

THE JOURNAL OF THE PHOTOGRAPHIC SOCIETY OF INDIA.

AN ILLUSTRATED MONTHLY JOURNAL.

Invaluable to all lovers of the Art of Photography.

A medium for the earliest information on all discoveries in Photography, Photographic Literature, Experience and News.

The Journal has a large and increasing circulation, is affiliated with Clubs or Amateur Societies all over India, Ceylon, Burma and the Straits Settlements, and has an extensive circulation out of India.

Each number of the Journal is illustrated with a Picture reproduced by a photo-mechanical process.

SUBSCRIPTION—Rs. 5 PER ANNUM.
Members of the Society, *free.*

THE RACING CALENDAR.
A FORTNIGHTLY CALENDAR.

Published in accordance with the Rules of Racing, under the authority of the Stewards of the Calcutta Turf Club.

A Record of all Race Performances in India, Racing Fixtures and Racing information, Meetings of the Calcutta Turf Club, Registration of Colours, Assumed Names of Owners, Jockeys' Licences, Unpaid Forfeit List, List of Defaulters, Change in Horses' Names, Horses and Ponies classed, aged and measured, and all information relating to Racing.

ANNUAL SUBSCRIPTION RS. 12.

THACKER, SPINK AND CO, CALCUTTA.

STANDARD WORKS ON INDIA.

THE JOURNAL OF INDIAN ART.—With full-page Coloured Illustrations. Folio 15 by 11. Parts 1 to 41 ready. Re. 1-10 each.

THE SACRED BOOKS OF THE EAST.—Translated by various Oriental Scholars. Edited by F. Max Muller. *List of Volumes on application.*

THE FAUNA OF BRITISH INDIA.—Including Ceylon and Burma. Published under the authority of the Secretary of State for India. Edited by W. T. Blanford, f.r.s., and Illustrated.

Mammalia.	By W. T. Blanford, f.r.s.	Rs. 17 0
Fishes, 2 vols.	By Dr. Francis Day	„ 31 4
Birds, 2 vols.	By F. W. Oates	„ 30 0
Reptilia and Batrachia.	By G. A. Boulenger	„ 17 2
Moths, 1 vol.	By F. Hampson	„ 17 2

THE INDIAN MUTINY, 1857-58.—Selections from the Letters, Despatches, and other State Papers preserved in the Military Department of the Government of India. Edited by George W. Forrest, b.a., Director of Records of the Government of India. With a Map and Plans. Vol. I, Dehli. Royal 8vo. Rs. 10.

WARREN HASTINGS.—Selection from the Letters, Despatches, and other State Papers preserved in the Foreign Department of the Government of India, 1772-1785. Edited by George W. Forrest, b.a. 3 vols. Fcap., cloth. Rs. 12.

THE ADMINISTRATION OF WARREN HASTINGS, 1772-1785.—Reviewed and Illustrated from Original Documents. By G. W. Forrest, b.a. 8vo, cloth. Rs. 4.

ANNALS OF RURAL BENGAL.—By W. W. Hunter, c.i.e., ll.d. 8vo. Rs. 6.

ILLUSTRATION OF SOME OF THE GRASSES OF THE SOUTHERN Punjab.—Being Photo-Lithograph Illustrations of some of the principal Grasses found at Hissar. With short descriptive letter-press. By William Coldstream, b.a., b.c.s. Illustrated with 39 Plates. Demy folio. Rs. 16.

ILLUSTRATIONS OF INDIAN FIELD SPORTS.—Selected and Reproduced from the Coloured Engravings first published in 1807 after designs by Captain Thomas Williamson, Bengal Army. Small oblong, handsome cloth cover. Printed in colours. Rs. 9.

THACKER, SPINK AND CO., CALCUTTA.

CONSTABLE'S ORIENTAL MISCELLANY.

BERNIER'S TRAVELS IN THE MOGUL EMPIRE.—An entirely new edition, with a Frontispiece printed in 18 colours on Japanese paper, other Illustrations, and Three Maps. By ARCHIBALD CONSTABLE, Mem. As. Soc., Bengal, F.S.A., Scot. Crown 8vo. pp. liv, 500. Rs. 5-2.

POPULAR READINGS IN SCIENCE.—By JOHN GALL, M.A., LL.B., late Professor of Mathematics and Physics, Canning College, Lucknow, and DAVID ROBERTSON, M.A., LL.B., B.SC. With 56 Diagrams, a Glossary of Technical Terms, and an Index. Crown 8vo. pp. 468. Rs. 4-4.

AURENG-ZEBE: A TRAGEDY.—By JOHN DRYDEN; and Book II of THE CHACE: a Poem by WILLIAM SOMERVILE. Edited, with Biographical Memoirs and Copious Notes, by K. DEIGHTON, B.A., editor of 'Select Plays of Shakespeare.' With a Portrait of Dryden, and a Coloured Reproduction of an Indian Painting of the Emperor Akbar Deer-stalking. Crown 8vo. pp. xiii, 222. Rs. 4-4.

LETTERS FROM A MAHRATTA CAMP.—By THOS. D. BROUGHTON. A new edition, with an Introduction by the Right Hon. Sir M. E. GRANT DUFF, G.C.S.I., F.R.S. Notes, Coloured and other Illustrations, very full Index, and a Map. Rs. 5-2.

STUDIES IN MOHAMMEDANISM.—Historical and Doctrinal, with a Chapter on Islam in England. By JOHN J. POOL. With a frontispiece and Index. Crown 8vo, cloth. Rs. 5-2.

"As a 'popular text-book,' dealing with some of the most picturesque aspects of Islam, it deserves more than ordinary attention."—*Times.*

THE GOLDEN BOOK OF INDIA.—A Biographical and Statistical Directory of the Ruling Princes, Chiefs, Nobles, and Titled and Decorated Personages of the Indian Empire; the dates of their birth and succession to the *guddi*; a concise account of their immediate predecessors and all the deeds of honour and valour of their house and family. Imp., red cloth, gilt. Rs. 35.

BOMBAY AND WESTERN INDIA.—By JAMES DOUGLAS. Dedicated to the Duke and Duchess of Connaught. With Maps and Plans, 13 full-page Photogravures, Collotype Reproductions from Old Documents one Coloured Reproduction of an Old Picture, and over 100 other Text Illustrations. 2 vols. Super-royal 8vo, cloth, extra, gilt top. Rs. 35.

THACKER, SPINK AND CO., CALCUTTA.

THACKER, SPINK & CO.'S UNIFORM SERIES.
ILLUSTRATED AND ELEGANTLY BOUND.

DEPARTMENTAL DITTIES AND OTHER VERSES.—By RUDYARD KIPLING. Seventh Edition. With additional Poems. Cloth. Rs. 3.

HINDU MYTHOLOGY: VEDIC AND PURANIC.—By the Rev. W. J. WILKINS, of the London Missionary Society, Calcutta. Profusely Illustrated. Rs. 7-8.

THE TRIBES ON MY FRONTIER.—An Indian Naturalist's Foreign Policy. By EHA. With 50 Illustrations by F. C. MACRAE. Imp. 16mo. Fourth Edition. Rs. 7.

A NATURAL HISTORY OF THE MAMMALIA OF INDIA, BURMAH, AND CEYLON. By R. A. STERNDALE, F.R.G.S., F.Z.S., &c. With 170 Illustrations. Imp. 16mo. Rs. 10.

HANDBOOK TO THE FERNS OF INDIA, CEYLON, AND THE MALAY PENINSULA. By Colonel R. H. BEDDOME. With 300 Illustrations by the author. Imp. 16mo. Rs. 10.

LAYS OF IND.—By ALIPH CHEEM. Comic, Satirical, and Descriptive Poems illustrative of Anglo-Indian Life. Seventh Edition. With 70 Illustrations. Cloth, elegant gilt edges. Rs. 7-8.

RIDING: ON THE FLAT AND ACROSS COUNTRY.—A Guide to Practical Horsemanship. By Captain M. H. HAYES. Illustrated by STURGESS and J. H. OSWALD-BROWN. Third Edition. Revised and Enlarged. Imp. 16mo. Rs. 7-8.

THE HORSE-WOMAN.—AN ILLUSTRATED GUIDE TO SIDE-SADDLE RIDING. By Mrs. HAYES, and Edited by Capt. M. H. HAYES. Uniform with "Riding: on the Flat and Across Country." Imp. 16mo. Rs. 7-8.

RIDING FOR LADIES, WITH HINTS ON THE STABLE.—A LADY'S HORSE BOOK. By Mrs. POWER O'DONOGHUE. With 75 Illustrations by A. CHANTREY CORBOULD. Rs. 7-8.

INDIAN RACING REMINISCENCES.—Being Entertaining Narratives and Anecdotes of Men, Horses, and Sport. By Captain M. H. HAYES. Illustrated with Portraits and Engravings. As. 6.

BEHIND THE BUNGALOW.—BY EHA, author of "Tribes on my Frontier." With 42 Illustrations by the Illustrator of "The Tribes on My Frontier." Fourth Edition. With Additional Illustrations. Imp. 16mo. Rs. 5.

THACKER, SPINK AND CO., CALCUTTA.